alternative media
and politics of resistance

Lynda Lee Kaid and Bruce Gronbeck
General Editors

Vol. 16

PETER LANG
New York • Washington, D.C./Baltimore • Bern
Frankfurt am Main • Berlin • Brussels • Vienna • Oxford

Joshua D. Atkinson

alternative media and politics of resistance

A Communication Perspective

PETER LANG
New York • Washington, D.C./Baltimore • Bern
Frankfurt am Main • Berlin • Brussels • Vienna • Oxford

Library of Congress Cataloging-in-Publication Data
Atkinson, Joshua D.
Alternative media and politics of resistance: a communication perspective /
Joshua D. Atkinson.
p. cm. — (Frontiers in political communication; v. 16)
Includes bibliographical references and index.
1. Alternative mass media. 2. Communication in social action.
3. Communication in politics. I. Title.
P96.A44A85 302.23—dc22 2009044581
ISBN 978-1-4331-0518-0 (hardcover)
ISBN 978-1-4331-0517-3 (paperback)
ISSN 1525-9730

Bibliographic information published by **Die Deutsche Nationalbibliothek**.
Die Deutsche Nationalbibliothek lists this publication in the "Deutsche
Nationalbibliografie"; detailed bibliographic data is available
on the Internet at http://dnb.d-nb.de/.

© 2010 Peter Lang Publishing, Inc., New York
29 Broadway, 18th floor, New York, NY 10006
www.peterlang.com

All rights reserved.
Reprint or reproduction, even partially, in all forms such as microfilm,
xerography, microfiche, microcard, and offset strictly prohibited.

Contents

Acknowledgements	ix
Preface	**xi**
Chapter 1: Introduction to the Past: **Social Movements and Alternative Media**	**1**
Social Movement Research	1
Alternative Media	13
Definitions and Arguments	20
Chapter 2: Resistance Performance	**25**
Audience and Performance	25
The Foundations of Resistance Performance: Power and Divergent Worldviews	34
Resistance Performance	37
Interconnectivity: The Multiplex	49
Conclusion	56
Chapter 3: Interactivity	**59**
Intercreative Capacity: User-to-Document Interactivity	61
Narrative Capacity: User-to-User Interactivity	70
Conclusion	79
Chapter 4: "Speaking Truth to Power" and "Amorality": The Reformist Quadrants	**81**
Alternative Media and Themes	82
Organizations and Communicative Performances	97

Conclusion	106
Chapter 5: Insurrections and Cafés: The Radical Quadrants	**109**
Alternative Media and Themes	110
"Organizations" and Communicative Performances	123
Conclusion	129
Chapter 6: Alternative Media World	**131**
Alternative Media World Defined	131
Alternative Media World in Political Communication: An Example	137
Conclusion	144
Conclusion	**147**
Social Movement Research	148
Alternative Media Research	150
Looking to the Future	152
Notes	**155**
References	**161**
Index	**175**

Acknowledgements

Alternative Media and Politics of Resistance represents the fruits of my academic labors over the past decade. This book would not have been possible without the help and support of four of the most important people in my life. First and foremost I would like to thank my beloved wife, Sandra Faulkner. Her love and dedication has been the pillar that supported me while writing this book. I would also like to thank my parents, Dan and Vicki, and my brother, Sam, for all of their love and support throughout my entire life. I could never have gotten where I am today without them.

I also feel that I need to give special thanks to a whole host of people who have supported me over the years. I would like to thank Debbie Dougherty, my advisor, who has been a model upon which I have based my career. I would like to thank Greg Armfield and Maria Dixon, who stood by my side throughout graduate school and never let me give up. I would like to thank Bernadette Calafell and Diane Grimes, who were both supportive friends and colleagues when others were not. And I would like to thank Jason Childress, who has always kept me in touch with reality (sort of). I would also like to thank Mary Savigar, Sophie Appel, and Laura Rawlins for all of their hard work helping me to prepare this project for publication.

Ultimately, I dedicate this book to my daughter, Mimi. I hope and pray that she will inherit a world that is guided by commitments to peace and prosperity for all.

Preface

At the dawn of the 21st century, many researchers concerned with political communication have sought to explore the role of "new social movements" in shaping the discourses and dialogues of the modern political landscape. Such attention should come as no surprise, as new social movements—movements that advocate for particular causes by shaping the political identity of audiences—have played an integral role in bringing issues like abortion and the environment into "mainstream" political debate. Prior to Operation Rescue's 1991 protests carried out in Wichita, Kansas, few politicians viewed abortion as an issue worthy of debate or pursuit. During the summer of 1991, Operation Rescue and other allied organizations used abortion clinics around Wichita as flashpoints to mobilize activists, who blockaded doorways and sidewalks; such actions led to the arrest of hundreds of those demonstrators (Bowers, Ochs, & Jensen, 1992). After those crucial protests, abortion became one of the most important issues that shaped Democratic and Republican political discourse for nearly a generation. Today, Randall Terry and other organizers of Operation Rescue use political events—such as the Supreme Court confirmation hearings of Judge Sonia Sotomayor and the town hall meetings on healthcare reform in August of 2009—as similar flashpoints to mobilize activists and keep attention focused on the topic of abortion.

Increasingly, it has come to the attention of scholars and advocates for social justice that change does not so much come from *within* government and power structures, as it comes from protestors, agitators, and resistors *outside* of those dominant power structures. Such is also clearly the case when looking backwards in time at movements like those for abolition, suffrage, and civil rights. Scholars such as Manuel Castells (1996; 2006) and Robert Huesca (2001) have demonstrated that modern movements for change, like the environmental movement and the pro-life movement, function more as networks than any predecessor movements that aimed to rid society of slavery or segregation. The network philosophy concerning these movements emphasized the important role that easily assessable and interactive media, like cheap homemade magazines (e.g., zines) and websites, have on shaping these movements. Rather than movements that are centralized or defined by singular personalities like Dr. Martin Luther King, Jr. or Susan B. Anthony, modern movements for change tend to be decentralized and less hierarchical due to the proliferation of media production devices and the Internet. Thus, scholars in multiple disciplines are beginning to recognize the importance of such assessable and interactive media in the new social movements that resist dominant power structures, as such media can deeply impact mainstream political discourse.

In the field of Communication, scholars have taken up the issue and made important contributions to academic literature published by the National Communication Association (NCA) and the International Communication Association (ICA), as well as several regional and interdisciplinary journals. Within the branch of Communication known as rhetoric, scholars such as Keven DeLuca (1999), Christine Harold (2004), Helene Shugart (2005), and Barbara Warnick (1998; 2007) have worked to explore issues of interactivity, intertextuality, and image found in media utilized by activists affiliated with new social movements. Other Communication scholars, such as Kirsty Best (2005) and Victor Pickard (2006a; 2006b) have worked to explore the role of narrative within the network metaphor, and how narrative creates interconnections between different social movement organizations. At the same time, scholars in the fields of Journalism and Media Studies such as Chris Atton (2002a; 2004), John Downing (1984; 2003a; 2003b), and Graham Meikle (2002) have worked to explore what Downing first termed "radical media" and what others have since described as "alternative media." By alternative media, these scholars were typically interested in media produced by noncommercial sources that sought to create some kind of social change or alter social roles. Essentially, these scholars were interested in the media produced and circulated by social movement organizations that sought to shape political identity, like those affiliated with the environmental movement. Unlike the research conducted in the field of Communication, the Journalism and Media scholars studied the features of alternative media, as well as the processes and politics of alternative media production.

For the most part, both lines of research have emerged separately and have rarely been connected by scholars in any of the before mentioned fields. The lone exception has been the research that I have conducted over the course of the past decade, and published over the past five years (see Atkinson, 2005a; Atkinson, 2005b; Atkinson, 2008; Atkinson, 2009a; Atkinson, 2009b; Atkinson & Dougherty, 2006). Within that line of research, I engaged in in-depth interviews and discussions with eighty activists and alternative media producers in three US cities and in Chiapas, Mexico, in order to demonstrate how activists and producers utilize alternative media in the construction and coordination of strategies of resistance against dominant power structures in society. Essentially, my research—and this resulting book—bring together both lines of research in the fields of Communication and Journalism/Media. Grounded in a social constructionist perspective, I have taken an active interest in the production of alternative media, as well as the ways in which activists make use of those media as they build and weave resistance in their public discourse and everyday lives.

Research Foundations
Alternative Media and the Politics of Resistance constitutes the fruits of my research over the past decade that has focused on the role of alternative media in the construction of resistance within new social movements, as well as in the performance of resistance by new social movement activists. From that research, five primary articles emerged in Communication and Mass Communication journals:

> Atkinson, J. (2005). Towards an understanding about complexities of alternative media: Portrayals of power in alternative media. *Qualitative Research Reports in Communication, 6,* 77-84.

> Atkinson, J., & Dougherty, D. (2006). Alternative media and social justice movements: The development of a resistance performance paradigm of audience analysis. *Western Journal of Communication, 70,* 64-88.

> Atkinson, J. (2008). Towards a model of interactivity in alternative media: A multilevel analysis of audiences and producers in a new social movement network. *Mass Communication & Society, 11,* 227-247.

> Atkinson, J. (2009a). Networked activism and the broken multiplex: Exploring fractures in the resistance performance paradigm. *Communication Studies, 60,* 49-65.

> Atkinson, J. (2009b) Networked activists in search of resistance: Exploring an alternative media pilgrimage across the boundaries and borderlands of globalization. *Communication, Culture, and Critique, 2,* 137-159.

The first article was published in 2005 in *Qualitative Research Reports in Communication* and explores the differing visions of power that are espoused by producers of alternative media through their work and the impact that such alternative media has on the worldviews of activists in the community that I called "Mystical City." The second article was a collaborative effort with Dr. Debbie Dougherty on the performance of resistance in "social justice movements." The article, published in 2006 in *Western Journal of Communication*, explored the concept of Resistance Performance Paradigm (RPP) in which activists' use of alternative media constructed differing "theatres" and a common "multiplex" through which Mystical City activists performed resistance. The 2008 article was published in *Mass Communication and Society* and explored the role of user-to-user interactivity in the production of alternative media content. Interviews with global and local producers of alternative media demonstrated how audience interactions with Mystical City producers established organizational support, while audience interactions with global producers helped to strengthen content found in alternative media sources like *Z Magazine* or Counterpunch.org. The *Communication Studies* article published in early 2009 was deeply rooted in the concept of RPP, but was based on interviews with activists and alternative media producers in a city located in the northeastern US, rather than my initial interview research with the activists in Mystical City. In this community, Erie City, I had noted that resistance coordinated by differing organizations did not emerge, despite the evidence of RPP that were revealed through interviews with activists and local producers of alternative media. My observations in Erie City led me to develop a new component of RPP—narrative capacity—which played an integral role in the construction coordinated resistance by organizations with opposing or differing worldviews. Finally, in a *Communication, Culture and Critique* article published in 2009, I explored the concept of the "alternative media world" in reference to activists who cross the boundaries between their own networks and into the worlds of marginalized communities for whom they advocate.

Research Sites and Research Participants
The research concerning resistance performance and alternative media was conducted at two primary research sites: Mystical City and Erie City. It should be noted that the names Mystical City and Erie City might prove to be a bit confusing for readers, but due to my promises of confidentiality to the participants I feel that I must adhere to the names that were used in the before mentioned five publications. Suffice it to say that Mystical City was a mid-sized city in the Midwestern section of the United States of America. The city was home to roughly 90,000 people, while 150,000 people lived in the larger metropolitan area. In addition to the population, the town was home to Mystical State University, a large research oriented university that typically enrolled over 20,000 students a year. In many ways, Mystical City is comparable to other Midwest college towns like Lawrence, Kansas, or Norman, Oklahoma. The name Mystical City was chosen to reflect the town because of the prevalence of the agitation strategy "polarization" performed by many of the activists in their demonstrations against dominant power structures. Such polarization constructed a kind of mythical storyline about the "noble us" against "villainous them" for many activists in the area. Through this storyline the town was perceived to be under siege by villainous corporations and government figures, and only through the efforts of the "noble us" could the city be saved. The research from Mystical City was conducted in the spring of 2003 and stands as the basis for the primary articles published in 2005, 2006, and 2008, as well as other articles published in *Communication Review* and *Popular Communication*. Overall, there were 35 research participants involved in the Mystical City research who were

affiliated with one of the many "social justice" organizations in the city, with 11 of those activists working to produce some form of alternative media.

Erie City was a larger town in the northeastern part of the United States of America, which was home to roughly 150,000 people within the city limits and 500,000 people in the metropolitan area. In addition, the town housed a mid-sized university called Great Lakes University, which typically enrolled 10,000 students a year. In many ways, Erie City is similar to other northeastern cities like Wooster, Massachusetts, near Boston. The name Erie City was chosen because of the town's relative proximity to Lake Erie, but also because of the eerie way in which the activists were in many respects similar to the activists in Mystical City, with the exception of the cohesive mythical storyline. Instead of cohesion, the activists in Erie City were quite fractured, with various activists and organizations suspicious of one another. The research from Erie City was conducted during the autumn of 2005, and is the basis for the 2009 article published in *Communication Studies*. Overall, there were 21 research participants who were members of one or more of the various social justice organizations within Erie City. Of those participants, nine were producers of alternative media. More information about the activists and organizations in both Mystical City and Erie City can be found in Chapters 2 and 3.

Two other research sites have proven integral for the expansion and refinement of my research concerning the role of alternative media in resistance performance: Chiapas, Mexico, and River City. Chiapas is the primary site for the conflict between the Zapatista movement and the government of Mexico. Many Zapatista "autonomous communities" emerged following the enactment of the North American Free Trade Agreement (NAFTA), and such communities consider themselves to be a part of the country of Mexico while independent of the Mexican government. Those Zapatista communities have become the subject of many alternative publications, broadcasts, and websites over the past fifteen years, which has led to an influx of activists from across the United States and Europe into those communities to be a part of their movement. In the summer of 2003, I travelled to four of the autonomous communities with six other activists in an endeavor to research and explore the efforts of such Western activists to work with the Zapatistas in their own marginalized communities. The Chiapas research served as the basis for the 2009 article in *Communication, Culture and Critique*. In addition, River City was a large town in the upper Midwest portion of the United States, home to 300,000 people in the city and 700,000 people in the metropolitan area. For the most part, River City is similar to Fort Wayne, Indiana, in terms of size and demographics. Overall, I interviewed ten research participants in the autumn of 2007 who were affiliated with a Latino/a community education organization. The research site has proven important as it has allowed me to gain more insight into the Reformist Lay quadrant of Resistance Performance (see Chapters 2 & 4), which had not been fully explored in my past research projects in Mystical City and Erie City.

There is also one final research "site" that should be noted, and that is the research concerning the production of alternative media at the "global level." While I was conducting interviews with activists and local alternative media producers in Mystical City, I simultaneously engaged in interviews with eight individuals who wrote and produced content for national and international alternative media titles, such as *The Nation*, ZNet, and Counterpunch.org. The research that I conducted concerning the global level alternative media producers supplemented the 2008 article that was published in *Mass Communication and Society*.

Research Methods

The research that I conducted with activists and producers of alternative media involved the use of "active interviewing", a technique developed by James Holstein and Jaber Gubrium (1995) that provides agency to research participants through broad questions. Essentially, the participant is given the ability to address a wide range of complex meanings by telling stories and weaving narratives by responding to very broad questions asked by the researcher, such as "Describe your role in [organization.]" In this way, the researcher and the participant work together to co-create the environment of the communication phenomenon from the perspective of the participant. The active interviews in Mystical City, Erie City, and River City were all conducted and tape-recorded at times and in settings chosen by the activist participants. The interviews with the global producers of alternative media were conducted and tape-recorded over the telephone at times designated by those participants. During the interviews, I would ask the activists and producers about (1) their opinions about dominant power structures in society (e.g., What are your opinions about the possibilities for corporate reform in society?), (2) their affiliations and work with "social justice" organizations (e.g., What organizations do you work with here in Erie City? What role do you play in that organization?), (3) their use of alternative media (e.g., What alternative media titles do you regularly use? Do you ever interact with any producers of alternative media? Do you ever write or produce any alternative media yourself?), and (4) demographics (e.g., What is your age?). The active interviews with the activists in the Chiapas research were embedded within a larger method called ethnographic narrative excavation, which was developed by Robert Krizek (2003) as a way to ask questions and conduct interviews with participants of short term, "non-routine public events." Essentially, ethnographic narrative excavation serves as a framework for conducting ethnography and interviews at research sites that only exist for short periods of time, like the two-week group journey into the Zapatista autonomous communities.

Alternative Media xv

In addition, I also engaged in qualitative content analysis of alternative media titles that were described by the activists through the active interviews. Qualitative content analysis is a method that is used in order to reveal themes contained within a text so as to demonstrate any latent meanings that are embedded therein (see Altheide, 1996; Krippendorff, 2004; Mayring, 2000). Such themes emerge through the establishment of thematic categories, which are constructed from theory or the guiding research questions (Mayring, 2000). In other words, if a researcher were searching for themes about resistance found within alternative media texts, they could search for examples of resistance that match theories of resistance established by researchers like Dennis Mumby (1988; 1997) or Robin Clair (1998), or they could search for examples of defiance of dominant power structures depicted within the text. Overall, I examined the content of eighty-seven articles and news stories from a variety of alternative media sources that were discussed by activists in Mystical City as important to their activism (e.g., *Z Magazine*, *Democracy Now!* radio, Indymedia.org). It should also be noted that qualitative content analysis also played an important role in the examination of anarchist zines, a project that was published in *Journal of Communication Inquiry* (2006). Although this was a minor project outside of the scope of the RPP research, the analysis of anarchist zines that I collected at the North American Anarchist Gathering provided valuable insight into the circulation of narratives by radical activists. Much of the information gleaned from that research plays an important role in Chapter 5, in the descriptions of alternative media utilized by radical activists.

Objectives of the Book
The five primary articles that emerged from my research were published as independent research projects, separate from one another. Within this volume I bring all of them together into a complete picture, much as I first conceptualized and investigated the role of alternative media in the construction and performance of resistance by activists. In the time between the project's inception, the interviews and qualitative content analysis, and the publication of each separate article, a few things have changed; those changes are reflected within this volume. The early articles (Atkinson, 2005a; Atkinson, 2005b; Atkinson & Dougherty, 2006) did not utilize the network metaphor in the establishment of RPP, nor in the conceptualization of resistance in alternative media used by activists. Trends in NCA journals, such as *Critical Studies in Media Communication*, demonstrated the rise of the metaphor in new social movement research starting in late 2005, and throughout 2006. With the emergence of the network metaphor in relation to interactive media networks like Indymedia.org (see Best, 2005; Pickard, 2006a; 2006b) I began to reanalyze some of the initial findings and the concept of RPP; such reconceptualization is prominently discussed in the later articles (Atkinson, 2008; 2009a; 2009b) as well as in the chapters of this

book. In addition to the network metaphor, the concept of Resistance Performance Paradigm has been renamed Resistance Performance (RP); at the end of the Atkinson and Dougherty (2006) research concerning RPP we hinted at the idea that the concept was in fact part of a larger paradigm of audience performance. I have assumed such a position in this book, which is discussed in greater detail in Chapter 2.

Ultimately, this book serves as a bridge between the fields of Communication, Journalism, and Media Studies—as well as differing branches within the field of Communication—in their efforts to study and understand new social movements and networked activism. Specifically, the book (1) outlines the history of new social movement research and research concerning alternative media carried out in the fields of Communication, Journalism, and Media Studies, (2) provides a theoretical framework that illustrates the role of alternative media in shaping communicative strategies utilized by activists and organizations that make up contemporary new social movement networks, (3) demonstrates the mosaic of alternative media content that shapes the construction and performance of resistance in different "quadrants" of the theoretical framework, and (4) illustrates the role of alternative media and activists' performance of resistance in the political landscape of the 21st century. These four goals are all informed by the work of rhetoricians and social scientists in the field of Communication, as well as scholars in the fields of Journalism and Media Studies, and those goals should also inform each of those fields. However, these four goals should have particular impact for scholars and students in the field of Communication, as the emphasis of my research has not been solely the alternative media used by activists or how activists produce alternative media. My research and writing have always sought to explore and address the ways in which alternative media informs activists' public performances of resistance against dominant power structures.

Chapter 1
Introduction to the Past: Social Movements and Alternative Media

The following chapter provides:

1) A brief history of research concerning social movements over the past fifty years by rhetoricians and social scientists.

2) A history of research concerning the subject of alternative media over the past thirty years.

3) An explanation of the problematic disconnect of both lines of research and the central argument at the heart of the book.

Social Movement Research

Serious and rigorous academic study of social movements began in the 1950s with the work of Leland Griffin, who conceptualized "historical movements" as attempts to create or abolish institutions in society through the art of rhetoric. The early years of social movement research were shaped by the debates that raged between Communication scholars, most notably rhetoricians such as Leland Griffin and Malcolm Sillars, and social scientists in the fields of Sociology and Social Psychology. Scholars in the field of Communication most often researched and analyzed social movements from a rhetorical paradigm based on concepts of meaning and discourse, whereas the social scientists approached the topic from an empirical paradigm grounded in the pursuit of effects and measurement. Later, the study of movements turned to the examination of "new social movements" that sought to establish political identity rather than the creation or abolition of social institutions, often through the use of images and visual rhetoric. At the end of the 20th century, Communication scholars began to incorporate the concept of network into research concerning new social movements. In the following section, I provide a survey of the many changes and challenges that have shaped the study of social movements and new social movements in the field of Communication. The following survey of academic articles and books is obviously not an exhaustive list of all of the research concerning social movements, but are notable as they have played an integral role in academic conceptualization of social movements. In addition, the works that appear in the following survey have played an important role in the concepts associated with Resistance Performance that are developed throughout the rest of this book.

Early Research: Rhetoric and Social Science
Early research in the field of Communication concerning social movements began with Leland Griffin's work that focused on the rhetoric of "historical movements." In his landmark essay published in the *Quarterly Journal of Speech*, Griffin (1952) classified different types of movements, as well as the different chronological phases of development for movements. According to Griffin, there are two types of movements that are found in society: pro-movements that seek to create or defend institutions and anti-movements that seek to remove or destroy institutions. In both cases, movements shift through cycles that are marked by three rhetorical periods: inception, rhetorical crisis, and consummation. At the period of inception, the movement is largely unknown and unseen by the general population, as "aggressor rhetoricians" emerge to take the forefront creating arguments for or against particular institutions in society. At the period of rhetorical crisis, defendants of the status quo take notice of the growing arguments made by the aggressor rhetoricians; the defendants begin to mobilize their own resources and arguments. It is at this point that an event occurs (e.g., a march, an arrest) that initiates a public and visible clash between the two groups, which inevitably disturbs "the balance between the groups which had existed in the mind of the collective audience" (p. 186). Such a clash marks the beginning of the end, as the movement then enters into the period of consummation. At this point in the movement's cycle, the aggressor rhetoricians abandon their work, as they feel that they have triumphed in their cause, their efforts have met with defeat, or they feel that there is a new cause to which they should attend.

Griffin's important conceptualization of the types and cycles of historical movements paved the way for future research concerning social movements, in both rhetoric and the social sciences. In fact, Griffin's 1952 article did more to advance the work of sociologists and social psychologists such as Neil Smelser (1962) and Ted Gurr (1970) than it did to advance the work of rhetoricians like John Bowers and Donovan Ochs (1971) and Theodore Windt (1972). Social scientists began to focus on collective behavior in social movements in terms of phases or "stages" that escalate in response to various political and social factors.[1] For instance, an essay written by Smelser demonstrated five stages of collective behavior that emerge during the course of a social movement: structural strain, growth and spread of beliefs, triggers for localized social action, mass mobilization, and social control. The collective action begins with the strain experienced by an initial group of social actors as they come to believe that something is wrong with society, and those beliefs mushroom outward beyond the initial group. As each stage unfolds, the collective behavior of the social movement participants grows and increases in intensity, leading to the final stage of the movement when authorities enact social control and stem the growth of the movement. Similarly, Gurr (1970) worked from the cyclical framework similar to Griffin in his research concerning political violence in collective behavior. In that research, Gurr claimed that the "turmoil" associated with the collective behavior of social movements moved through different stages: protest to localized rebellion. The stage of turmoil was marked by the intensity of political violence perpetrated by social movement actors. The focus on attitudes, beliefs, and behaviors on the part of the social scientists such as Smelser and Gurr diverted attention away from the discourse of agitators and defenders that had been central to the rhetorical research of Griffin. Such a diversion fomented division between rhetoricians and social scientists and created tension between the two camps.

Through the 1970s, many notable Communication scholars worked to draw research concerning social movements away from attitudes and behaviors and back to the subject of discourse and meaning created by activists and protesters. John Bowers and Donovan Ochs' book *Rhetoric of Agitation and Control* (1971) was a notable publication in this regard as the researchers documented categorical rhetorical strategies and tactics utilized by protesters to agitate for widespread social change such as promulgation, solidification, polarization, nonviolent resistance, and confrontation.[2] Promulgation constituted tactics such as handing out pamphlets and mass meetings, all of which are carried out with the intention to win over large-scale public support beyond the movement and recruit new members. The strategy of solidification entailed tactics such as singing songs and displaying symbols used to reinforce a sense of cohesion among protesters. Polarization entailed tactics that bifurcate the world into "us against them" through the use of emotionally charged "flag issues" (e.g., abortion = murder) or "flag individuals" (e.g., George W. Bush = Hitler) in speeches and everyday language utilized by protesters. Nonviolent resistance constituted tactics that violate laws that protesters deem to be socially unjust. The point of nonviolent resistance is typically to provoke establishment control on the protesters, thus demonstrating the unjust nature of such laws. Finally, confrontation is a strategy that entailed violent or obscene actions that would provoke an attack by establishment figures; such attacks would help protesters to demonstrate the unjust nature of the entire socio-political structure. According to Bowers and Ochs, these strategies often unfold in a linear fashion; movements seek to gain support through promulgation, and then move to solidification. Such attention to strategies once again drew scholarly attention to the rhetoric woven by protesters and social movement actors and paved the way for research that provided additional insight into rhetorical strategies and evaluated the effectiveness of such strategies in creating social change. Many rhetoricians built on the rhetorical strategies and tactics described in *Rhetoric of Agitation and Control*, like Theodore Windt (1972), who addressed the concept of diatribe in social movements. In his article published in the *Quarterly Journal of Speech*, Windt explained diatribe as shocking and/or vulgar rhetoric that is often employed by social movement actors who reject "traditional" strategies for persuasion, such as promulgation. It is often the position of protesters and activists that traditional forms of persuasion are corrupt, as they have been developed by the very power structures to which they are opposed. Such diatribe often grabs the attention of onlookers and audiences, but fails to persuade due to the lack of solutions or alternative ideologies within the discourse.

In response to the literature developed by both social scientists and rhetoricians, Michael McGee (1975; 1980a; 1980b) advanced the claim that such research had focused too much on social movement as "phenomenon" and neglected "meaning" in articles published in the *Quarterly Journal of Speech* and the *Central States Speech Journal*.[3] According to McGee, both social scientists and rhetoricians had focused their attention too much on the numbers of individuals *within* social movements and their management/use of resources and did not address the more important development of meanings that emerged *outside* of social movements. In effect, social movement was not a culmination of actions taken by agitators and protesters, as much as it was the transformation and shifting of meanings through rhetoric utilized by the social movement. Such rhetoric constructed meanings that affected the discourse across society about topics like war, race, and gender. The shifts transpired as the rhetoric utilized by social movements challenged specific ideographs—which stood as the building blocks of ideological assumptions—and integrated new meanings into those ideographs; hence social movement occurred. Such critiques by McGee led rhetoricians such as Malcolm Sillars (1980), Leland Griffin (1980), and Stephen Lucas (1980) to reassess the state of social movement research, especially research within their own rhetorical paradigm. Each in turn addressed that early work concerning social movements had fit more within a social scientific framework due to the focus on cycles and events; the research of rhetoricians like Bowers and Ochs even fit within such a framework. In an article published in the *Southern Speech Communication Journal*, Sillars (1980) addressed problems concerning methods for defining and analyzing social movements in past research, and sought to redefine social movements by "casting the widest net" rhetorically. In his article, Sillars noted significant problems with past research concerning social movements strategies, which had in turn led to the development of an inaccurate conceptualization of social movements. In particular, past research by Communication scholars, as well as social scientists, had focused solely on the strategies that took place at "major" events during the course of a movement (e.g., protests, marches), the intentions behind movement strategies, and the cause-effect impact of such strategies on attitudes and opinions. These problems emphasize a linear mode for conceptualizing social movements, which hold the potential to blind scholars to a variety of issues and elements within movements. For instance, if one conceptualizes the civil rights movement in terms of Smelser's theory of collective behavior, with speeches and protests spreading beliefs and mobilizing national actions, the internal divisions between different camps within the movement can easily be overlooked. Instead, Sillars suggests that movements should be defined in the widest sense, through observation of the multiple rhetorical strategies that are used to shape the "social environment." In the article, he does not suggest a total abandonment of major events and cause-effect impacts, but proposes that scholars also examine additional concepts that can shape perceptions on a topic within the social environment, such as nonverbal communication, interpersonal communication, performance, and written arguments. Such concepts often do not unfold according to the linear cause-effect framework that emerged from past research. Interestingly, Griffin (1980), who had first taken up the issue of social movements in 1952 and started the proverbial ball rolling, also worked toward a new definition of social movements in terms of discourse and meaning. In an article published in the *Central States Communication Journal*, he reassessed his original research concerning social movements. Instead of conceptualizing a social movement as a cycle marked by historical events, Griffin claimed that movements serve a dialectic function in society as they allow for debate about policies and institutions. Essentially, social movements and counter-movements, which respond to arguments developed by aggressor rhetoricians during the period of inception, engage in a discourse that expands the amount of information in society on a given topic.

In a similar vein to Sillars' and Griffin's articles that focused on redefining social movements, Stephen Lucas (1980) worked to establish a non-linear conceptualization of movements in an article published in the *Central States Speech Journal*. In that article, he called for reconciliation between the paradigms of rhetoric and social science, as both had lost sight of social movements and needed to realize that their research can complement one another. Lucas proposed that scholars from both paradigms examine movements by "explicating the cumulative metamorphosis of discourse in response to emerging exigencies imposed from within and without of the movement" (p. 263). Essentially, he called for researchers across both paradigms to recognize that social movements stood as a collection of different discourses that played out over time. Both camps should embrace the findings of the other and ask questions about the discourses that emerge in response to problems and challenges that arise within and around a movement. The work of Sillars, Griffin, and Lucas helped to shift the focus of research concerning social movements in the field of Communication away from phases and events and toward the discourses utilized by agents within movements that addressed the "social environment" and reacted to various exigencies; such discourse works to shift and transform prevailing ideographs in society about war, gender, and industry.

Later research by rhetoricians in the field of Communication reflected this shift in social movements studies. For instance, Charles Stewart (1980) demonstrated the different functions of rhetoric utilized by social movements in an essay published in the *Central States Speech Journal*. In that essay, Stewart claimed that rhetoric transformed perceptions about history and society, prescribed solutions for problems, and mobilized audiences to take action. Justin Gustainis and Dan Hahn (1988) examined the rhetorical strategies utilized by anti-Vietnam War protesters, many of which fell within Sillars "wider net" and focused beyond the major event and cause-effect oriented framework of past research. Anti-capitalist beliefs, nudist lifestyles, and drug use were all examined as rhetorical strategies employed by activists to change the social environment in regards to the war in Vietnam. Their research helped to dispel the notion that the anti-Vietnam War protests brought around the end of the war, as such strategies proved to be negative for the social environment and actually reinforced ideographs about American interventionism, as well as support for the Vietnam War. In an article published in the *Quarterly Journal of Speech*, Kathryn Olson and G. Thomas Goodnight (1994) demonstrated the role of social movements in building controversies that span both public and private spheres. In their essay, Olson and Goodnight illustrate how the arguments of anti-fur activists spawn responses from pro-fur advocates, providing more information to general audiences across the nation. The available information altered the social environment by extending the controversy from the private sphere, where people made consumer choices about fur, to the public sphere, where people's consumer choices are on display. Later, Donna Kowal (2000) worked to categorize the various rhetorical strategies utilized by activists of the American and British suffrage movements in an article published in *Communication Quarterly*. The two emergent categories, militant and adjustive, were based on Kowal's examination of major events such as marches and protests, as well as lifestyles of activists. Militant strategies are those major actions and activist lifestyles that are combative and confrontational in their approach to social change. Conversely, adjustive strategies are those major actions, interpersonal behaviors, and lifestyles that are "orderly" and do not (overtly) threaten authority figures. In her book *Peaceful Persuasion*, Ellen Gorsevski (2004) explained that strategic utterances that are often dismissed as "inarticulate" or "loose," such as graffiti or mass riots, construct a "rhetorical climate" that demands a response; the act of response constitutes the emergence of a social movement.

In the early years of social movement research, rhetoricians within the field of Communication first engaged the topic as Griffin examined the cycles of historical movements. Later, social scientists in the fields of Sociology and Social Psychology built on the framework of cycles by emphasizing behaviors and cause-effect relationships that occurred through various social movement phases. Such emphasis on phases and behavior dominated the focus of social movement research, including research conducted by rhetoricians like Bowers and Ochs. Finally, rhetoricians such as Sillars and Lucas worked to shift the emphasis of social movement research from phases and behavior to discourse and exigencies in the social environment. Such an emphasis dominated the study of social movements in the field of Communication until the 1990s. At that point, many within the field began to adopt the concepts of rhetoric, image, and identity in their research concerning "new social movements."

New Social Movements
The origin of the new social movement concept began with Alain Touraine (1978) in his book *The Voice and the Eye: An Analysis of Social Movements*. From Touraine's work, the term has come to describe contemporary social movements that work to shape political identities or challenge social roles and norms (e.g., DeLuca, 1999; Huesca, 2001; Touraine, 1978). Through activists' use of interactive technology, radical performance, and image politics such movements tend to be smaller, non-hierarchical, and more decentralized than the social movements that had been the subject of rhetorical and social scientific research throughout the 1960s, 1970s, and 1980s (DeLuca, 1999; Huesca, 2001; Shugart, 2005). In addition, such social movements tend to focus on the establishment of political identity, rather than on the creation or abolition of institutions in society as described by Griffin (1952).

In his book, Touraine, a Sociologist, described the emergence of the new social movements from the decline of "older" social movements that had focused on the rights of workers. The decline of older movements and emergence of new movements comes as Western society "shifts" from an industrial society defined by relationships of production (e.g., owners of industry and manual labor), towards a "programmed" society founded on education and the management of information within and between organizations. Earlier movements of the industrial society pressured authority figures in government to enact legislation that would address problems that stemmed from exploitation of workers that was often carried out by the state. Such movements began to decline as unions and other pressure groups for workers' rights became integrated into various economic institutions and government agencies. As these workers' rights-oriented movements faded away with the shift towards the programmed society of information management, other movements arose in their place, such as liberal movements that aimed to speak on behalf of the "voiceless" and populist movements that sought to stem the tides of national and international change. Eventually, Touraine claims that these new social movements emerged, which work as mechanisms that "denunciate power":

> The denunciation of power dismisses the image of society as a system, with its own language, or as an instrument of repression, and instead it chooses to set out from the event, i.e. the drama, the conflict, the clash of interests, and the sway of the dominator of the dominated who argues, resists, counterattacks or negotiates. (p. 21)

For Touraine, the new social movements of the post-industrial programmed society are those movements that work to address problems of power inequity in society. Professionals who hold particular knowledge about power structures in society, and are aware of the problems that stem from those structures, often organize such movements. In order to address those problems, these professionals work to build bridges with the very people who are forced to the "sidelines" of society by power inequities. The professionals within the new social movements are not so much concerned with the passing of legislation or material gains, as much as they are concerned with shaping political identity and lifestyles of those on the sidelines in order to make them more active participants in the fight against the power structure; such activity could be marching and protesting, or voting at the ballot box. As a social scientist, Touraine was interested in the "collective action of actors" who are "fighting for the social control of historicity" (p. 26) and cultural orientations. Essentially, his focus was on the actions carried out by new social movement actors in their efforts to shape political identity of audiences and onlookers.

Because of the emphasis on organization, structure, and social action by scholars like Touraine, few rhetoricians within the field of Communication looked to the concept of new social movements and their emphasis on political identity until the 1990s. In his book *Image Politics*, Keven DeLuca (1999) built on the previously discussed research of McGee (1975; 1980a; 1980b) as he critiqued the work of social scientists, such as Touraine and Alberto Melucci. Like Sillars before, DeLuca claimed that the social scientific framework of previous research concerning new social movements shifts academic attention away from the rhetorical strategies that social movement actors use to frame particular topics and influence the political identities of mainstream audiences. In particular, he was interested in the images used by activists to win over popular support and create polarization of an issue. In his book, DeLuca examined numerous images utilized by environmental activists—such as photographs featuring Green Peace activists confronting Soviet whaling ships—used to challenge traditional ideographs concerning industrialism and consumerism and affect the identity of mainstream audiences about issues such as whaling and logging. Later, other Communication scholars engaged in a similar study of image, such as Helene Shugart (2005), who examined the "coming out" of Ellen DeGeneres and Rosie O'Donnell as a form of "poster child politics." According to Shugart, the coming out of the two celebrities made both so-called poster children for the gay rights movement. O'Donnell proved to be a less affective poster child for the movement, as dominant narratives about her prior to coming out cast her as childlike and maternal. The combination of these two prior narratives with her coming out relegated the issue of gay adoption to the margins of the mainstream once more.

In addition to the emphasis on image, other rhetoricians in the field of Communication worked to address the efforts of new social movement activists to bridge the gaps between those with knowledge and those on the periphery of society by examining activist performance. For such Communication scholars, performance is conceptualized as mode for public discourse about social issues that draws attention while communicating the identity and knowledge of those who perform. Such performance can include, but is not limited to, oratory, informal speech, songs, dance, gestures, and play (Calafell, 2007; Conquergood, 1985; 1991; Denzin, 1997; Langellier, 1983). For instance, Phaedra Pezzullo (2003) conducted an ethnographic investigation of activist "tours" to marginalized communities, which was published in *Text and Performance Quarterly*. Specifically, Pezzullo took part in a series of bus tours sponsored by Sierra Club that took activists into a part of Louisiana called "Cancer Alley" that had been ravaged by poor environmental policies. In the essay, Pezzullo demonstrated how the drivers of the bus, along with the members of the marginalized communities of Cancer Alley, wove stories to the activists on the bus about crimes committed by corporations that poisoned the environment around various towns through which they travelled. The bus tour served an important role in bridging the communities and the activists, as the stories told by the bus drivers, activists, and communities members served as performances that constructed a shared memory for all. The shared memory emphasized all of those people who were missing in the communities due to cancers and illness from corporate negligence in the area, as well as what was present in the despoiled aftermath. In addition, Bernadette Calafell (2007) examined the role of Latina/o performance in the construction of bridges between multiple communities in her book *Latina/o Communication Studies*. One of her subjects was the performance of Robert Lopez, aka El Vez, a Latino Elvis Presley impersonator who attempts to shape audience perceptions about political issues like immigration through improvised Elvis songs and Elvis-like dance. Calafell found that the performance of El Vez involved the rhetorical strategies of disidentification and poaching. Through the simultaneous acceptance and rejection of certain racial stereotypes in his Elvis-like dance routine and songs (e.g., hypersexuality) El Vez is able to hide his critiques of political issues and power structures from certain audiences while emphasizing it to others. Conveniently, his poaching of the Elvis narrative provides a familiar backdrop for his disidentification, which helps to additionally camouflage his critique, and makes the message less hostile to those adverse audiences who might happen to pick up on the critique. Ultimately, his performance works to build a bridge between Latino/a diasporas so that they might build an understanding about the different power structures that keep them at the periphery of power in the United States.

Ultimately, the concept of the new social movement rose with Touraine's assessment of movements in the post-industrial age of the programmed society. With emphasis in society on the necessity for education and knowledge rather than production, movements began to emphasize political identity rather than legislative changes or policy. Similar to the research concerning the social movements from the 1950s to the 1980s, a rift developed between social scientists and rhetoricians on the topic of new social movements. For social scientists, including those social scientists within the field of Communication, the new social movements are a confluence of organization, structure, and social action. Conversely, rhetoricians, like DeLuca, claim that new social movements are constructed from the images and performances utilized by activists, which challenge and transform dominant ideographs in society. Interestingly, the rift is no longer between those within the field of Communication and the social scientists outside, but rather has become embedded within the field of Communication itself. I plan to address this rift, and how the concepts of alternative media and Resistance Performance can help to bridge that rift, in the final chapter of this book.

The Network Turn
Recent media and communication scholarship has adopted Evan's (1972) network concept in order to conceptualize the small, decentralized structure of new social movements (e.g., Arquilla & Ronfeldt, 2001; Castells, 1996; Best, 2005; Pickard, 2006a; 2006b; Stengrim, 2005). Through the network metaphor, new social movements have come to be conceptualized as diffused power structures where participants pass information to one another through multiple channels of communication to coordinate temporary communities that focus on accomplishing temporary goals. Such structures are referred to as *new social movement networks*, while the passing of information and building temporary communities is referred to as *networked activism*.

The network metaphor was first developed from the research of social scientists, such as William Evan (1972), who examined organizations and interorganizational communication in society. Evan categorized the three forms of networks, and thus organizations, that had emerged from experimental research concerning networks: the chain, the wheel, and the all-channel. In each case, lines of communication connect a series of nodes. The chain network involves a single string of communication that passes through each node in a line; such a network is similar to a bucket line that involves people passing water from one person to another, on down the line. The wheel network (also referred to as the star network) involves multiple nodes grouped around a single node; the lines of communication extend outward from the center node to the surrounding nodes. The all-channel is structured much like the wheel network, except that each node within a group has a line of communication to all other nodes. Ultimately, Evan claimed that the shape of the network affected the information circulated within and between organizations, which in turn could impact the efficiency of the organization. John Arquilla and David Ronfeldt (2001) later adopted the concept of network in their research concerning "netwars." In their edited volume *Networks and Netwars*, Arquilla and Ronfeldt explained how, under Evan's original classification of three forms, the all-channel network was a rarity within "traditional" organizations, as such networks are seldom dispersed or diverse enough to justify the use of such a form. However, the all-channel network has become more of a reality with the advent of the Internet and interactive media; such a network has become the optimal form for dispersed transnational groups. In particular, Arquilla and Ronfeldt claim that radical ideological organizations, like anarchists and terrorists, have been at the forefront of adopting the all-channel network as it functions like a headless beast that cannot be easily suppressed or dispersed by authorities. In addition, scholars such as Manuel Castells (1996; 2006) and Robert Huesca (2001) speculated about the role of new social movements in the "networked society." In his book *Power of Identity*, Castells (1996) addressed how new social movements have taken the forefront of shaping political identity due to deficiencies of traditional institutions that have arisen in the age of the networked society. According to Castells, the networked society has emerged at the end of the 20th century as interactive media has constructed "placeless" and "timeless" social spaces. Because of the asynchronous nature of interactive media, traditional institutions that are grounded in time and space, like the Democratic and Republican parties, no longer shape political identity. In the past, the time spent car-pooling to meetings and conventions shaped political identity just as much, if not more than, the platforms and messages of the two parties at those conventions. With the advent of interactive media, fewer people now engage in such identity shaping activities; one can easily watch both party conventions on YouTube in their pajamas. Instead, Huesca claims that many people now turn to new social movements, as small size and decentralized nature of such movements conforms to the placelessness and timelessness of the networked society.

The concept of new social movement networks was further developed by the research of Communication scholars such as Kirsty Best (2005), Laura Stengrim (2005), and Victor Pickard (2006a; 2006b). In an essay published in *Communication and Critical/Cultural Studies*, Best cited the concept of mesomobilization, which was first developed by Alan Scott and John Street (2001), as the foundation for what she called networked activism. Best explained mesomobilization as a multitude of different groups that come together for a single purpose; such a process, she said, was characteristic of the contemporary "globalization movement." When one looks at major actions such as the 1999 WTO protests in Seattle or the 2003 FTAA protests in Miami one sees a variety of different groups, each dedicated to a different cause, that come together for one similar issue. Essentially, this is the basis for networked activism, in which "networks of networks" begin to emerge:

> Individual protests draw in a variety of participants, and websites such as Protest.net act as hubs of interest, action and information. By forming provisional collective projects, the globalization movement activates temporary, local forms of communication that maintain agonism between different interpretations, while extending a logic of identity which, as many critics have pointed out, tends to be overly particularized. (p. 227)

According to Best, websites provide activists information about protests and other such events. Protests and activist events become the focal points for the construction of collective, yet agonistic identities of resistance. Networked activism entails the process of activists reaching beyond their immediate organizations, and often beyond their immediate communities, to other organizations that share a few similar beliefs or opinions on an issue. In this way, the different organizations are able to build a collective identity that is pluralistic because of their similar conceptualizations of the issues. Such pluralism allows for new social movements to be more democratic, as described by Huesca. However, the differing interpretations associated with individual groups often create agonisms, or political conflicts that can disrupt long-term communities of resistance. For that reason, the networks of networks often address only temporary goals (like organizing a protest against one institution) rather than long-term goals for the future (like establishing an altogether new institution).

In addition, Stengrim (2005) and Pickard (2006a; 2006b) have advanced the concept of new social movement networks through their critical examinations of the Indymedia network.[4] In an article published in *Communication and Critical/Cultural Studies*, Stengrim (2005) claimed that the multiple Indymedia sites operated around the globe are integral to new social movements, as they enable "activists to appropriate the technologies of globalization to promote access to citizen produced content" (p. 283), which allows for citizen-centered manufacture of information and culture. Through such a process, activists can construct a democratic dialogue that challenges corporate media power. Along a similar vein, Pickard (2006a) examined the various narratives of democratic dialogue circulated through the Indymedia network in an essay published in *Media, Culture and Society*. In that article,

Pickard found that there were two themes associated with the narratives that activists posted on Indymedia sites and in listservs: "be the media" and "principles of unity." Both themes were so vague and broad that a wide variety of different activists felt welcomed into the network and, in turn, became involved in the network; such access and involvement provided those activists with a sense of trust and loyalty for their fellow activists and the larger network. Pickard (2006b) also provided a valuable critique of the Indymedia network in an essay published in *Critical Studies in Media Communication*, in which he illustrated problems, or "tyrannies," associated with the interactive technology of the website. Pickard (2006b) claimed that the rigid ideologies of activists, elites masked by structuralessness, and the tensions that emerge from vague editorial policies can limit the network's ability to "level all hierarchies" (p. 23) inside and outside of a network.

Ultimately, the emergence of the network metaphor helped to illustrate new social movements as a collection of nodes connected by lines of communication, usually the Internet, which aids in the decentralization and small size described by Castells and Huesca. Likewise, the metaphor contributes to the concept of mesomobilization, which gives rise to the networked activism described by Best. As the concepts of network and networked activism have taken the forefront in the study of new social movements and the politics of resistance, it has become increasingly important to examine the interactive technologies and media that are integral for networked activism. Although those technologies and media have not become the focus of research in the field of Communication, other scholars have taken an interest in such topics. Most notably, in the fields of Journalism and Media Studies, scholars have engaged in rigorous research concerning alternative media.

Alternative Media

The term alternative media has proven to be slippery at best. Over the years, researchers have examined different aspects of alternative media. Starting in the early 1980s, David Armstrong (1981) explored the rise of alternative media from the politics of social movements, while John Downing (1984) profiled different alternative media around the world. Later, scholars in the fields of Journalism and Media Studies worked to address the shifting forms of alternative media, as well as the politics of production. Recently, Communication scholars have taken an interest in alternative media, usually in regards to interactivity and rhetorical strategies utilized in interactive formats online.

David Armstrong's (1981) book *A Trumpet to Arms* stands as one of the first attempts to study alternative media. In the book, Armstrong, a former editor for the *Berkley Barb* and writer for KPFA radio in Berkley, chronicles the "underground press" from 1964 to the late 1970s, as well as its role as a kind of bullhorn for social movements. The book focuses on alternative magazines, radio stations, novels, and independent films that emerged during the turbulent era of the '60s and '70s. Throughout the book, he explains the political perspectives espoused by different alternative media titles and the personalities who produced them. According to Armstrong, writers and artists such as Max Scherr, Ken Kesey, Robert Crumb, and Gloria Steinem were integral in the development of "underground" magazines and newspapers such as *Rat, Zap, Berkley Barb, Mother Jones,* and *Off Our Backs*, as well as radio stations like KPFA and WBAI in New York. The creative personalities behind the alternative media acted as voices that helped to mobilize particular social movements in America, such as the free speech and Yippie movement, anti-Vietnam war movement, and women's liberation. One of Armstrong's numerous examples included his explanation of the history of early feminist magazines in the United States. He explained how Mary King and Casey Hayden, two feminist activists in the "peace and freedom movements," circulated a letter to numerous women in 1965 that explained the problematic and oppressive marginalization of women within social movements, like the movement against the war in Vietnam. The letter created a firestorm that sparked many feminist activists to collaborate on various alternative publications like *Off Our Backs* and *It Ain't Me Babe*, which featured exclusive stories about women taking prominent roles in politics and scathing reviews of male political figures. Later, John Downing (1984) offered his own examination of alternative media by profiling print publications and radio stations around the world in his book *Radical Media*. The profiles written by Downing included basic information concerning the location, date of inception, number of staff, circulation, finance, and in the case of magazines and newspapers, how often the title appeared (e.g., weekly, bi-monthly). Downing also provided information about the content, as he included a basic thematic analysis of the topics and issues that tended to be the focus of each alternative media title. In all, *Radical Media* profiled fourteen alternative publications, film companies, and radio stations around the United States and Europe. Ultimately, Armstrong's and Downing's research stands as the first significant work to understand the alternative media, a subject that had long been neglected. Together, they demonstrated the important role of alternative media in social movements and provided a surface understanding of what constitutes alternative media; namely, print and radio content developed by social movement actors.

Journalism and Media Studies
The early work of Armstrong and Downing set the stage for the research concerning alternative media that would emerge in the fields of Journalism and Media Studies. The first to take on the task of building on the research of the 1980s was in fact John Downing, when he teamed up with Tamara Ford, Genève Gil, and Laura Stein to write an updated version of *Radical Media* in

2001. The work of Downing and company preceded important research published by Journalism and Media scholars like Chris Atton (2002a; 2002b; 2003; 2004), Graham Meikle (2002), John Caldwell (2003), and Jennifer Rauch (2007). Such research within the fields of Journalism and Media Studies often involved sophisticated discussions concerning (1) how best to define alternative media and (2) the processes and politics of alternative media production.

Defining Alternative Media. In the updated version of *Radical Media*, Downing, Ford, Gil, and Stein (2001) build on the profiles presented in the earlier version by incorporating theories of power and hegemony, which give rise to a broad "tapestry" of alternative media in a variety of different forms. In the book, Downing et al. explain that alternative media is not merely a voice for social movements, but also a form of resistance to hegemonic power structures in society. It is true that such resistance often involves the political presence of social movements. However, resistance cannot be limited to movements, as resistance to hegemony can be carried out in the daily lives of ordinary people, which can aid in the production of a broad tapestry of different alternative media. Downing et al. explain that this tapestry can entail print and radio, like those alternative media profiled in the 1984 version of the book, as well as songs, graffiti, street theatre, dress, and "mind bombs" like woodcuts and murals. Essentially, alternative media represents a response to oppressive and hegemonic power by activists, and a creative outlet for marginalized people; the alternative media exist in whatever formats are available to the producers. For instance, Downing et al. cite the Mothers of Plaza de Mayo, a group of Argentinean women who had lost their children during the military junta of the late 1970s. In order to keep the public memory of the missing alive, the women would converge at the Plaza de Mayo wearing diapers as head scarves and holding photos of their missing children. In the face of the oppressive military junta, such actions constituted a means for the mothers to keep the public memory of their lost children alive; the diapers and photographs were the only resources available to the women. In this way, media become "alternative" whenever they provide a form of resistance.

John Caldwell (2003) further complicated the definition of alternative media in his ethnographic study published in *Media, Culture and Society* about "media on the margins" used in migrant worker camps of southern California. In his article, Caldwell described his work to introduce alternative media to the Latino workers in the camps situated near some of the most expensive homes in southern California. The goal of the project had been to provide the workers with media equipment so that they could produce materials that would give voice to their marginalized position, thus making them more visible in the political economy of southern California. Interestingly, Caldwell found that many of the workers had in fact cobbled together their own "alternative media" from VHS and audio equipment poached from the garbage cast out of the nearby opulent homes. Within the community, the workers circulated video and cassette tapes that featured subject matters like "media marketing" and "domestic pet care" that they had found in the discarded garbage of the nearby elites. Such materials helped the workers to gain a better understanding of the cultural borders around them and their employers who lived across those borders. In this case, alternative media functioned in the way that Downing et al. had described in 2001, as the Latino workers utilized poached media equipment in their efforts to not only resist hegemony, but to understand the power structures that lived just next door. For Caldwell, media are "alternative" when they are used by traditionally marginalized groups to understand oppressive power structures or to gain voice in society.

Chris Atton's books *Alternative Media* (2002a) and *An Alternative Internet* (2004), as well as Graham Meikle's (2002) book *Future Active*, provided additional insight into the definition of alternative media. Atton and Meikle both veer away from the broad tapestry of alternative media developed by Downing et al. and Caldwell, while also avoiding the more rigid definition that developed from Armstrong's and Downing's earlier work of the 1980s. Instead, they approached alternative media as tendencies and "potential approaches available to any media outlet" (Meikle, p. 60). The term alternative media is a reference to practices in which media producers maintain independence from large media conglomerates and promote "horizontal linkages between their audiences" (Meikle, p. 60). As Atton (2002a) explained, the alternative media "typically go beyond simply providing a platform for radical or alternative points of view: they emphasize the organization of media to enable wider social participation in their creation, production and dissemination than is possible for mass media" (p. 25) Although such tendencies apply to print and radio, both scholars were particularly interested in the Internet, as that medium had not been seriously addressed in past alternative media research. According to Meikle, the capacity for interactivity associated with the Internet created greater potential for producers of websites, such as Indymedia, to engage in those approaches. Essentially, these tendencies lead to alternative media content—in print, radio, and the Internet—that is characterized by a multiplicity of voices that are typically pushed out of the mainstream media, which espouse dissonant or radical views about society and social issues. Websites like Indymedia and McSpotlight, radio stations like Radio B92 in Serbia, and zines like SchNEWS are independently run media outlets that appear to audiences as a mosaic of voices that are not typically represented in the mainstream, often engaged in dissonant dialogue. In this sense, the processes of production, as well as the content that is produced, make media "alternative."

One of the more recent studies that provided a definition for alternative media has been the research of Jennifer Rauch (2007) published in the journal *Media Culture and Society*, which explored the interpretive strategies used by audiences to read alternative media. In her research, Rauch demonstrated how activists' interpretive strategies—a concept developed by Stanley Fish (1980a; 1980b) and extended to audience research by Thomas Lindloff (1988)—shaped whether media were "mainstream" or "alternative." Essentially, Rauch argued that alternative media is not so much an issue of content or the organizational practices of production, as much as it is the interpretive strategies through which audiences read it and experience pleasure in building distinctions between mainstream and alternative media. For audiences, media are alternative when they read it as divergent from the mainstream. In her article, Rauch cited examples of audiences who read news produced by traditional agencies like the British Broadcasting Company (BBC) as alternative, while they read news published by the New York Times and MSNBC as mainstream. For Rauch, the media take the form of "alternative" because of the interpretive strategies used by the audience to read the text.

Ultimately, the early research presented by Armstrong and Downing presented a rigid picture of alternative media as media produced by social movement actors. Later, Journalism and Media scholars worked from the assumption that such a definition was a good start, but required greater attention to additional factors. Downing, Ford, Gil, and Stein returned to the topic and provided a much broader definition steeped in issues of power and resistance. Caldwell defined alternative media in terms of function, while Rauch's definition of alternative media rested with the audience. Atton and Meikle provided a definition that was based on the organization of the media production, which blurred the line between audience and producer and held important implications for the alternative media content. Ultimately, this attention to organizational factors led many Journalism and Media scholars to place enormous emphasis on the processes of production.

Production. Atton and Meikle both emerged at the forefront of research concerning alternative media production as their definition of the subject focused on organizational tendencies. According to Atton (2002a), alternative media are not produced in what Jurgen Habermas (1974; 1989) called the public and private spheres, but are instead relegated to a "ghetto sphere." Atton claims that corporate conglomerates have taken control of the private sphere, which inherently corrupts the discourse of mainstream news that is circulated in the public sphere. Consequently, producers of alternative media, particularly zines, operate within a sphere that, although public, is "underdeveloped" because of a lack of available resources; corporate conglomerates have accumulated most of those resources, while low circulation of alternative publications leave producers economically strained. The strain forces alternative publications to rely on a number of organizational tactics such as decentralization of production, anti-copyright policies, and reliance on "movement intellectuals." The decentralization of production allows for multiple people to play important roles simultaneously (e.g., editor and writer), so that as circumstances develop different people can step up and fill in any voids in the process that might develop from week to week or month to month. Producers also embrace "anti-copyright" policies, in which the producers encourage readers to photocopy and circulate the publications without permission. In addition, producers utilize content written by what Atton calls "movement intellectuals" such as Hakim Bey and Noam Chomsky, who are widely recognized across academia and by activists involved in a variety of new social movements. The writing of these intellectuals provides a high level of credibility because of their connection to academic circles, while simultaneously ensuring increased sales because of their popularity in new social movements. When alternative media producers effectively use these tactics, Atton claims that the ghetto sphere can be transformed into an "alternative public sphere" in which public address and debate about social issues is conducted independent of the corporate controlled private sphere and the corrupted public sphere.

Research concerning alternative media has also engaged in detailed examinations of open publishing technologies associated with what Atton (2004) calls an "alternative Internet." According to Atton, websites that engage in different approaches to "doing media" and offer up content that stands in contrast to the status quo constitute the alternative Internet. These websites may not actually present politically charged content, but their manner of collecting and circulating information construct a process and content that are alternative to the mainstream of corporate conglomerates. According to Meikle (2002), the Internet has moved through two phases that he calls version 1.0 and version 2.0. Internet 1.0 constitutes fully interactive, or "intercreative," websites that utilize open publishing technologies that allow for audience feedback and co-production of the sites, such as Indymedia.org. Internet 2.0, on the other hand, are websites that are not intercreative as they do not utilize open publishing, and emphasize instead the marketing of products and political candidates to mass audiences. Essentially, Meikle sees the evolution of the Internet as "backing into the future" in which corporations and traditional institutions have eliminated the intercreative qualities in order to control content and messages. Conversely, new social movement activists have embraced Internet 1.0 sites for two primary reasons. First, the open publishing technologies of 1.0 websites provide an opportunity for the activists to voice opinions that would not otherwise make it into mainstream media. Second, the engagement with open technologies helps activists to feel that they are involved in some kind of demonstration against corporate and government power structures. It is important to note that both Atton (2002a; 2004) and Meikle (2002) claim that taking part in open publishing and what Atton calls "radical online journalism" allows activists to be involved in movement politics in ways that they cannot through traditional political parties and institutions. The act of engagement with websites via open publishing and radical online journalism represent a transformational action that shapes the nature of protest from mass mobilization to the circulation of information and construction of knowledge, which in turn shapes the political identity of the participants. Atton and Meikle have not been alone in their examination of alternative websites. In *Contesting Media Power* (2003), a volume edited by Nick Couldry and James Curran, several Journalism and Media scholars came together to explore resistance to corporate controlled media and alternative media. For instance, Downing (2003a) claims that the production of news through Indymedia has been governed by three principles of socialist anarchism: disengagement from institutions, an anti-capitalist spirit, and an emphasis on involvement through direct action. James Curran (2003) explained the benefits associated with online journalism: lower costs, global readership, and avoidance of "market gatekeepers."

In addition, many Journalism and Media scholars have explored the production of alternative websites as an activist tactic designed to protest topics or disrupt the logic of dominant power structures in various books and edited volumes. In the edited volume *Cyberactivism* (2003), scholars such as Sandor Vegh, Larry Elin, and Maria Garrido and Alexander Halavais weigh in on the tactical value of alternative publications and websites. Vegh classified "hacktivism," or online activism, by three forms: advocacy of ideas and issues, mobilization for protests, and online actions like hijacking web traffic through fake websites and defacing websites. Elin claims that alternative websites constitute a gateway that helps ordinary citizens to access "virtual political communities" of activism, in which people learn new forms of social capital associated with social justice activism. The social capital that people learn in the virtual communities can be transferred to the physical world, and constitutes the basis for their worldviews concerning institutions like the WTO. Garrido and Halavais illustrated how the Zapatista movement of Chiapas, Mexico, utilized the Internet after their 1994 uprising in order to build an international "social network." The alternative websites created by the Zapatistas and their sympathizers not only allow for the movement to tell its story to international audiences, but it also allows for the movement to attain "closeness" to human rights and global support organizations.

Communication
Some Communication scholars have begun to explore the concept of media activism over the past decade, although few of those studies have referred to the concept of alternative media. Instead, these Communication scholars have focused their attention on "activist websites" and "media activism." For instance, Lynn Owens and Kendall Palmer (2003) published an essay in *Critical Studies in Media Communication* that examined the phenomenon of "funneling" associated with activist websites. According to Owens and Palmer, acts of vandalism and violence committed by anarchists often attract

attention from the mainstream media. Such mainstream media attention was often negative yet vague, which led mainstream audiences to use online search engines in order to access information about the anarchists, thus "funneling" them to anarchist websites like Infoshop. In a later article published in *Critical Studies in Media Communication*, Christine Harold (2004) examined the concept of "pranking rhetoric" and its role in media activism. According to Harold, pranking is a form of rhetorical protest in which activists appropriate and redirect the tools of commercial media. Such protest rises above the parody associated with mock advertisements circulated through alternative forums like *Adbusters* magazine, as "pranks" are designed to draw media attention and disrupt the authority of those who control the corporations that own such media. For instance, the Biotic Baking Brigade would throw pies in the faces of industry leaders (e.g., Milton Friedman, Bill Gates), which would immediately draw the gaze of news cameras and journalists. Such an action disrupts the authority of those industry leaders, and thus, momentarily, disrupts the logic of the free market for audiences who witness the action in mainstream news. In addition, Barbara Warnick's (2007) book *Rhetoric Online* explores the concepts of interactivity and intertextuality as integral characteristics associated with activist websites like MoveOn.org, JibJab.com, and the *Adbusters* website. The interactivity of some of these sites allowed audience involvement in the creation and circulation of certain political messages. In addition, intertextual strategies, such as parody, allowed producers to fuse multiple texts, and multiple political situations and problems, into a single message; such strategies allow for producers to target multiple audiences at once.

Over the past decade, Communication scholars have conducted research concerning the rhetoric of pranking, the interplay between mainstream media and activist websites, and the interactive/intertextual characteristics of "activist media" and "media activism." Such research has provided valuable insights concerning the role of media in new social movements, but has largely been disconnected from the research concerning alternative media conducted by scholars in the fields of Journalism and Media Studies. If the field of Communication is to play an important role in the study of media utilized by new social movements, it is important to build a body of literature that brings together and synthesizes the concepts of new social movement, networks, and alternative media.

Definitions and Arguments

Over the years, Communication scholars such as Huesca, Best, DeLuca, and Pezzullo have taken the forefront of social movement studies, as they have explored the rhetoric of image in new social movements and the dynamics of networked activism. Meanwhile, Journalism and Media Studies scholars such as Atton, Downing, and Meikle have made significant contributions to the study of the alternative media utilized by contemporary political and social movements that often resist or contest policies concerning "globalization." In their research, Journalism and Media scholars have explored the features of alternative media, as well as the processes of alternative media production. Headway has been made in the exploration of alternative media within the field of Communication, as scholars such as Owens and Palmer, Harold, and Warnick have examined the characteristics found on the activist websites and the rhetorical strategies utilized by activists engaged in consciousness-raising. However, little has been done to actually bridge these similar lines of research. The remaining chapters in this book synthesize concepts of new social movement networks, networked activism, performance, and alternative media in order to illustrate a humanistic Communication perspective of Resistance Performance. Such a perspective can stand as a common bridge between the fields of Communication, Journalism, and Media Studies that illustrates the role of alternative media in the construction of communicative performances of political resistance against dominant power structures in contemporary society.

New Social Movement Networks and Performance
The following chapters entail the following assumptions about new social movements: (1) that new social movements exist as networks and (2) activism entails rhetorical performance.

New social movement networks. Corresponding with past research in the field of Communication, the following chapters assume that new social movements exist as networks in which activists build temporary communities around broad narratives (Huesca, 2001; Best, 2005; Pickard, 2006a; 2006b; Stengrim, 2005). Essentially, activists work within organizations that are dedicated to one or two social justice issues, often working to circulate a broad narrative about those issues. Social justice organizations often learn about one another, and where they stand on particular issues through the circulation of these broad narratives. Such social justice organizations will occasionally converge with other social justice organizations that are dedicated to similar, yet different, social justice issues in order to stage a unified protest against some institution or entity that has presented a threat to the broad narratives circulated by the social justice organizations.

Activism and performance. The following chapters also correspond to past Communication research concerning the concept of performance (Conquergood, 1985; 1991; Denzin, 1997; Langellier, 1983) and the role of performance in new social movement activism (Calafell, 2007; Pezzullo, 2003). The strategies of promulgation, solidification, and polarization discussed by Bowers and Ochs (1971) emerge in new social movements as performances. Marches, songs, dancing, graffiti, and theatre are all activist performances that are used to engage in a public discourse about issues of social justice in society, as well as to create bridges between their organizations and surrounding communities. These performances demonstrate to observers the political identity of the activists, as well as the activists' knowledge about particular social justice issues. Ultimately, the performances coalesce into image events (DeLuca, 1999), which can be photographed and circulated in order to draw widespread attention to a social justice issue and potentially challenge dominant ideographs in society.

Alternative Media
Throughout the following chapters, media are determined to be "alternative" if they adhere to one of three definitions that have been established in past Journalism and Media Studies literature: (1) alternative content, (2) interpretive strategies of audiences, and/or (3) alternative production.

Alternative Content and Interpretive Strategies. In terms of the first two definitions, many of the alternative media titles covered in this book entail content produced by non-commercial entities that entail written texts, photographs, audio and video that challenge power structures and attempt to transform social roles. The term typically includes websites such as CounterPunch.org, radio programs such as *Democracy Now!*, and print publications such as magazines like *Adbusters* and anarchist zines like *After the Fall*. I note that such titles are "typically" alternative, as the interpretive strategies utilized by the audience to read such media play an important role. Audiences may not recognize certain titles as challenging power structures, while others do. For this reason, radio programs such as NPR's *All Things Considered* or magazines such as *The Nation*, which are more commercially oriented and hierarchically structured than the previously mentioned titles, can constitute alternative media. Therefore, many of the alternative media that appear throughout the book are those that are recognized by audiences to have themes about challenging power structures and transforming social roles.

Production. In terms of the final definition, many of the titles described in the following chapters also correspond to past research in Journalism and Media Studies concerning the production of alternative media. Specifically, many of the alternative media titles described herein are produced independently of corporate media conglomerates, and often under economically constrained conditions. Because of conglomerate independence and economic strain, the alternative media producers typically utilize two primary strategies: content from movement intellectuals and audience input to supplement content (Atton, 2002a; 2004; Curran, 2003; Meikle, 2002). First, alternative publications and websites often rely on content that is submitted by movement intellectuals like Hakim Bey and Noam Chomsky who can provide high quality material. Such figures are recognized across different new social movements, social justice organizations, and academic fields, which guarantees large audiences. In addition, producers utilize the Internet in order to solicit content from audiences either directly into the title (as in the case of Indymedia.org), as running commentary about previously produced content (as in the case of Commondreams.org), or to solicit articles and letters to the editor that can be published in a print form (as in the case of *Adbusters* and *Z Magazine*). The alternative media title, then, highlights content written/created by a movement intellectual and is supplemented by additional content written/created by activist audiences.

Utilizing the concepts of new social movement networks and activist performance Chapter 2 explains the concept of Resistance Performance, which illustrates the emergence of new social movement networks as sites for the performance of political resistance against dominant power structures in society. Chapter 3 explores the role of alternative media content in the convergence of multiple sites of political performance, as well as the role of alternative media production in the construction of those sites. Chapters 4-5 examine the content of alternative media used by activists in past research, and explain the role of different alternative media titles and their specific themes in the construction of communicative performances of resistance within activist networks. Finally, Chapter 6 provides insights and commentary about the "alternative media world" that emerges from Resistance Performance. The final chapter of the book describes the implications of the Resistance Performance concept for research concerning social movements, new social movements and alternative media.

Chapter 2
Resistance Performance

The following chapter provides:

1) An introduction to the Spectacle/Performance Paradigm (SPP) followed by arguments for an Audience Performance Paradigm (APP), and the need for this paradigm in alternative media and new social movement research.

2) The foundations of Resistance Performance (RP): concepts of power found in alternative media content and the divergent worldviews of activists.

3) A detailed explication of three initial categories that give rise to RP: Critical Worldviews, Alternative Media Interactions, and Communicative Resistance.

4) An illustration of the emergent "Multiplex" of coordinated performance, which interconnects RP within a community.

Audience and Performance

Integral to the conceptualization of the role of alternative media in new social movement networks is the concept of audience performance. Audience research has moved through three distinctive phases over the decades: effects based Behavioral Paradigm, meaning-oriented Incorporation/Resistance Paradigm, and performance based Spectacle/Performance Paradigm. Each of these phases have been explicated and described in detail by Nicholas Abercrombie and Brian Longhurst in their book *Audiences* (1998) and by Andy Ruddock in his book *Understanding Audiences* (2001). The Behavioral Paradigm (BP) emerged from a multitude of media effects studies that approached the media and audience from a "stimulus-response" perspective. The BP assumes direct or limited effects of media messages on audiences, which are a collection of individuals. Examples of BP conceptualizations of audience can be found in early research concerning two-step flow and limited media effects (e.g., Lazarsfeld, Berelson, & Gaudet, 1949), as well as later cultivation research (e.g., Gerbner, Gross, Morgan, & Singorelli, 1980a; 1980b). Such effects driven research has often been criticized because of the apparent lack of audience agency embedded within the paradigm (e.g., Gitlin, 1978; Hall, 1980). These critiques gave rise to what Abercrombie and Longhurst called the Incorporation/Resistance Paradigm. According to Abercrombie and Longhurst:

> The Incorporation/Resistance paradigm defines the problem of audience research as whether audience members are incorporated in the dominant ideology by their participation in media activity or whether, to the contrary, they are resistant to that incorporation. (p. 15)

Researchers working under the assumptions of IRP focused on the ways in which audiences interpret or "read" media texts and how audiences reconstruct and reinforce dominant ideologies through such interpretation and reading. Reader-response, encoding/decoding, and cultural studies are all theories that have emerged from research conducted under the assumptions of the IRP conceptualization of audiences. For instance, Stuart Hall (1980) and John Fiske (1987) addressed the different ways in which audiences could "read" and make sense of mediated texts (preferred, negotiated, oppositional, or resistive readings). In addition, scholars such as Thomas Lindloff (1988) and David Machin and Michael Carrithers (1996) utilized Stanley Fish's (1980a; 1980b) concept of the interpretive community to address the strategies that audiences use to construct, or encode, meaning within mediated texts. Such positions addressed the primary problem associated with the BP, by providing audiences with their own agency for meaning making in their relations with media.

However, IRP was not without criticism, as postmodern scholars began to question the importance of consumption and pleasure in the audience experience. Cultural studies scholars such as Ien Ang (1985), Henry Jenkins (1992), and Joli Jensen (1992) have argued that interpretive, or IRP, visions of audience usually envision the enthusiastic "fans" of television programs and movies as unfortunate individuals who have been deceived or fooled by the ideological and hegemonic forces circulated and reinforced through the media. Ruddock (2001) contends that postmodern scholars have, in turn, viewed such enthusiastic fans as the core for "fan cultures" that develop around programs like *Dallas* or *Star Trek*. Such fan cultures constitute "parasocial" worlds that are constructed, not only by the media content, but also through pleasurable activities on the part of the fans. Writing "fan literature" and attending fan conventions are activities that postmodernists claim are largely ignored under IRP, and they need to be examined in order to understand the role of media in the "everyday life" of audiences in contemporary society. Such activities are important, as they allow audiences to take media content and utilize it in ways that are outside the dominant ideologies in society, even though many of those dominant ideologies are embedded within the content.

Spectacle Performance

In order to address the problems of consumption and pleasure, scholars began to view audiences in terms of their relationship with performances found in the media, as well as audiences' performances within the context of the spectacles around them. Abercrombie and Longhurst (1998) engaged in an examination of research situated from this new perspective and declared the emergent paradigm of audience research the Spectacle/Performance Paradigm (SPP).

The concept of spectacle was pioneered by Guy Debord in his book *The Society of the Spectacle* (1967) and his later *Comments on the Society of the Spectacle* (1988). Inherent in Debord's writing is the idea that everything in society is presented to people in the form of images and fable-like narratives that become infused into the fabric of "everyday life." Images and fables that are constructed for the purpose of capitalist enterprises gather together and combine into spectacles that attract the gaze of observers. Such a process of infusion frames both the human body and inanimate objects in the media as engaged in elaborate performances that should be gazed on and possessed. As bodies and objects in the media become perceived as performance, they become spectacles as well; such bodies and objects stand as a continual display of surfaces for the pleasure of audiences, often with little or no detail present. In this way, all bodies and objects across capitalist societies have the potential to become spectacles themselves. In a sense, the spectacles that play out in the media teach the audience how to view the world, how to take pleasure in the world, and how to perform. Images take the forefront in everyday life, while life seems to be altered and warped into artwork that can be possessed and, in fact, consumed. In his book *Subculture*, Dick Hebdige (1979) built on Debord by explaining how fashion and styles found in popular culture, clothing trends, music, and movies play an important role in the development of youth cultures within the spectacle-laden world. According to Hebdige, young people take bits and pieces of spectacles swirling about society and use them to carve out subcultures in which they can build and express identities that they feel are their own. Examples of such spectacle-oriented identity in society would be children who demand *Star Wars* birthday cakes that feature Yoda instead of Obi-Wan Kenobi, school children who choose the Power Puff Girl backpack over the Barbie backpack, young women who style their hair just like Jennifer Aniston in *Friends*, and young men who search out clothes similar to those worn by Brad Pitt in *Fight Club*.

Ultimately, the concept of spectacle has aided in research concerning topics such as the construction of landscape and cityscape and the role of celebrities in fan culture. In the case of landscape/cityscape, William Sadler and Ekateriana Haskins (2005) illustrated how the images of landmarks like the Statue of Liberty, districts like Times Square, and living and working spaces in New York City that were circulated through television programs like *Seinfeld* create a "postcard effect" that draws the tourists' gaze. The images of landmarks anchor the program to a particular location (e.g., New York), and the districts and living/working spaces frame the fables and narratives that emerge during the course of the program. The result is a spectacle that stands as the New York cityscape, a place that people want to possess and consume. In regards to celebrity or stardom, Nick Couldry (2000; 2003) addressed the distinction between two disparate worlds that have arisen due to the advent of broadcast media: the media world and the ordinary world. The media world is the place that is deemed by people to be special because it is the culmination of sites where movie and news producers have fixed the gaze of their cameras, and subsequently directed the gaze of society. Conversely, the ordinary world is the boring place, where average people pump gas, go to work, and raise their children. The separation of the media world and the ordinary world is maintained through a series of media rituals on the part of audiences; none are quite as important as the rituals associated with celebrity/stardom. Celebrities gain their position because they have been on television programs, in the movies, or the subject of news reports, which are all sites that are the media world; the attention of all of those eyes and cameras make the celebrities special. Because of their specialness, then, those celebrities are accorded certain rituals by the people from the ordinary world when the two come into contact. Signing autographs and posing for photographs are all rituals that take place, which reinforce the specialness of the celebrity, and the distinction between the bland ordinary world and the spectacle-laden media world.

Performance, the second concept associated with SPP, in large part emerged from the dramaturgical perspective pioneered by Erving Goffman. In his books *Presentation of the Self in Everyday Life* (1956), *Behavior in Public Places* (1963), and *Relations in Public* (1971) Goffman described the social behaviors of people in terms of dramas that unfold on the stage. In this way, interactions with other people and institutions constitute a performance, which Goffman defined as "all activity of an individual which occurs during a period marked by his continuous presence before a particular set of observers and which has some influence on the observers" (Goffman, 1956, p. 19); this very definition of performance was cited by Abercrombie and Longhurst in their formation of SPP. From this perspective, interactions as performance entail tactics and strategies necessary to draw the gaze of observers, as well as to gain compliance of any observers of a performance. In his book *Verbal Art as Performance*, Richard Bauman (1977) noted the different verbal components of performance such as figurative language, parallelism, and appeal to tradition serve as strategies that could be used to draw attention to the performer and gain compliance from observers. In addition, scholars who explored the concept of performance also turned to cultural studies in order to build on the research of Goffman and others. In his books *Performance Theory* (1977) and *Future of Ritual* (1993) Richard Schechner explained that the postcolonial world is a place in which "cultures are colliding, interfering with, and fertilizing each other" (Schechner, 1993, p. 21); performance in this context stands as an expression of cultural and individual identity. Scholars who worked from such a cultural studies perspective, such as Judith Butler (1990) and Vivian Patraka (1996; 1999), incorporated the human body and space in their conceptualizations of performance. The movement of the body, coupled with verbal acts such as narrative, illustrates immediacy, presence, absence, the past, and the future. In essence, the co-performances of people in everyday life aid in the social construction of reality described by Peter Berger and Thomas Luckman (1966); performance helps people to understand the world and themselves. For instance, Pezzullo (2003), whose research was discussed in Chapter 1, explored the role of performance in activist bus tours of "Cancer Alley." Sitting together on the bus, telling tales and listening to the tales of members of the various communities in Cancer Alley, helped to construct a shared memory of what had happened to that stretch of Louisiana, a memory shared by the activists and the communities.

The notion of SPP has provided an excellent account of the performances of audience in "everyday life" and made significant contributions to debates and research concerning mainstream audiences' interactions with mainstream media and performance (e.g., Couldry, 2004; Downing, 2003b; Gray, 2005; Hills, 2005; Holmes, 2004; Kellner, 1995; Longhurst, Bagnall, & Savage, 2004; Murphy & Kraidy, 2003; Sandvoss, 2005). Within the SPP, spectacle and narcissism are interwoven with the notion of the "diffused audience," which is significantly different from "simple" or "mass audiences." A simple audience is one that is structured in the sense that there are fixed roles for the audience and the media performers. The simple audience's attendance at a performance constitutes a kind of ceremony, which implies an amount of physical and social distance between the audience and the performance that plays out before them on stage or screen. An example of a simple audience would be when a person attends the premiere of a film and sits quietly in their seat watching the narrative unfold. In this scenario, the audience member adheres to their fixed role of audience, separate from the performance of actors that plays out on the screen. A mass audience is an audience that is removed from performances in society because they take place in the distance. Instead of a ceremonial attendance of the performance as in the case of the simple audience, the mass audience observes most media performances as spectacle that occurs in the far-off background. Essentially, media performances constantly swirl about everywhere because we live in a consumer driven, media saturated society. Because of media saturation, the mass audience has to be selective about which content they will observe and pays low attention to most media content around them. In addition, because of the extreme distance between the mass audience and performers, the audience has no impact on such performances. An example of the mass audience would be co-workers who go to a bar to have a drink and discuss their day at the office. In the background of the bar, music might be playing while a large screen television shows ESPN. The co-workers will engage in their discussions about office politics, while only occasionally paying scant attention to the media messages that are playing out around them.

In contrast, because of its focus on both spectacle and performance, the diffused audience is central to the SPP. Much like the mass audience, the diffused audience exists in a media-saturated environment. However, in the case of the SPP, performance becomes so pervasive that the diffused audience takes part in the performance, blurring the boundary between audience and performance. This is similar to the crafting of a spectacle-laden identity described by Hebdige. Media become a resource that audiences can use to formulate their performances in "everyday" activities, and their life transforms into a "constant performance" (Abercrombie & Longhurst, 1998, p. 73) in which diffused audience members perceive themselves as performers as well as audience.

> So deeply infused into everyday life is performance that we are unaware of it in ourselves or in others. Life is a constant performance; we are audience and performer at the same time; everybody is an audience all the time. Performance is not a discrete event. (p. 73)

It is important to note that the diffused audience does not replace the previous two forms; instead, the three forms intermingle. Sometimes people assume more rigid "audience" roles that keep them separated from other performances in society; at other times, performances are part of the background and paid little attention; and at still other times, the audience becomes a part of performances. Abercrombie and Longhurst provide the example of a football game to demonstrate such fluidity. A person might go to a football game and ceremonially attend to the events that play out on the field as a fixed audience sitting in the stands. After the game, the person might then go home and turn on ESPN's *Sports Center* to watch a recap of all of the games played that day. During commercial breaks and commentary on baseball, the person might pick up the phone and call their parents, fold laundry, and feed their dog. Finally, the person might go online to NFL.com to buy the jersey of their favorite football player. By purchasing the jersey, the person is blurring the boundary between themselves and the performances of that athlete as they are portrayed on the field and on ESPN.

The diffused audience stands at the intersection of everyday life and the innumerable media messages pervading into their lives. At this intersection, spectacular images in the media coalesce together to form a mediascape where the audience can engage in narcissistic performance. The mediascape constitutes a world that is pieced together by audiences through their attendance to the fragmented spectacles that are circulated through society via the media. According to Abercrombie and Longhurst, the diffused audience is driven by the concepts of spectacle and narcissism. As discussed previously, spectacle emerges from the gathering and coalescing of images and fable-like narratives swirling about society, which draw the gaze and demand that people possess and consume such spectacle; such spectacle teaches people how to live and perform. Narcissism, the other aspect of the diffused audience discussed by Abercrombie and Longhurst, is the self-centered or self-oriented nature of the individual that comes from a long affiliation with spectacle. According to Marc Porter and Isacc Catt (1993) narcissism is the inability of the individual to make a differentiation between themselves and the outside world. Either the individuals see the world as an extension of themselves, or they see themselves as a component of the world. Abercrombie and Longhurst further characterize narcissism as a state in which one has no sense of the past or the future, they worship celebrity, and are preoccupied with instant gratification. Spectacle combined with narcissism guides diffused audiences toward conceptions of how to perform in everyday life. The individual is self-centered and exists in a world in which everything can be possessed, including the individual and her or his performances. Essentially, spectacle and narcissism are related in that the more spectacle that audiences attend to in their media consumption the more they blur the line between themselves and spectacle driven performances in society, which increases the risk of becoming narcissistic.

One final point about the diffused audience discussed by Abercrombie and Longhurst involves the aspect of media production; the diffused audience performs in the spectacle and narcissism of modern society through their level of media consumption or production. Typically, diffused audiences seek to make their fanship or enthusiasm known through their use of media. Some audiences obsess about celebrities, television programs, or activities (e.g., hunting), and seek those things out through heavy use of general or specialized media. Other fans become so engrossed in celebrities or activities that they engage in minor media production about the subject. Abercrombie and Longhurst called such audiences petty producers, as they contribute to the media or literature on the subject by producing some form of content, such as fan zines (e.g., the Pearl Jam newsletter) or websites (e.g., a *Sopranos* fan website). Therefore, an audience continuum exists based on media use that ranges from consumer to petty producer, along which most people in modern society fit. Whether audiences perform as petty producers often depends on the extent of their interests in particular media topics.

Audience Performance, Resistance, and New Social Movements
As important as SPP has been for insight into the performance of audiences, the concept has only addressed the issues of "everyday life" as it applies to prosperous audiences within a thriving capitalist society and economic system. Unfortunately, the intersection of "everyday life" and media as conceptualized through the SPP creates problems for the assessment of audiences who fall outside of such notions of everyday life; in particular, how can scholars study audiences who are part of subcultures that resist a thriving economic system, such as many of the activists affiliated with contemporary new social movements (Atkinson, 2005b)? Although Abercrombie and Longhurst did provide a discussion about the performance of subcultures, they limited their discussion to how "cultists" and "fans" become subcultures—subcultures saturated in mainstream media. This is problematic, however, because it means that the SPP downplays the notions of power and resistance in terms of media and audiences. SPP audiences seem to become part of the dominant structure without question; the more involved they are in spectacle, the more narcissistic they become. The problem is compounded when the SPP is used to look at contemporary new social movements because of the critical perspectives espoused by organizations found within many networks, and the content of the alternative media used by members of those organizations (see Atkinson & Dougherty, 2006; Atkinson, 2005b; Atton, 2002a; Downing, 2003b). Past research has demonstrated that critical perspectives are frequently used in alternative magazines, such as *The Nation*, alternative radio programs, such as *Democracy Now!*, and alternative websites, such as Indymedia.org (e.g. Atkinson, 2005a; 2005b; Atkinson & Dougherty, 2006; Atton, 2002a; 2004; Downing, 2003b; Downing et al., 2001; Pickard, 2006b). These critical perspectives are found in alternative media content that is produced by new social movement advocates, who often urge readers and audiences to resist the consumption-oriented spectacle that Abercrombie and Longhurst described as integral to the performances of diffused audiences (Atkinson & Dougherty 2006; Atkinson, 2009a; Atton, 2002a; Downing et al., 2001).

One way to address the problems associated with SPP is to turn to theories concerning resistance. In the field of Communication, research concerning resistance has provided insight into responses to physical oppression, but has focused mostly on responses to socially constructed contexts of oppression built through interactions. In regards to the latter, many Communication scholars have often sought to build on Antonio Gramsci (1971) and his work concerning hegemony, in which he emphasized the individual's role in their own oppression. Essentially, Gramsci noted that ideological assumptions in society, such as capitalism and consumerism, were only partially enforced by dominant elites in society. Heavy-handed enforcement of ideological assumptions by the elites would usually be counterproductive, as it would usually result in a backlash against those elites by the masses; such an argument has also been raised by Louis Althusser (1971) and Max Horkheimer and Theodor Adorno (1972). Oppression, then, was a "two-way street" in which elites promoted certain ideological assumptions on the one hand, and individuals in a society took part in their own oppression by participating in the ideological assumptions that had been promoted across the social spectrum by those elites. Such participation often stems from the individual's desire to fit in and feel "normal." Such notions of hegemony have been supported by Michel Foucault's (1975) conceptualization of discipline and punishment, as he had conceptualized society as a prison. According to Foucault, social discourse constructs various classifications, or "cells," into which people become categorized; people often fit within many different categories at once (e.g., Caucasian, male, professor). Once a person becomes categorized, discourse is used by that individual, as well as others around them, to keep the person within those categorical cells. Therefore, many Communication scholars, like Dennis Mumby (1988; 1997), conceptualize resistance as a response to the combination of ideological assumptions and hegemonic reproduction of those ideological assumptions through interactions with other people and institutional structures.

Resistance associated with alternative media audiences conforms to notions of resistance identified by past Communication scholars; specifically, resistance does not occur in a void but in a socially constructed context of oppression built through interactions (Aptheker, 1989; Clair, 1998; Mumby, 1997). Consequently, it seems likely that an alternative form of audience performance occurs for audiences of alternative media, a performance in which power, ideology, and resistance are the primary components. This is not to say that spectacle does not play a role in such performances; indeed, past social movement research has demonstrated the importance of spectacular imagery for social movement tactics such as diatribe (e.g., Windt, 1972), pranking (e.g., Harold, 2004), and counter-culture lifestyles like nudity and drug use (e.g., Gustainis & Hahn, 1988). Although spectacles for general audiences are accomplished for its own sake, for audiences who are affiliated with new social movements, spectacle is subordinated to a message of resistance. For these audience members, resistance is center stage, with spectacle simply a means to an end. Therefore, the rest of this chapter proposes an alternate interpretation of Abercrombie and Longhurst's SPP that is integral to the following discussion concerning alternative media and new social movements, as well as for the remaining chapters in the book. The analysis of past research that addressed the problems of consumption and pleasure conducted by Abercrombie and Longhurst has demonstrated an Audience Performance Paradigm (APP) and not a Spectacle/Performance Paradigm (SPP). At the heart of this paradigm is the fact that audiences construct mediascapes at the intersection of multiple mainstream media and "everyday life" and engage in media-oriented performances that range from consumption to petty production. Such mainstream media are woven from spectacles that aid in the construction and reconstruction of the dominant ideologies associated with consumerism and capitalism. It is these spectacles from which audiences learn about the world and how to engage in performance; it is also these spectacles with which audiences perform within their mediascapes. If we were to think about the APP as a continuum, the notion of Spectacle Performance (SP) developed from past research concerning audiences and mainstream media sits at one end. At the other end of the continuum rests the concept of Resistance Performance (RP), a concept that will be developed throughout the rest of this chapter.

The Foundations of Resistance Performance:
Power and Divergent Worldviews

The notion of RP differs from Abercrombie and Longhurst's SP, in that audiences engage in performances that acknowledge the spectacle-laden nature of media and attempt to resist the dominant power structures in society that produce those spectacles. That is not to say that the performance of resistance observed in past research does not entail images and spectacle, or that activists who engage in those performances of resistance are immune from the problems of narcissism discussed by Abercrombie and Longhurst, as well as Porter and Catt. Indeed, the spectacles in alternative media serve as a backdrop for activist communities, against which activists perform resistance. The foundation for RP lies in the images and narratives circulated through alternative media produced at the national/international level, or global level, which often entail multiple conceptualizations of "power." Conceptualizations of power found in alternative media content (e.g., *Z Magazine, Democracy Now!*, Indymedia.org) aid in the construction and reinforcement of worldviews concerning power and social justice in society, and set the stage for Resistance Performance.[1]

Typically, alternative media content portrays power in society, and how power is wielded by elites, in one of two forms: traditional power and hegemonic power. The category of "traditional" power reflects control over material, often physical, resources such as money and arms (e.g., Fairhurst & Sarr, 1996; Pfeffer, 1992) and is pervasive in articles found in magazines such as *The Nation* and in commentary posted on websites like Indymedia.org and Infoshop.org. The category emerges from portrayals of government and corporate forces as controlling various aspects of society through their domination of resources, leaving little hope for democratic change or reform on the part of "the people." *The Nation* article "Inverted Totalitarianism" by Sheldon Wolin (2003) serves as an example of content found in alternative media that reflects traditional power. The article describes the culture of fear created in the United States by corporations:

> Inverted totalitarianism has its own means of promoting generalized fear; not only by sudden "alerts" and periodic announcements about recently discovered terrorist cells or the arrest of shadowy figures or the publicized heavy-handed treatment of aliens and the Devil's Island that is Guantánamo Bay or the sudden fascination with interrogation methods that employ or border on torture, but by a pervasive atmosphere of fear abetted by a corporate economy of ruthless downsizing, withdrawal or reduction of pension and health benefits; a corporate political system that relentlessly threatens to privatize Social Security and the modest health benefits available, especially to the poor. (p. 14)

Wolin's portrayal of power emphasizes material resources, such as money and healthcare benefits, as integral to power. In other words, through the domination of money and other such resources, corporations create a political environment by threatening people with the elimination of those resources. The fear that people feel concerning the loss of such resources helps such corporations to dominate the decision-making processes of society.

Conversely, hegemonic power reflects the notion of hegemonic oppression described by Antonio Gramsci (1971) and developed in Communication literature by scholars such as Stan Deetz (1992) and Dennis Mumby (1988; 1997); the concept involves elite groups manipulating ideological assumptions in society while the subordinate groups willingly participate in those assumptions. Hegemonic power is found in Internet forums such as the Amnesty International website and bulletins emailed by MoveOn.org, on the radio program *Democracy Now!*, and in magazines like *The Progressive*, and *Z Magazine*. The category emerges from portrayals of corporate domination of the media and public opinion. These alternative media sources claim that corporations use the media to shape government and society to suit the interests of a small group of elites. In a sense, the producers often make the claim that media resources are used to convince the general population that particular roles and behaviors are commonplace and normal. A *Z Magazine* article by Edward Herman (2003) provides an illustration of this conceptualization of power:

> Saddam [Hussein] was demonized quite effectively—not a difficult task—but the media also accomplished the more difficult task of deflecting attention from the earlier alliance with and support of the demon. The mainstream media have not said that an agreement between the United States and Saddam is impossible; they refuse to discuss and reflect on the one that existed for an extended period of time. The picture of Donald Rumsfeld shaking hands with Saddam Hussein in December 1983, as he helped cement an alliance with the demon, was not shown on the TV networks or published in the New York Times or Philadelphia Inquirer.

In this excerpt, Herman claims that the mainstream media had hidden some aspects of the US relationship with Saddam Hussein and brought others to the forefront. The implication is that the mainstream media helped to dictate and shape ideological assumptions concerning Iraq, weapons of mass destruction, and the role of the US in world affairs.

Bulletins emailed by MoveOn.org also reflect a vision of corporate domination of the media and manipulation of society. In a series of MoveOn.org bulletins, the threat of neo-conservative power to American democracy loomed as the FCC moved towards further deregulation of media ownership rules in 2003. In an article entitled "Showdown at the FCC" emailed through the MoveOn listserv, Jeffrey Chester and Don Hazen claim the following:

> According to experts cited by the Los Angeles Times, if the media moguls get what they want, only a dozen or so companies will own most U.S. stations, giving them even more control over the marketplace of ideas than they already have. Jeff Chester of the Center for Digital Democracy explains, "The ownership rules on the FCC chopping block have been developed over the last 50 years. They have been an important safeguard ensuring the public's basic First Amendment rights. The rationale for these policies is that they help provide for a diverse media marketplace of ideas, essential for a democracy. They have not been perfect. But the rules have helped constrain the power of the corporate media giants."

In this excerpt, the producers claim that, as of the writing of the bulletin, only a small group of neo-conservatives hold the potential to influence millions of people through the use of corporate media; further deregulation by the FCC could prove dire, as neo-conservatives would have a much larger bullhorn to voice their opinions to the American public and shape ideological assumptions in society concerning a variety of issues.

The two categories about corporate power in the pages and pixels of alternative media do not exist in a vacuum, but are often reflected in the ways in which activists describe corporations and discuss dominant power structures in society. Some activists (who were audiences of alternative media) express traditional visions of power as they talk about corporations and governments in terms of resources and materials, whereas hegemonic visions of power emerged when other activists discussed power structures in society. For instance, Activist #8 related the following about corporations and their abuse of workers:

> Corporations by their very nature abuse workers and so the only way you could have corporate reform or corporate responsibility is for the workers to own the means of their production. And so—and I don't see that happening. Not in my lifetime. I don't think you can have corporate reform as long as you accept the notion that it's okay to abuse the workers and use them as just a means of production, which is how they're used.

Many activists, such as Activist #8, see corporate power in traditional terms of production and resources: corporations control the means of production (e.g., resources) in an abusive manner and refuse to relinquish control. In fact, human beings, within this viewpoint, can be objectified and seen as resources. For other activists, corporations and power structures in society are hegemonic, in that they shape ideological assumptions and allow people to follow those assumptions on their own. This is not to say that the traditional visions of power are absent when they discuss or describe corporate power or other power structures in society. However, many activists look beyond resources to the hegemonic vision of power. For instance, Activist #23 said the following about corporations:

> To put it simply—well, I think that—see consumerism is—and the sale of things in general feeds on several different things that have come out of our society that are people—individual people. Like the way things are advertised to us as far as like, they market things based on hope and fear. And those are two very strong emotions in people. Like people fear that if they don't use a certain product they won't be a certain way. You know they won't be accepted by other people. And then they have the hope that if they do buy this product they will be that way. So the way corporations in general are—I don't want to say corporations in general, but the way advertising markets those products to us is really—well it's—I think it has a negative effect on our society as a whole.

According to Activist #23 corporations control resources, much like the description provided by Activist #8. However, such corporate control also dictated the ideological assumptions in society and subsequently the roles that individuals play in their families and communities. This is not to say that activists like Activist #8 are ignorant of issues of hegemony. Such activists are well versed in the concepts of hegemony and ideology, and acknowledge the role of those concepts in society. However, they emphasize the conceptualization of traditional power in their discussions concerning power structures in society. In part, the reason for such a preference lies within the emergence of theatre-like communities from RP.

Resistance Performance

The concept of Resistance Performance emerges from five categories that construct a conceptual framework for understanding activists, organizations, and networks associated with new social movements as "theatres" in which networked activists perform resistance for the gaze of outsiders, as well as for their compatriot activists. The five categories are: (1) Critical Worldviews, (2) Alternative Media Interaction, (3) Communicative Resistance, (4) Intercreative Capacity, and (5) Narrative Capacity.[2] The initial two categories intersect to construct four spaces that are integral for the performance of resistance. Such performance on the part of activists constitutes the third category, which emerged from discussions by activists concerning their attempts to publicly confront, challenge, or change those dominant power structures. The first three categories, which will be discussed in the following pages, serve as a theoretical framework for conceptualizing the role of activists' worldviews and use of alternative media in the construction and interconnection of spaces for the performance of resistance. The final categories play an integral role in the production of alternative media and interconnectivity of different groups and organizations and will be discussed in the following chapter.

Critical Worldviews
The category of Critical Worldviews encapsulates beliefs and attitudes held by activists about dominant power structures in society. The dominant power structures are oftentimes corporations, which many activists feel are the driving forces behind political policies concerning trade, globalization, and wars. However, corporations are not the sole power structure discussed by activists, as many anarchist and anti-capitalist activists reference the government and religious institutions in their discussions about power and social justice. The category of Critical Worldviews can be conceptualized as a continuum that ranges from "radical" to "reformist." Activists who engage in *radical* discussions about power often demonstrate an intense distrust of those institutions and people that wield such power; such radical discussions demonize those institutions and people. Ultimately, corporations like Nike or Wal-Mart, the United States government, "mainstream" political parties, and religious institutions are portrayed in these radical worldviews as "evil." In contrast, *reformist* discussions about power by activists depict institutions and people who wield power as oftentimes problematic, but legitimate. Such activists believe that although institutions, like corporations, are responsible for many ills and problems in the world, those same institutions can be reformed with time and effort. The concepts of radical and reformist are simplified positions that function within the political spectrum developed by Clinton Rossiter (1962) in his book *Conservativism in America*. In that book, Rossiter claimed that political worldviews took the shape of a circle, with far left and far right viewpoints meeting at a point of the circle that is opposite of centrist "conservative" political views. The concepts of radical and reformist are not intended to demonstrate an entire spectrum of worldviews within a particular community. Instead, they are used to describe sections of a political spectrum within one community (e.g., radical and reformist sections of a leftist community). The Critical Worldview Continuum of radical to reformist was best explained by Activist #11:

> Well, in Mystical City, there's usually almost two camps. There's sort of those within, who are looking for institutional reform, and there are those

who are for an all-new system to be put into place. It's more complex than that because there's always hundreds of people who want to give it time. But say that there's the anarchist movement, and within Amnesty International we go and we lobby the government. We push for prison reform and policy reform. That's what we have to do is this kind of thing. These things are already there. We're trying to change to make them better. The [anarchist movement] is sort of just like—these systems are inherently corrupt, which I somewhat agree with.

According to Activist #11, there, thus, were two faces of left-leaning activism that operated in and around the immediate local community. First, there were the reformists who held a worldview in which working within the boundaries of the established political systems could reform corporations, which was the "side" where this person saw himself. Then, there were the far-left radicals who held a worldview in which the entire system is far too corrupt and no amount of overhaul or reform will make corporations work for the benefit of individuals or communities. The Critical Worldview Continuum is represented on Figure 1 (p. 43) as a line that extends from left (radical) to right (reformist). Discussions on the part of activists about dominant power structures that utilize radical, anarchist, or extremist jargon or ideas are positioned to the left side of this line; those discussions that use jargon or ideas that focus on the possibility for reform of dominant institutions are positioned to the right side of this line.

In his book *Image Politics*, DeLuca (1999) offers Green Peace and Earth First! as radical activist organizations. Activists affiliated with both organizations held a worldview in which the industrial use of the environment by corporations and governments, and the subsequent harm to wildlife from such use, are all unnecessary evils. However, the problems do not merely stem from the actions of the corporations and governments, but from the very ideologies in society concerning industrialism and progress. "Belief in progress is contemporary common sense. Progress has become the taken-for-granted background of Western culture through a historical and political process" (p. 46). In this sense, the ideologies themselves constitute the power structure that is first and foremost targeted by Green Peace and Earth First!, and such a power structure must be altogether altered or defeated in order to save the planet, not just merely reformed. Conversely, Barbara Warnick's (2007) book *Rhetoric Online* offers a description of MoveOn.org as an example of an organization in which the members are primarily reformist activists. Wes Boyd and Jean Blades founded the organization in 1998 to address the problem that the Monica Lewinsky scandal posed to politics in the United States. Warnick notes that the organization circulated "an online petition calling for Congress to censure President Clinton and move on to deal with the issues facing the nation" (pp. 77-78). In this instance, the members of MoveOn hold a view of the dominant power structure (e.g., Congress and the US government) as legitimate; such a structure can be persuaded or "reformed" through efforts on the part of individuals and groups in society.

Alternative Media Interaction

The category of Alternative Media Interaction describes how activists use alternative media. As stated previously in Chapter 1, alternative media is defined in terms of content (e.g., Armstrong, 1981; Atkinson, 2005a; Downing et al., 2001), processes of production (e.g., Atton, 2002a; 2004; Meikle, 2002) and the interpretation of the audience (Rauch, 2007). Alternative media are those media that focus on challenging power structures and changing social roles rather than making profit, and are read by audiences as outside of the domain of mainstream media. As with the Critical Worldviews category, the interactions that activists have with alternative media can be conceptualized as a continuum that ranges from lay to participatory; concepts developed by Norman Denzin (1997) in his book *Interpretive Ethnography*. *Lay* interactions involve passive consumption of alternative media on the part of users for personal information, entertainment, reinforcement of their values, or to gain a sense of community. *Participatory* interactions, on the other hand, actively contribute to alternative media through some form of user-to-document interactivity (see McMillan, 2002; Warnick, 2007), a topic that will be discussed in greater detail in Chapter 3. In many ways, the participatory interactions are similar to Abercrombie and Longhurst's notion of petty production, except that the participatory interaction is not confined solely to media production. Activists who engage in participatory interactions also often provide feedback and suggestions via email or face-to-face communication to alternative media producers—at the local and/or global levels—about content that the producers have created. Such participation, whether through production or interaction, has proven to be integral to the formation of political identity as Castells (1996; 2004; 2006), Huesca (2001), and Meikle (2002) have explored such participation in new social movements. Essentially, participation with interactive and alternative media formats allows for the formation of political identity in the absence of traditional institutions that do not fit into the lives of people embedded in the networked society. Activist #26 serves as an example of a participatory activist in his explanation about how he frequently interacted with global producers of alternative media to gain additional information concerning particular topics: "I try to find out more about who has actual information about a subject. I correspond with people who usually are authors or intellectuals who are writing articles on the issues that interest me." In addition, participatory interactions by activists involve petty production of zines and articles for websites such as Indymedia.org. Activists #3 and #10 both serve as examples of such participatory petty production, as those activists explained the following:

> *Activist #3*: [I try to] voice my thoughts and my feelings and combine with other activists to make our voices heard on the streets, and to publish anti-consumerist literature and things like that. That's what I've done thus far. There's a collective zine that my friends and I have put together. It's more of an anti-oppression zine. It's called Proclamations of Wimmin, and it's basically a collection of articles and things concerning patriarchy, which is also part of the society that we live in today.

> *Activist #10*: A lot of times what happens is you post a story up [on the Internet] or a comment—like you can always post a comment on Indymedia. They have an open-wire publishing thing where you can just click right on it and type whatever you want—like a response to something or whatever. And it prints up on the front page. But in order to do a story you have to go through this whole process and all this other stuff. But I just basically use the open wire publishing, you know? Like what I had to write about [George W. Bush] or corporations like Monsanto or actions we want to do around town or stuff like that.

Overall, participatory activists, like the three activists mentioned above, demonstrate the blurring of audience and producer described by Atton (2002a; 2003; 2004). Such activists are not just audiences of alternative media; they also interact with the global and local producers of alternative media, as well as engage in petty production of their own. Such activists rarely, if ever, produce content for major alternative media sources like *Adbusters* magazine or *Democracy Now!* radio. Instead, these activists contribute by posting comments to articles on online forums like Indymedia, produce small zines with their home computer and printing equipment, and provide suggestions and feedback to producers about alternative media content.

In her article published in *Communication and Critical/Cultural Studies*, Stengrim (2005) provides an excellent description of the "citizen journalists" affiliated with the Indymedia network, which serves as an example of participatory activists:

> A collective of citizen journalists, Indymedia produces radio, newspaper, and Web content to be posted online or published locally. It would have been antithetical for fair trade and anti-corporate activists to allow the institutions they oppose to cover the [demonstrations against the World Trade Organization]; Independent Media Centers (IMCs) thus emerged in Seattle and Washington, DC to provide from-the-streets coverage of each city's respective protest events. (pp. 281-282)

Essentially, the activists who work with the Indymedia network are constantly providing content for the over-arching website, or any one of the several local level websites, in order to provide information about protests and demonstrations across the country. Such activists are consistently working to produce some kind of content for the site, whether text, video, radio, or photographs. Conversely, Thomas Olesen (2005) provides examples of lay audiences in his discussion of various pro-Zapatista organizations, like the Mexico Solidarity Network, in his book *International Zapatismo*. Many of the activists within the organization are participatory, in that they regularly produce content for the website and listserv about the Zapatistas and their activities in Chiapas, Mexico (more on the Zapatistas in Chapter 6). However, the participatory activists are a minority, as most of the activists are recipients of the media produced by the few producers; such recipients use the information forwarded along to them to organize local protests and pro-Zapatista solidarity actions. The alternative media content serves as a source of information for such activists, with little interaction with the producers at the center of the organization. The organizing of protests and engagement in actions of solidarity by such lay activists stand as social interactions that are integral for the development of political identity in new social movements.

As with the category of Critical Worldviews, the Alternative Media Interaction category is represented in Figure 1 as a line, in this case, a vertical line. Alternative Media Interactions that involve consumption on the part of the user, and little, if any, feedback or petty production constitute lay performances and are situated near the bottom of the line. Interactions that involve alternative media production and/or feedback to alternative media producers are considered "participatory" and are positioned toward the top of the line. The Critical Worldviews and the Alternative Media Interaction Continua converge to create four activist quadrants: Radical Participatory, Reformist Participatory, Reformist Lay, and Radical Lay (see Figure 1).

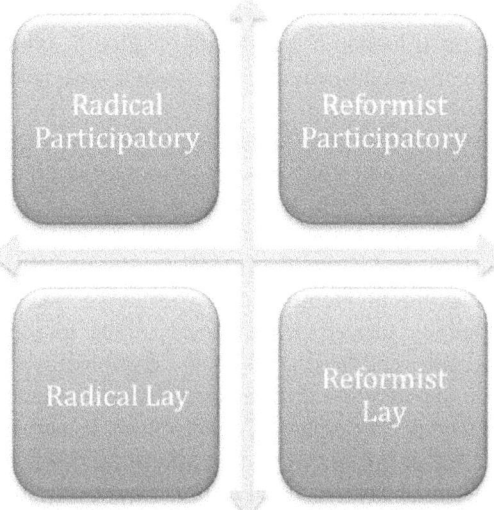

Figure 1. Four Emergent Quadrants.

The Radical Participatory quadrant entails activists who hold radical worldviews about dominant power structures and engage in interactions with alternative media producers and/or engage in petty production of alternative media. Activists positioned within the Reformist Participatory quadrant express opinions that the power structures in society are problematic but could be reformed, as well as interact with global level alternative media producers and petty production of alternative media content. In the Reformist Lay quadrant, activists express reformist views, but do not create any alternative media content or interact with global producers. Finally, the activists that fall within the Radical Lay quadrant espouse radical views about power structures in society, and do not engage in any production or alternative media interactions.

The four quadrants can aid in the conceptualization of the different activists found in a particular region. For instance, Mystical City was a Midwestern community of 90,000 people and home to a large state university of 20,000 students; the community was also home to numerous left-leaning, social justice-oriented organizations that had emerged throughout the 1980s and 1990s. The activists who were members of these organizations displayed either radical or reformist worldviews about power and social justice, and they regularly used alternative media titles in order to gather information and/or to express their radical or reformist worldviews. For instance, the Student Action Committee was a group formed on the campus of Mystical State University that focused much of their attention and efforts on corporate exploitation of workers and the environment. The members of the organization read and circulated articles and information found in *The Nation*, and on Infoshop.org and Indymedia.org, which were often based in traditional conceptualizations of corporate and government power. Such themes about corporations in the content corresponded with and reinforced their anarchist worldviews concerning the domination of resources by world governments and transnational corporations. In addition to their reading and circulation of information, most of the members also regularly submitted articles and commentary to online forums such as Infoshop.org and the local Indymedia site. Such participation is integral as it helps to further cement a political identity in the spaceless place of the networked society described by Castells and Huescea. Due to the radical worldviews of the members, coupled with their participatory use of alternative media, most of the activists affiliated with the Student Action Committee fit into the Radical Participatory quadrant. Activists involved with another organization, Peace Alliance, often worked to coordinate anti-war demonstrations as efforts to win over widespread support against the wars in Iraq and Afghanistan. The consensus among the Peace Alliance activists was that if the "general public" were made aware of the criminal nature of these wars, changes would occur (reformist worldview). Such a worldview corresponded with the descriptions of hegemonic power of dominant power structures found in *The Progressive* and *Z Magazine* and programs on National Public Radio, alternative media read and circulated by members of the organization. In their efforts to sway the general public, many of the activists aided in the publication of a monthly newsletter and regularly submitted materials for a local listserv (participatory interactions). For these reasons, most of the Peace Alliance activists fit the quadrant of Reformist Participatory. Activists involved with an environmental organization, Midwest Forests, often discussed corporations as villainous tools of a corrupt government (radical worldview) and read articles and materials circulated by global organizations such as Green Peace (lay interactions); such activists fit into the Radical Lay quadrant.

Similarly, Erie City was a community in the US northeast with a population of 150,000 people, and home to a large university of 10,000 students. As in the case of Mystical City, several social justice organizations emerged in the city throughout the second half of the 20th century. Most notable among those organizations were the Erie City Urban Partnership and the Olive Branch Association (OBA). The activists affiliated with the Erie City Urban Partnership focused their attention and efforts on predatory lending practices in some of the impoverished neighborhoods of the community. Most of the activists affiliated with the organization believed that the entire system of banks and lending in the US was built to exploit the poor and disenfranchised; the entire structure was morally bankrupt (radical worldview). The members of the Erie City Urban Partnership regularly read and circulated alternative media titles such as Indymedia.org and *The Nation*.

In addition, many of the members of the group worked to produce their own zines and newsletters about predatory lending and the corrupt financial system of the US, as well as videos on the subject for YouTube and other Internet sites (participatory interactions). Meanwhile, the OBA was similar to the Peace Alliance in Mystical City, in that the organization coordinated and carried out protests and marches against the Iraq War. The membership of the OBA believed that if people were made aware of the variety of different problems created by the war, public support would completely evaporate (reformist). The OBA activists were not only avid readers of articles found on ZNet, AlterNet, and in the pages of *The Progressive*, but many activists were involved in writing articles and commentary for the organization's monthly newsletter and multiple listservs (participatory interactions).

The descriptions of power found in alternative media produced at the global level construct a backdrop where activists co-construct worldviews as they engage in social interactions and use alternative media within local communities. In respect to the first two categories, the quadrants serve as spaces where activists that are similar to one another (i.e., radical or reformist) can circulate narratives necessary for networked activism as described in the research of Best (2005), Pickard (2006a; 2006b), and Stengrim (2005). At the local level in communities like Mystical City and Erie City, participatory activists circulate narratives that reflect organizational and/or personal worldviews about power and social justice through locally produced alternative media (e.g., zines, newsletters, community radio, listservs), while lay activists circulate narratives through social interactions (e.g., meetings, protests, face-to-face encounters). As other activists discover those narratives, they are able to gain a deeper understanding about the differing worldviews throughout their community. Whenever an activist encounters a narrative that they feel is similar to narratives that they are circulating (either through alternative media interactions or social interactions), that activist often develops a sense of trust and loyalty toward the source of the narrative. In that case, the activists may develop a loose affiliation, work together to develop an organization so as to perform resistance together, or join organizations of which one or the other is already a member. In this way, then, activist networks are developed and grow within communities like Mystical City and Erie City. Activists who fall within the four quadrants circulate personal and/or organizational narratives through alternative media and social interactions, they learn of one another "out there" in the community, and come together to form organizations and affiliations. Keep in mind that organizations themselves are not classified within one quadrant or another, as there are often combinations of participatory and lay activists within an organization. For instance, many university campuses across the United States have local level Amnesty International chapters. Within such chapters, there are usually one or two activists who engage in participatory actions as they produce materials (e.g., blogs and listservs) and comment on materials on activist websites, like the Amnesty International website. Most of the other members, however, use alternative media, like the Amnesty International website, in a lay fashion. Conversely, some peace and justice organizations, like Peace Action, entail a large number of participatory activists who work on organizational publications and listservs in the community. Some of the members utilize alternative media in a lay fashion, but many, if not most, of the activists engage in some aspect of alternative media production. In terms of radical versus reformist, however, there is usually little crossover. Few radical activists are involved in local level Sierra Club and MoveOn organizations. Chapter 4 and 5 will further illustrate the relationship between the participatory and lay quadrants.

Communicative Resistance
The third category of RP involves the performance of resistance against problems that stem from dominant power structures, such as corporations, governmental agencies, and religious institutions. The different categories of power depicted within alternative media and the first two categories of RP set the stage for the third category. The intersection of worldviews, interactions with alternative media, and portrayals of power in alternative media allow for the emergence of the four quadrants described in the previous section. These four quadrants stand as "theatres" in which activists engage in public discourse, or performances, that draw attention while also communicating identity and knowledge about issues of power and social justice. These performances include a variety of different actions, such as oratory, chanting, songs, gestures, play, and pranks (Calafell, 2007; Conquergood, 1985; 1991; Denzin, 1997; Harold, 2004; Langellier, 1983). As stated in Chapter 1, protest strategies such as promulgation, solidification, and polarization discussed by Bowers and Ochs (1971) constitute such performance, all of which can coalesce into image events (e.g., DeLuca, 1999) that can be photographed and circulated within and across theatre-quadrants through alternative media.

The category of Communicative Resistance refers to activists' strategies (e.g., promulgation) and tactics (e.g., handing out pamphlets) that they use to publicly approach dominant power structures that they perceive to be problematic, such as corporations like Wal-Mart or Monsanto. Donna Kowal's (2000) categories of "adjustive" and "militant" tactics, discussed briefly in Chapter 1, prove useful for conceptualizing Communicative Resistance of activists. Kowal defined *adjustive tactics* as actions that do not violate laws and are deemed to be socially acceptable by average people. "Orderly public speeches, parades, picketing, and other non-violent actions" (p. 241) are all examples of adjustive resistance. Conversely, *militant tactics* are confrontational and aggressive actions that break societal rules and threaten dominant groups. Such resistance can prove to be hegemonic as the actions provide authorities with evidence that the current domination structures are necessary (Clair, 1998; Pierce & Dougherty, 2002). In addition, militant tactics can be problematic as they may threaten other activists who align themselves with those who perpetrate the confrontational actions. Militant performances include confrontations that involve clashes with law enforcement officers (e.g., storming police lines or throwing objects at officers), actions that violate city ordinances (e.g., blocking traffic or blocking entrances to buildings) or vandalism (e.g., graffiti or destruction of corporate property). Such tactics are often utilized in order to serve the larger strategy of polarization described by Bowers and Ochs. Activist #9 serves as an example of an activist who broke laws as a means to publicly challenge dominant power structures.

> The last [anti-Iraq war] march is a great example of [militancy] where a few—I've heard estimates of 30 to 50 people—in its peak marched in the street when there was a sidewalk march. There were [activists] who were really upset about that because they viewed it as giving the movement a bad look. These people that didn't think people should march in the streets, and, of course, the people in the streets viewed it as, you know, "This is what we want to do if we really are concerned about stopping the war. We need to not just do what the government is allowing us to do. They're the ones perpetrating the war. Of course they're not going to allow us to do anything effective, so we have to do things that aren't allowed."

According to this activist, the government was the driving force behind the war in Iraq; small things like stopping traffic and congesting infrastructure could interfere with the war effort. Several other activists who took part in this activity were arrested, as those actions were a violation of the law. According to Kowal (2000), militant tactics often depend on "audiences and historical moments" (p. 241). Not only are laws and ordinances violated by such actions in a historical moment, but other activists may be upset because they believe that the militant protest by such activists would anger the mainstream public or destroy the credibility of like minded activists and protesters everywhere.

Conversely, adjustive performances include moderate forms of protest or activism in a peaceful manner so as to not anger authorities or other activists. Such performances include educational workshops or speeches aimed at educating the public about problems associated with dominant power structures. In addition, sanctioned and lawful demonstrations such as marches and rallies would likewise constitute adjustive tactics. These performances are often utilized in order to accomplish the larger strategy of promulgation described by Bowers and Ochs. Activist #24, who explained some of the strategies utilized by one organization that she works with in order to confront the problems associated with corporations, offers an example of adjustive performance:

We have a really wide base of support. And so sometimes we have to be concerned about upsetting the wrong members with the wrong issues. I mean not too much, but occasionally...So one thing is of course education. That's what Peace Alliance works on a lot. Education. You know we have classes and programs, speakers and things like that. And it's important to lobby by educating people about bills and things like that, asking people to become active also.

For many activists, like Activist #24, it is important to maintain a widespread base of support across a community. For this reason, it becomes increasingly important to address issues in an adjustive manner that will not offend people who might become part of a widespread base. In addition, it is also important not to offend any authority figures (e.g., business leaders, community leaders, church figures, as well as the police) in order to maintain credibility with people who are already part of the wide base of support.

John Sanchez and Mary Stuckey's (2000) descriptions of the different tactics carried out by the American Indian Movement (AIM) serve as good illustrations of militant performances. In 1969, a group called "Indians of All Tribes" seized control of Alcatraz in San Francisco Bay, and held the island for nineteen months. During that time, the Indians of All Tribes established what they called the Bureau of Caucasian Affairs, and offered to buy the island from the US government for some glass beads and cloth. Although the performance provided an effective critique of the colonization of the Americas by Europeans and their descendants, the actions were in clear violation of the law and put the group at odds with the Nixon Administration and the US government. In addition, many argue that the militant action reinforced negative stereotypes about Native Americans and alienated activists who preferred more adjustive performances. Conversely, Downing, Ford, Gil, and Stein (2001) illustrated the actions taken by the Mothers of the Plaza de Mayo, which can help to demonstrate adjustive performances on the part of activists. During the Argentinean military junta from 1976 to 1982, tens of thousands of citizens were killed or disappeared. As any opposition to the junta during that time resulted in imprisonment or worse, the citizenry could not draw any attention to the abuses perpetuated by their own government. The lone exception was a group of mothers and grandmothers who had lost children to the vicious military crackdown; they gathered regularly in the Plaza de Mayo wearing diapers as headscarves and carrying about photographs of the deceased or missing loved ones. Such a performance broke no laws and did not alienate any potential supporters, while demonstrating to those who could see that there were people missing from the lives of the women.

As with the categories of Critical Worldviews and Alternative Media Interaction, Communicative Resistance can be visualized as a continuum, one that runs perpendicular to the intersection of the Critical Worldviews and the Alternative Media Interaction (see Figure 2). Tactics of Communicative Resistance that break laws or violate group norms are considered to be militant and are situated toward the top of the line, while performances that involve education and/or lawful protest tactics are considered to be adjustive and placed near the bottom. Typically, activists situated within the Radical Participatory quadrant approve of and engage in militant actions. Activists positioned within the Reformist Participatory and Reformist Lay quadrants often adhere to adjustive tactics like community education and picketing. Activists within the Radical Lay quadrant express an appreciation and admiration for militant tactics, but do not always engage in such performances.

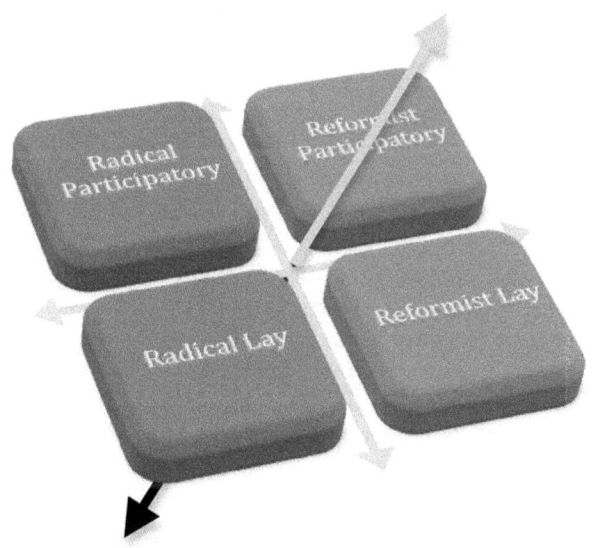

Figure 2. Communicative Resistance: Militant vs. Adjustive Tactics.

Interconnectivity: The Multiplex

The concept of the Multiplex is integral to RP, as it represents a fifth space where activists perform Communicative Resistance with activists from other theatre-like quadrants. Activists in each quadrant construct the Multiplex from themes that emerge from the culmination of all alternative media used across all of the quadrants within a network and from information in local level listservs and on the website Commondreams.org. Essentially, the

Multiplexes are large-scale co-performances of resistance by multiple activists and activist organizations. Like the name suggests, it is one large space, like a theatre multiplex, that houses many theatres that are showing different movies. Examples of the Multiplex concept would be mass demonstrations like the 1999 World Trade Organization (WTO) protests in Seattle, the 2003 Free Trade Area of the Americas (FTAA) protests in Miami, and demonstrations at the Republican and Democratic National Conventions in 2000, 2004, and 2008. In a more local sense, the Multiplex also includes large anti-war rallies and marches, Earth Day celebrations, and sexual assault awareness rallies like Take Back the Night. In each case, there are activists from all four quadrants involved in those actions, radical and reformist alike. The Multiplex is a stage in which activists of all stripes and different organizations come together to temporarily resist a power structure that they perceive to be a common threat.

Essentially, most activists use alternative media titles that are specific to their own quadrant (e.g., MoveOn.org) and a few alternative media sources that are used by everyone in the network (e.g., local level listserv/publication). The alternative media that is specific to a particular quadrant may be different from one quadrant to the next, but those alternative media titles usually entail similar conceptualizations of power and social justice; Chapters 4 and 5 will demonstrate how alternative media like *The Progressive* and *Z Magazine* contain similar themes about power. Analysis of alternative media content in past research has examined important themes that (1) emerged from *all* of the alternative media used across all four theatre-like quadrants in particular communities and (2) themes that emerged from alternative media that was specific to each individual quadrant.[3] In the analysis of all of the alternative media that were used in all of the quadrants, common themes about social justice emerged that proved to be quite broad. Such broad, social justice-oriented themes were an integral component for interconnections that gave rise to a Multiplex of coordinated RP. In addition, alternative media sources that are used by everyone in a network, like local listservs, serve an important role as they complement the emergent common themes. The following pages describe such a phenomenon, while the themes that emerged from the individual quadrants will be covered in Chapters 4 and 5.

Common Visions and Commondreams

Qualitative content analysis has demonstrated the use of broad, nebulous themes in alternative media utilized across all four theatre-like quadrants in multiple communities. In other words, broad themes emerge when looking at all of the alternative media used across an entire activist network. Across a diverse network that includes the four quadrants of RP, broad themes about "human rights" and "democracy" are often found within all of the alternative media used by activists. Overall, these themes operate as *common visions and goals* that are circulated throughout an entire network and help to link together all of the quadrants that make up that network. Not only do common themes link the theatre-like quadrants together, but also the themes establish the Multiplex that constitutes an additional space in the network where activists from differing theatre-like quadrants can coordinate performances of resistance together. In reference to the theme of "human rights," many alternative media sources contend that there has been an erosion of the rights that were established in the United Nations' (2004) Universal Declaration of Human Rights, due in large part to the profit orientation of corporations. For example, in *The Nation* article "Offering Hope—at a Price" Greider (2003) described the impact of the profit-driven pharmaceutical industry on human rights. In that article, Greider discussed how the drug industry "does not expend resources to develop medicines that might be an enormous boon for public health but offer little prospect for commercial gain" (p. 27). Instead, drug industry produces designer medicines, such as Viagra, that garner large profits for the industry, rather than medicines that can be used to treat diseases, such as malaria or yellow fever. Essentially, the corporate profit orientation interferes with issues of medicine and the well-being of all people that are integral to the Universal Declaration of Human Rights. The importance of democracy also emerges as a common theme in many alternative media sources, as content often explains how corporate profit orientation has undermined democracy. In *The Progressive* article "Holding the Line at the [Federal Communications Commission]" McChesney & Nichols (2003) claimed that corporations had gained unprecedented domination of media outlets in the United States, which has led to corporate domination of public debate about social issues like health care, taxes, and the war in Iraq. To rectify this problem, the authors discussed how US citizens should take democracy back into their hands and contact officials, such as progressives within the Federal Communications Commission (FCC), to voice their concerns about corporate domination of media.

Such themes are similar to the narratives described by Pickard (2006a), which emerged from his analysis of emails and news stories circulated through the Indymedia network. According to Pickard, there are two primary narrative types circulated through the network: "be the media" and "principles of unity." Both narrative types are nebulous and vague, in that they are defined by relatively simple concepts. "Be the media" is a narrative that calls for media democracy in opposition to the domination of the mainstream media by corporate conglomerates; such media domination by corporations silences and marginalizes alternative voices that are not a part of the corporate sphere. In order to oppose those corporate forces, many narratives suggest that it is necessary for ordinary citizen journalists to produce their own media content and add their voice to the public sphere. "Principles of unity," the second narrative type, calls for dialogue and consensus among members of the network, so as to avoid the marginalization and silence imposed by corporate conglomerations. Ultimately, the themes and narratives that have emerged from past research concerning alternative media and new social movement networks have proven to be quite nebulous and vague, based in concepts that almost everyone would accept as important and good. Who would be against democracy or human rights? Who could claim that citizen operated media and unity are bad? The nebulous nature of these themes and narratives makes them acceptable to all.

In addition to themes that emerge from cross-quadrant alternative media, the emergent Multiplex is dependent on alternative media that are used by all of the activists in each of the four quadrants of a network: "clearinghouse" websites and locally produced listservs and/or publications. A clearinghouse website is a site, usually produced at the national/international level, that entails articles from a wide variety of different alternative media sources. Commondreams.org is one such clearinghouse used by left-leaning activists in communities like Mystical City and Erie City. The content of Commondreams.org entails articles from all of the different alternative media sources, as well as links to those sources (e.g., *The Nation*, Indymedia.org). The content and the links provide all of the activists within a network, radical and reformist, with a glimpse into the worldviews and performances of resistance within the context of each of the other theatre-like quadrants. In other words, Radical Participatory activists using Commondreams.org are able to get a small look into the worldviews and performances associated with the Reformist Lay quadrant and vice versa.

In reference to a second source that is often used across all four quadrants, the listservs and many news publications produced by organizations are used to circulate information about social justice events in and around a community, which provides opportunities for activists to meet and socialize together. The following excerpt comes from an email sent out throughout a common listserv used by activists throughout the Mystical City network in June of 2003; the email serves as an example of the circulation information about sites for social interaction:

> We invite you to join us this and every Wednesday anytime between 4:15 and 5:45 p.m. for the weekly Peace Protest at Main St. and State Ave. Come for as much of the time as you can. Several of our regular participants have left town for the summer. Don't let our neighbors get the impression that the peace movement has disappeared. Help us remind folks that our concerns are substantial and our commitment to raising them is ongoing. Please join us for this highly visible effort.

Ultimately, events such as the one mentioned above allow for activists on the listserv to meet and interact with one another. Such interactions have been described by scholars as important for the social construction of reality (see Anderson, 1996; Berger & Luckman, 1966; Searle, 1995). This point is illustrated through the example of Activist #11, a Reformist Lay activist, who regularly read such emails and, hence, knew about social justice oriented events (e.g., protests, demonstrations, educational seminars) that were occurring in the area. As Activist #11 stated:

> If there's something [discussed on the listserv] that I'm interested in, I'll go to a meeting. A lot of the work I do is locally based and so if I want to put in my input on something or I want to learn about something, I'll go to a meeting and I'll talk about [that subject] there.

In addition to the primary function described above, the listserv also accomplishes a second function, circulation of common visions and goals, as the listserv is also used to forward articles and blog material that had been published in alternative media produced through global level networks (e.g., Indymedia). Therefore, the information about protests, as well as common visions and goals, are passed along on listservs and can temporarily link the four quadrants together into a larger site (see Figure 3). Within such a forum, the activists can express their worldviews or perform resistance, oftentimes within the context of common visions and goals concerning the themes of human rights and democracy.

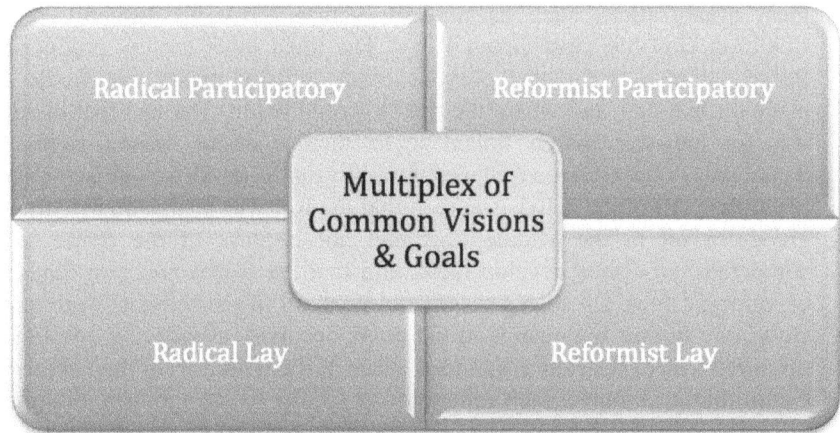

Figure 3. Emergent Multiplex.

Coordinated Performance of Resistance
The performances of diffused audiences of mainstream media described by Abercrombie and Longhurst (1998) were co-performances with consumer-oriented spectacle, which resulted in the emergence of narcissism on the part of the audience. Conversely, coordinated performances of resistance by activists from different quadrants are constructed from the categories of RP discussed previously, coupled with the common visions and goals that

emerge from alternative media used across all four theatre-like quadrants. The common visions and goals underlying most alternative media content (especially clearinghouse websites like Commondreams.org) provide a momentary context in which radical and reformist worldviews about a topic (e.g., the war in Iraq) can interconnect and perform resistance. It should also be noted that in many ways, the interconnected Multiplex of coordinated resistance proves to be similar to Best (2005) and Pickard's (2006a; 2006b) description of temporary communities and networked activism that emerge from the circulation of broad and often nebulous narratives by global level networks like Indymedia or Amnesty International. The circulation of broad narratives concerning human rights and democracy allow for the construction of a collective identity that prove to be temporary; agonisms concerning worldviews often dissolve such identity.

Take, for instance, activists' discussions concerning an anti-Iraq war march in Mystical City. The anti-war march provides an excellent example of resistance performed by activists from differing theatre-quadrants, but coordinated within the Multiplex constructed from common visions and goals. All of the social justice activists and organizations in Mystical City were aware of the February 15, 2003, event because it was discussed many times on the Peace Alliance listserv and was mentioned in the meetings of local organizations such as Student Action Network, Peaceful Peoples Coalition, and the local Green Party. The local level listserv produced by Peace Alliance discussed the event as an anti-war march that would take place on that day, and where the march would begin. The fact that the event was an anti-war march linked it to themes about human rights and democracy, which created interest for activists to perform within the larger Multiplex. All of the activists agreed that the war was instigated by corporate greed for oil in the Middle East and not because of the desire to see democratic processes develop there, and that the war would cost thousands of innocent lives. On such a vision and goal, all of the activists were united. However, during the march, dissolution occurred as activists viewed the performances of resistance that took place at the march from their respective theatre-like quadrants. Such separation is similar to the agonistic dissolution of temporary communities described by Best. Activist #9 and Activist #10—both Radical Participatory activists—described their militant performance of "taking to the streets" as appropriate actions for confronting the war in Iraq. For the Radical Participatory activists, marching in the street and blocking traffic was necessary to make their voices heard in the din of corporate-dominated spectacle. Activist #10 addressed the role of such a militant tactic:

> There were a lot of people that felt threatened that there were some people taking to the street—that weren't on the sidewalks. And I know that I was specifically concerned about why people were so threatened, why people were so angry with us. And so I guess the feedback we provide is like,

"Hey! We're not trying to hurt anybody or fuck with anybody's flow or anything. We're just trying to mobilize people and empower them."

These activists felt that such a performance physically impeded the war efforts, and placed some measure of power in their hands. Radical Lay activists also found marching in the streets to be appropriate, but only one person—Activist #7—actually engaged in that performance.

In regards to the Reformist Participatory and Reformist Lay activists, the militant performances of radicals during the march appeared inappropriate from their respective theatre-like quadrants. A Reformist Lay activist, Activist #4, claimed to like the radicals, but also expressed concern about their militant performances:

> I think I like a lot of the stuff—and I support a lot of the stuff that they're about. Sometimes I think maybe they alienate people just because sometimes they're almost like—a lot of them I know hold anarchist views, and sometimes I think they almost pigeonhole themselves, whether intentionally or inadvertently. But I think I agree with what they're doing. I think having them is pretty important for the cause on a couple of different levels because they're pretty active in doing things like protests and stuff. And also, in a way, they're kind of at a point where they're probably the most left-wing organization on campus.

Although there was some respect and even admiration for the militant radicals, reformist-minded activists, such as Activist #4, believed that the militant performances "pigeonholed" the radicals and "alienated" people. Other reformist activists described the militant performances in similar terms, pointing out that the actions of the radicals were counterproductive to any and all efforts against the war. For instance, Activist #16, a Reformist Lay activist, characterized her comprehension about the different approaches to corporate corruption by individuals in Mystical City as follows:

> [Radicals] are more anarchy and no war. I think [Activist #25] and [Activist #22] both take kind of a middle of the road, sort of trying to get that middle-class bourgeoisie over where everybody always says—you hear this all the time, "If you can convince the middle class, *it* will happen." So [the middle class] have the power to sort of sway the whole masses...I think certain crowds understand that better and the [radicals] want to see the World Bank scheduled to be smashed on Saturday at five, and that's not going to happen that way.

According to Activist #16, as well as other reformist-oriented activists, identifying with the middle class and the general population would make a nebulous "it" happen. The Reformist Participatory and Reformist Lay activists watched the militant performances from their respective theatre-like quadrants and saw actions that would offend the middle-class, "bourgeoisie" public. Consequently, they believed the mainstream public would refuse to listen to any anti-war messages altogether, including those adjustive performances by the reformist activists.

Conclusion

The preceding chapter demonstrates two kinds of new social movement networks that exist at different levels: global networks and local networks.[4] Stengrim and Pickard's research (as well as Castells and Huesca) describe networks in which global level organizations, like Indymedia, are able to use the Internet to interconnect nodes around the globe and circulate narratives about power and social justice. In this way, Indymedia is an all-channel network (Arquilla & Ronfeldt, 2001; Evan, 1972) that is comprised of several different Independent Media Centers, each one with its own website, and each website connected to all of the others, as well as to the overarching Indymedia.org site. The Internet not only allows for multiple nodes of a single organization to interconnect, but also allows for different global level organizations to mesomobilize and build temporary communities of protest. At the local level, in communities around the world, various activists "plug into" one or more global networks through alternative media. In some cases, such plugging in may entail merely a lay reading (e.g., checking into a website to read articles) or may entail additional participatory actions (e.g., commentary about online articles, open-publishing). In both cases, the worldviews and use of alternative media construct for the activist, and activists with whom they engage, a theatre in which they publicly perform resistance against dominant power structures. In turn, many participatory activists assemble and maintain organizations through the circulation of narratives that they have found in the global level alternative media within the area, which draws other activists, participatory and lay alike. The worldviews of activists in those organizations, then, often mirror narratives about power found in alternative media produced and circulated by those global networks. Essentially, the four theatre-like quadrants constitute a local level network that often spans an entire community. In addition, at least one participatory organization acts as a "hub" for the network, producing some form of alternative media, such as a listserv or newsletter, which is circulated among the other activists and organizations through the theatre-like quadrants that make up the network. Such alternative media is integral for the emergence of the temporary Multiplex of coordinated performance.

Take, for instance, the case of Mystical City (see Atkinson, 2008; 2009a; Atkinson & Dougherty, 2006). The primary media produced in Mystical City were the Peace Alliance listserv and the *Peace Alliance Observer*, a monthly newsletter about social justice activities in Mystical City that was circulated to a mailing list of 6000 in the metropolitan area. Both media were important because of two functions that they served. One function was to make articles about broad concepts such as "human rights" and "democracy" available to activists affiliated with the overarching network. In addition, the Peace Alliance collaborated with other activist newspapers in Mystical City, forwarding articles about "human rights" and "democracy" to the editors for inclusion in those papers. The second function was to circulate information about social justice demonstrations in Mystical City, providing opportunities for activists to engage in coordinated performances of resistance. Peace Alliance also worked with a community radio station to produce a community calendar that provided information about social justice events and demonstrations. In these two functions Peace Alliance served as the hub of the network, providing to activists information that was necessary for the emergence of the Multiplex of common visions and goals of RP. In the case of Peace Alliance, the steering committee members who produced the listserv and newsletter performed resistance within the context of the Reformist Participatory quadrant. The demonstrations and social justice that emerged from those functions were in response to some "threat" to the broad narratives circulated through the listserv and newsletter; activists across the four quadrants of the Mystical network were able come together into temporary protest communities to oppose the threat. The opportunities for dialogue, performance, and reading of alternative media presented within the Mystical City network allowed for the development of political identity, which is not so much the case with traditional institutions like the Republican and Democratic parties (e.g., Castells, 1996; 2004; 2006; Huesca, 2001).

Therefore, new social movements, such as the peace movement and the environmental movement, tend to be small in scale and decentralized with few, if any, recognizable leaders at the global level as they circulate narratives in alternative media that reflect traditional or hegemonic visions of power. At the global level, these movements exist as a series of nodes interconnected by websites, YouTube communities, and Facebook profiles. In local communities, organizations affiliated with these movements emerge, each holding only a few dozen members at most and shifting roles among those members. Because of their small size and decentralized nature, these local level organizations enable citizens who are concerned about particular issues, such as war and peace, a forum where they can communicate with others. At the local level, in places like Mystical City citizens cannot easily participate in dialogue about controversial political issues, like the war in Iraq or the impact of corporate crime on the environment, within the frameworks of traditional institutions like the Democratic and Republican parties. The lack of dialogue contributes to the erosion of political identity described by Castells (1996) and Huesca (2001). In order to fill the void, citizens are often able to turn to a network of local organizations influenced by global level new social movement networks, like the Indymedia network.

Chapter 3 explores the role of interactivity within the framework of RP. In particular, the chapter examines the role of interactivity within local level networks, and describes two types of interactivity as categories important for RP. First, global connectivity, which entails the role of user-to-document interactivity in the production of alternative media, will be explicated and explored. In addition, the chapter describes the narrative capacity of communities and networks, which entails user-to-user interactivity through local level media, as a category important for the construction of the Multiplex of coordinated performance of resistance.

Chapter 3
Interactivity

The following chapter provides:

1) A description of the fourth category of RP, Intercreative Capacity, which entails the role of user-to-document interactivity in the production of alternative media.

2) A description of the fifth category of RP, Narrative Capacity, which entails the role of user-to-user interactivity in the construction of the Multiplex of coordinated performance.

The previous chapter illustrated the framework of Resistance Performance, which entails the emergence of four activist quadrants and a Multiplex of coordinated performance. Essentially, the first two categories, Critical Worldviews and Alternative Media Interaction, construct the four quadrants that serve as theatres in which activists engage in the third category of Communicative Resistance. The type of resistance, militant or adjustive, is usually dependant on activists' worldviews and the backdrop of alternative media content, which will be covered in more detail in Chapters 4 and 5. From their respective quadrants, activists circulate narratives about power, social justice, and resistance that are based on personal experience, organizations with which they are affiliated, or news stories produced by global level networks. The circulation of such narratives allow for organizations to form and grow, which stands as the construction of local level networks. Citizens and activists alike could become politically involved in controversial topics through those networks, which could in turn counteract the voids in political identity created by the networked society, as described by Castells and Huesca. Chapter 3 illustrates the important role that local level networks play in the interactive production of alternative media at both the local and global levels. In addition, the chapter expands upon the theoretical framework of RP by taking a closer look at the role of interactivity within local networks, and notes the importance of such interactivity in the construction of the Multiplex. Therefore, the following chapter explores the fourth and fifth categories of RP: Intercreative Capacity, Narrative Capacity.

As discussed in the previous chapter, Denzin made significant contributions to research concerning audience performance that corresponds with Abercrombie and Longhurst's SP, by conceptualizing audience performances with media and texts as "lay" or "participatory." By lay, Denzin (1997) meant that the audience merely seeks information or enjoyment from the performances that they observe in a text. In contrast, the participatory audience engages with the performances they observe "as co-performers or critics (in the postperformance phase) of the performance" (p. 101). Essentially, the participatory audience adds to performances through their interactions with either alternative media content or alternative media producers. As a concept, interactivity associated with media has been defined in a variety of ways. Research has defined interactivity as audience reactions to transmissions from a sender (e.g., Rafaeli, 1988; Sundar, Kalyanaraman, & Brown, 2003; Turrow, 1977), and it has been understood as audience engagement with texts (e.g., Endres & Warnick, 2004; Warnick, Xenos, Endres, & Gastil, 2005). In fact, George Landow (2006) has claimed that the concepts of interactive and interactivity have "been used so often and so badly that they have little exact meaning anymore" (p. 41), and that few media are actually interactive; true interactivity only occurs when audiences co-create media content along with producers (see Landlow, 2006; Meikle, 2002).

Despite such conflict concerning interactivity, Sally McMillan (2002) noted three definitions for media-related interactivity that have emerged in Communication and Media literature: (1) user-to-system, (2) user-to-user, and (3) user-to-document. User-to-system refers to interactions between new media users and their technological systems, similar to interactions with Google or Yahoo! on one's computer (e.g., Durlak, 1987; Kiousis, 2002). User-to-user refers to interactions between two or more people through new media systems, such as conversations using email or Instant Messenger (e.g., Puopolo, 2001; Stromer-Galley, 2000). For instance, mass communication research exploring user-to-user interactivity has demonstrated the concept of "flaming," which asserts that individuals are more likely to engage in critical interactions or provocative remarks online than in face-to-face settings (e.g., Bernthal, 1995; Cosentio, 1994; O'Sullivan & Flanagin, 2003). Finally, user-to-document interaction "occurs when users modify site texts, or when real-time feedback collected from receivers is used by the source to modify the message" (Endres & Warnick, 2004, p. 325). By such a definition for media-related interactivity, the audience is capable of adding directly to or modifying media content, as with websites like Indymedia.org (e.g., Kidd, 2003; Meikle, 2002). In addition, this definition applies to interactions between audiences and producers that result in the modification or enhancement of media content (e.g., Armstrong, 1981; Atton, 2002a; Eliasoph, 1988). Ultimately, user-to-document interactivity is not about using "interactive" media like Google or Instant Messenger as much as it is about a process in which audiences play a creative role in the production of media content (Berners-Lee, 1999; Landlow, 2006). Meikle (2002) calls interactions in which audiences have a hand in the creation of media content "intercreativity." In the following sections, interactivity is conceptualized in terms of the latter two forms: user-to-document and user-to-user.

Intercreative Capacity: User-to-Document Interactivity

The fourth category associated with RP, Intercreative Capacity, emerges from user-to-document interactivity, discussed above, in two ways. First, user-to-document interactivity, in the form of audience feedback, proves to be integral for the production of alternative media within local level networks. Second, user-to-document interactivity—again, feedback—between participatory activists in local networks and producers affiliated with global level networks plays an important role in the production of global level alternative media. Essentially, the capacity for local networks to provide feedback to alternative media producers at the local and global levels constitutes an important component of the RP framework. As in the case of the first three categories discussed in Chapter 2, the category of Intercreative Capacity focuses on local level activists. Different from those previous categories, however, is the fact that this category also involves alternative media producers from global level networks.[1] The category of Intercreative Capacity is based, in large part, on the *nature of audience interactions*, which deals with two different types of interactions between audiences and producers that have been observed in past research: activists' interactions with producers concerning either *encouragement* or *content*. Local level producers often receive simplistic encouragement in face-to-face interactions, whereas the producers affiliated with global networks most likely receive critical interactions about their content via email. The following pages provide details concerning the encouragement and content-oriented interactions and examine the role of those interactions in the production of alternative media.

Interactivity and Local Producers of Alternative Media
The local producers of alternative media content associated with organizations within local level networks often claim to have regular interactions with their (participatory) audiences in the local community; the interactions are often described as face-to-face and encouragement-oriented. Activists who fall within both the Radical Participatory and Reformist Participatory theatre-quadrants of RP—as lay activists rarely, if ever, engage in alternative media production or interactions with alternative media producers—initiate such audience interactions. In those situations, the participatory activists often meet the local level producers in face-to-face

situations, and provide to the producers encouragement and appreciation for their work on a listserv, or any of the other alternative media (e.g., zines, pamphlets, community radio broadcasts). For instance, Activist #22, who worked on a local level listserv, described her interactions with audiences who approached her while she would do volunteer work in the community:

> We don't get a whole lot of feedback as far as letters to the editor, or things like that, but like people who come into the store a lot. And I work in the store too, so I get to interact in that way. And you know people are like, "That was a great article you had," or, "I really appreciate your writing."

Local level producers often describe similar situations in which they meet their audience, often activists, in public places. In those situations, the interactions rarely, if ever, go beyond a simple greeting and commentary in which the audience would tell them that they were doing a "terrific job" and to "keep up the good work."

Participatory activists, radical and reformist alike, reiterate such face-to-face, encouragement-oriented interactions when they describe their own interactions with local alternative media producers. Activist #13, a faculty member who worked as a community organizer, discussed "suggestions" that he would make to Activist #25, who worked on the local listserv and hosted a community radio program:

> *Activist #13*: I'll see [Activist #25] at rush hour protests on a fairly regular basis. We don't get into long discussions on things. I will make suggestions. I'm not involved in Peace Alliance planning sessions at this point.
>
> *Interviewer*: What kind of suggestions do you make?
>
> *Activist #13*: [Pause]. Usually it's just encouragement about what he's doing.

When asked about the "suggestions" that he made, Activist #13 reported encouraging comments rather than actual suggestions about alternative media format or content. Other activists consider buying products sold by organizations that produce alternative media to be an interaction that "encourages" the local producers. For instance, Activist #18, a self-described "radical cheerleader," claimed, "I guess I have shopped at the Social Justice Cubbyhole [operated by Peace Alliance] and I've definitely supported them a lot. I think that's a great indication that they're a really good source."

The encouragement proves to be important as local producers usually value the encouragement that they receive from the audience. Activist #24, a community educator and a local producer of a community newspaper, discussed how such encouragement made her "feel good":

> I think [the encouragement] did make me feel good about [writing]. Like I said, I'd like to write more…But I have had other people who I didn't know

were sympathetic—like to sweatshop stuff—say, "Oh, I saw your article on sweatshops," and just start talking about the issue. And so that kind of surprised me.

Activist #24 also indicated that audience encouragement made her feel good about her work with the community newspaper when she discussed a recent article she had written about a protest, "I got a lot of good feedback from people who were like, 'Wow! I really liked that article.' It really made me feel good about [my work] and that sort of thing." Such encouragement-oriented interactions are similar to the concept of "positive feedback." Past research by Deanna Geddes and Frank Linnehan (1996) illustrated two feedback types in organizations: positive and negative. "Positive feedback tends to produce mindless thinking patterns during decision making, in contrast to the mindful information processing following negative feedback" (p. 339). Positive feedback is simplistic because there is little guidance to the recipient of the feedback, whereas negative feedback is complex because it aids the recipient to reflect on the subject matter. The encouragement interactions were similar to positive feedback as they produced little guidance about the alternative media content. For instance, Activist #23, a writer for the same community newspaper discussed above, stated the following about his interactions with audiences, "The positive stuff mostly doesn't do much. It just makes me think, 'oh okay they like this.' Glad I wrote it kind of thing. It doesn't influence the work."

Instead, the simplistic encouragement-oriented interactions seemed to function as discursive closures described by Stan Deetz (1992) and Robin Clair (1998). According to Clair, "certain forms of discourse act to distort power relations, disguise inequity, sequester resistant discourses, and ultimately close emancipatory forms of communication" (p. 38) through communicative practices such as naturalization, topical avoidance, subjectification of experience, and legitimation. Indeed, the findings suggest that the encouragement-oriented interactions constitute topical avoidance, in which individuals felt that discussion of their own feelings or perceptions was prohibited (see Deetz, 1992). Activist #16 was a volunteer for a local level organization, and worked with producers of a community newspaper; she described how she avoided drawing attention to problems she perceived in articles within that community newspaper for fear of a "hierarchical thing":

> I try to make my opinion known at the Cubbyhole. Maybe sometimes I'm not as publicly as vocal as I should be. And I tend to go home and tell my boyfriend about it or tell my friends about it. It's really hard for me because of that hierarchical thing I was talking about before where there's sort of "our way or the highway" feeling once in a great while. Not that I don't feel I'm free to speak my mind, but I get that kind of fear when—they're kind of in charge and I have a hard time expressing myself.

Many activists in similar situations, radical and reformist, echo the perception that their opinions might be prohibited by some "hierarchical thing," and so problems that they perceive with the content are never acknowledged in their interactions with the local producers. Interestingly, DeLuca (1999) noted how most radical social movement organizations, like Green Peace and Earth First!, often reject hierarchy. It is true that many organizations with primarily radical activists as members, on the surface, are often described as nonhierarchical with no official leaders. However, hierarchy does exist as a component of those organizations in terms of the deep structures that develop through the preconscious assumptions held concerning what actions or behaviors are deemed to be appropriate or inappropriate (e.g., Giddens, 1984; Weick, 1979); such deep structure is maintained by way of rewards and punishments (see Gramsci, 1971). Because of deep structures that emerge in groups like Green Peace, hierarchy develops without any codified rules or laws, as certain individuals emerge who maintain the deep structure of the organization.

Interestingly, the local producers also report instances of simplistic encouragement as topical avoidance. Activist #24, the community educator, felt that there were problems with the way Activist #25 operated his local radio program:

> There's something that I've thought about talking to [Activist #25] about but I haven't gotten around to it yet. So I don't know if this counts, but I feel like he does this thing sometimes where if somebody calls up [on the radio show] who is obviously of a different opinion of him, he kind of talks over them and doesn't let them express themselves and it's not respectful really. But that's something that I want to figure out. A way to tell him without offending him... I think I try to like not step on people's toes in general. So I think I try to be respectful in general.

Rather than discussing format and content of the radio show and risk "stepping on people's toes," many activists engage in self-censorship to avoid the topic and instead provide "respectful" encouragement; in such situations the local producers are complimented for their "good job" and for picking "good topics." Essentially, such work on the part of activists to avoid critiques via simple encouragement represents an adherence to hierarchy, even within organizations dominated by radical members; the encouragement avoids the potential for upsetting the deep structure and upsetting those who reinforce the deep structure through punishment.

Essentially, user-to-document interactivity plays a dual role in the production of alternative media in local level new social movement networks. First, the participants (audiences and local producers alike) often avoid discussions about perceived problems with the alternative media content in their face-to-face interactions with local producers, and instead provide encouragement for the "good work" of the producers. Such discursive avoidance is similar to Pickard's (2006b) discursive "tyrannies" of ideology, structuralessness, and editor that emerged in past research concerning the limitations on new social movement networks as they sought to "level hierarchies" inside and outside of the network. Oftentimes, audience perceptions about a "hierarchical thing" seem to limit their role in the network as their interactions about alternative media are limited to simple encouragement, leaving local producers blind to potential problems that their audiences perceive in the content. Second, the encouragement interactions constitute an important element necessary for the establishment of perceived organizational support. Perceived organizational support occurs when members of an organization feel that their effort and loyalty are worthwhile (see Allen, 1995). Top-down (e.g., Allen, 1995; Rhoades & Eisenberger, 2002) and bottom-up (e.g., Shanock & Eisenberger, 2006) interactions between different levels of an organization are both important for high perceptions of organizational support. The encouragement often helps local producers to feel their work on alternative media in the network is important and appreciated.

Global Production: Interactions about Content
The global producers of alternative media are often scholars, activists, and/or writers who contribute content to Internet, print, and radio alternative media sources that are accessible to national and international audiences.[2] Because of their work with websites like Commondreams.org and magazines like *The Nation*, such producers were a part of the global networks discussed in the Chapter 2. Global producers often claim to engage in interactions with audiences via the Internet; the "nature of interactions" is usually focused on content. The content-oriented interactions are similar to the negative feedback and "mindful processing" described by Geddes and Linnehan (1996). This is not the simple encouragement that gives rise to "mindless thinking patterns," as the notion of negative feedback refers to questions and/or suggestions about content to a producer. Often audiences sought clarification on matters in the alternative media content. According to Global Producer #1:

> Well, most [interactions are] just inquiries. "Where can I find—you said so-and-so, where can I find something about it?" Or, "I want…" When I'm giving talks I constantly try at least to say, "Look, I don't want you to believe me, I want you to check it out." And I'll often get requests from people that want to check it out.

Because of the content-oriented interactions from audiences, Global Producer #1, as well as other global producers, often experiences the need to provide details about their content, such as sources and dates that can be verified. Similar requests were made of Global Producer #7, who coordinated articles and information on the World Wide Outreach website:

> I get everything from "how do I get more information" to "how do I get involved" to "you guys suck." It's really the whole gambit of responses. But most of them are sympathetic. People who disagree with us generally don't take the time to write in. Mostly it's people like yourself who are writing for more information about what we do and how to get involved.

Such complex audience interactions about content play an important role in the production of alternative media at the global level. According to Global Producer #4, interactions with audiences provide information about audience opinions and audience interpretations of his content in sources such as *The Nation*:

> I mean it actually helps my work because it helps give me some understanding of who's out there. I mean its data. It's not a random sample, but it is data about how—I know something about how one hundred people think about some things. And I sometimes try to understand the patterns in the mail like this. And yeah—I mean it's in a small way a piece of instruction for me. But do I change the way I write and think. I mean if somebody makes an argument that I've gotten—I'm just giving this as an example because I got a lot of mail this week. I'd say maybe three or four people made points that I felt were intelligent and probably right. So I stand corrected on—I mean if I write more on the subject I will take these responses into account for sure.

Global Producer #4 explained that his interactions with audiences in many ways provided him with "data" about the social climate and potential audiences—a kind of audience analysis. He knew which topics he should address and how to address them based on such audience interactions. Ultimately, he looked for "patterns" in the opinions of his audience to shape his work and to gauge the impact of his work. The content-oriented interactions held additional implications for the global producers. According to Global Producer #3, a regular contributor to *The New Left Review* and Commondreams.org, audience interactions helped guide him to topics for his work:

> Someone had written me that what something that [a friend] and I had written was something like this book by an activist in South Africa. So I read that book and I wrote [South African activist] and I met the people who's working with him and then—and [the meeting] definitely frames what I'm writing now.

In this instance, one person emailed Global Producer #3 ideas that aided his work writing content that would later be used in alternative media produced by and circulated from a global level network. In addition, Global Producer

#7 reported that some audience interactions pointed out problems on the World Wide Outreach website:

> I mean the comments we get are that stuff is maybe too hard to find. So we can definitely take in that feedback and we redesigned the new website, which we're hoping to launch in the next couple of weeks. We hope it is more user friendly.

According to Global Producer #7, audience interactions were crucial to revealing "hard to find" flaws with the website, which helped him to redesign the website and address audience needs. Therefore, the email interactions with audiences are considerably different from the simple encouragement experienced by the local producers. The content-oriented interactions provide global producers with the opportunity to revisit and build on their own content and arguments.

Interestingly, the audiences who discuss content-related interactions with global producers are typically local level producers. Rarely, if ever, do non-producing activists report any user-to-document interactivity with global producers. Activist #25, a Reformist Participatory activist who produced an organizational listserv and a community radio broadcast, explained how he interacted with global producers:

> I've occasionally sent an email asking for clarification on something I heard on *Democracy Now!*, or asked for more information, or passed on a source or something. I actually just sent something to *Democracy Now!* yesterday suggesting they might do something on the Mystical City Republican Central Committee Chair who just resigned and put out an anti-war statement.

In this case, Activist #25 emailed a suggestion along to Amy Goodman of *Democracy Now!* The activist was never aware of any action taken by Goodman or the other producers of *Democracy Now!* to include the topic in any of their broadcasts. Similarly, Activist #23 often took the time to email producers of content for *Z Magazine* when she felt that they had missed important facts:

> *Activist #22*: Sometimes if I feel strongly about it. I'll send an email or write a letter or something like that. In general I just kind of take it as it comes.
>
> *Author*: What are those things that you felt strongly about?
>
> *Activist #22*: Mainly something like leaving a group out of a list or something like that.

The suggestions made by both Activist #22 and Activist #25 were similar to content-oriented interactions described by global producers. In both examples the activists either asked for clarifications about where to find more information on a topic, addressed problems that they found in the content, or made suggestions about where to look for information and contacts.

Essentially, the global producers claim that they often engage in interactions with their audiences via email about alternative media content. In addition, local producers often describe email interactivity about content between themselves within their own local networks and global producers of alternative media. Such insights from audiences and producers help to provide a glimpse into a process of interactions between the global producers and their audiences, which help the global producers to assess their work and in some instances make changes to content. As global producers have demonstrated, interactions with audiences often lead to clarification on positions, on facts, and even provide greater insight into audiences and topics. However, it should be noted that the findings from past research do not demonstrate *direct* interactivity between the two levels as the global producers in many of those cases were unaware of details about the audiences who interacted with them about content (e.g., location, organization affiliation), and the local producers did not report emailing any of the global producers who took part in such research. Past research only demonstrates that producers in local level networks often interact with the global level, and that global producers often interact with their audiences.

Production Level(s) and Interactivity
The concepts of encouragement and content-oriented feedback in user-to-document interactivity with local and global producers of alternative media hold two important implications. First, the findings help to establish a multilevel model that illustrates the integral role of interactivity between the global and local levels in the intercreative production of alternative media (see Figure 1). At the top of this model is the global production level where alternative media content (solid line) is produced by individual creators and made accessible to audiences through sources like Commondreams.org and *Z Magazine*. The local producers also create content (solid line), which audiences often access through newsletters, listservs, and community radio. The audience level uses content from both local and global producers, and in turn interacts with the local level producers providing them encouragement (dotted line). Finally, the local producers interact with the individual global producers, providing comments about global producers' work (dashed line).

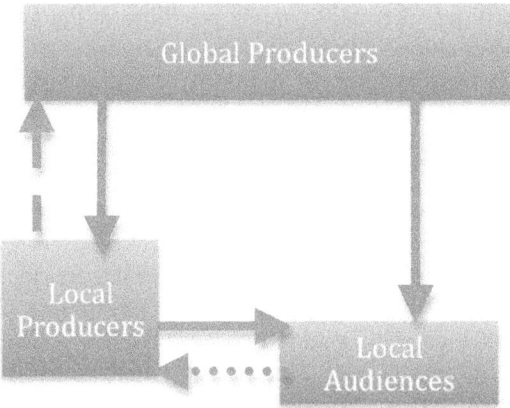

Figure 1. Model of Interactivity in Alternative Media Production.

Second, this model builds on the theoretical implications about the role of interactive alternative media within the concept of RP established in the previous chapter. Specifically, this interactivity model demonstrates the importance of interactive audiences and producers in the construction of alternative media texts that portray traditional and hegemonic power, which are integral for the emergence of RP. Essentially, participatory activists' interactions with alternative media producers at the local level builds and maintains a "blinded" support network that *potentially* aids in interactive production of alternative media at the global level. The model builds on research concerning the circulation of broad narratives and themes like "be the media" between activists through listservs and discussion boards (Best, 2005; Pickard, 2006a; 2006b; Stengrim, 2005), as well as research concerning discursive closures of the tyrannies of ideology, structuralessness, and editor associated with the technologies and ideologies of new social movement networks (see Pickard, 2006b).

Ultimately, an intercreative relationship between the global level and the local level emerges from the provision of feedback between audiences and producers. Audiences and activists in local networks utilize alternative media produced by individuals affiliated with nodes of global networks. Such content helps those activists and their organizations to develop a sense about the nature of power in society, which serves as the basis for the Communicative Performances described in Chapter 2. In addition, the content from globally produced alternative media serves as the source for the broad themes of "human rights" and "democracy" associated with the Multiplex. The encouragement-oriented interactions between activists and local producers create a sense of organizational support for those participatory local producers throughout the local network. With such support, the local producers are able to accomplish two tasks: circulate information and critique alternative media produced at the global level. The circulation of information allows for the emergence of the Multiplex described in the previous chapter. In addition, the critique provided to global producers helps them to strengthen their alternative media content, which is then circulated to audiences and activists in local networks.

Narrative Capacity: User-to-User Interactivity

The three categories associated with RP outlined in the previous chapter play an important role in the emergence of the temporary Multiplex of coordinated performance. The worldviews and use of alternative media set the stage for the emergence of theatres in which activists engaged in Communicative Resistance. Narratives circulated by organizations and communities through user-to-user interactive media, such as listservs, aided in the emergence of the Multiplex in which differing communities could coordinate Communicative Resistance together. In addition to those first three categories, Narrative Capacity, the fifth category, constitutes the capacity of a network to efficiently circulate narratives to activists through interactive media, such as listservs. This fifth category of RP is one that can either aid or hinder the emergence of the overarching Multiplex of coordinated performance. This category emerged from interviews with activists in the northeastern community of Erie City.[3] Ultimately, all of the important categories of RP that had been observed in past research were observed in the Erie City network. In addition, there was one Reformist Participatory organization, the Olive Branch Association (OBA), which served as a "hub" at the center of the network; this organization produced a listserv and a newsletter that was circulated throughout all of the theatre-like quadrants of Erie City. However, despite the similarity to past RP research, the activists of the Erie City network never reported examples of a Multiplex of coordinated resistance emerging within their network. Instead, many Reformist Participatory activists who were direct members of the OBA frequently spoke of taking part in protests and actions coordinated by the OBA, while most activists who fell within the other three quadrants (and even some affiliated with the Reformist Participatory quadrant) described a reluctance to take part in those actions. Essentially, activists outside of the OBA were rarely involved in that organization's actions, even though most of those activists reported using the OBA listserv as a source of information about social justice issues and events in Erie City, as well as frequently engaging in face-to-face interactions with OBA members and the OBA steering committee at various sites across Erie City. The fact that many activists used the hub organization's listserv and interacted with members of that organization, but were reluctant to take part in actions organized by the hub, represented a significant hindrance for the emergence of the Multiplex.

Interviews with Erie City activists revealed two categorical problems that seemed to hinder the emergence of a Multiplex in which coordinated resistance could be performed by different activists and organizations in the network. Such problems were manifested in the network as "fractures" because they were divisive in nature, involving two competing visions about the OBA. These problematic fractures emerged in activists' discussions concerning the social justice issues addressed by the OBA, and the protest actions orchestrated by the OBA.

Fracture #1: Issues. The first fracture stemmed from divergent visions about the social justice issues addressed by the OBA in its protests and events. Specifically, this category encapsulated the beliefs among activists that the OBA was either "open" to a wide variety of social justice issues, or that the OBA was "restricted" solely to the topic of the wars in Iraq and Afghanistan. The activists who discussed the organization as *open to diverse issues* claimed that the OBA was a place in which activists could bring any idea to the steering committee and receive support to move their idea to action. Activist #38, a member of the OBA steering committee, stated the following:

> People look at our mission statement, which talks about trying to create a society that is based on mutual cooperation and respect rather than oppression and hierarchy. I think people who are working on corporate globalization and economic stuff or racism feel like they can fit into the OBA.

From this excerpt, Activist #38 felt that the broad mission of the OBA allowed activists all over Erie City to come to the organization and address a diverse range of social justice issues. She described the organization as a place where activists concerned with racism or economics could go to "fit in" and work on those issues. Activist #35, owner of an "alternative" bookstore in downtown Erie City, noted that the OBA conducts workshops on a wide range of social justice issues such as sustainable lifestyles, how to recycle, "the nuclear message" and "what [then-President George W.] Bush is really saying." Activist #42, who worked with an Erie City Latina/o community center, said that lately the OBA "had been working with the immigration issues" and protesting the construction of a sewage treatment plant in the predominantly African-American quarter of Erie City. Each of these activists felt that the OBA was a place that was broad in its mission to social justice, allowing for the organization to address a wide range of social justice issues.

Conversely, activists who discussed the OBA as *restricted on issues* claimed that the organization's sole interest was anti-war issues and little else. For instance, Activist #33, an organizer who worked with the Erie City

Urban Partnership, described the different kinds of "social justice movements" found in Erie City:

> There's sort of the peace and justice movements that coalesce around not really local issues. Bigger issues about war and peace…[OBA's] work tends to be more symbolic. [OBA will] hold a rally. Big deal. War is bad. Yeah! Okay. There doesn't seem to be a strategy to move it forward.

In this excerpt, Activist #33 complained that some social justice movements in Erie City were only concerned with "issues about war and peace" and nothing else; he included the OBA in this category. Activist #33, as well as other activists, claimed that the OBA occasionally made "awkward" attempts to dabble in local issues with groups like the Partnership. However, they felt that such dabbling was only a charade used to draw attention to the OBAs "symbolic" work against war. Activist #43, owner and operator of an "independent African-American newspaper" in Erie City, claimed that the OBA protests against the sewage plant previously mentioned were only organized to get "African-Americans to stand in the picture and smile." According to Activist #43, the OBA had no intention of ever stopping the construction of the sewage plant or empowering the people in those communities. The attention paid to the issue was merely a photo opportunity to help the OBA demonstrate that they were a racially diverse anti-war organization.

Fracture #2: Actions. The second fracture stemmed from contrasting views about the nature of the OBA protest actions and events. In particular, this category entailed the opinion among activists that the OBA protest actions were inclusive and allowed for anyone to partake, or exclusive to a select group of activist "elites." Those activists who discussed the actions as *inclusive* claimed that the OBA reached outward to bring in as many perspectives as possible. For instance, Activist #29, who had worked on the steering committee in the past, said the following:

> I think the OBA has been working hard to use its broad focus to—to welcome people from different backgrounds. And even though the OBA is still primarily a white organization they've made some incredible progress connecting with the Muslim community.

In this excerpt, Activist #29 acknowledged that the OBA had been limited and narrow in terms of the background of their membership, but they had worked to "connect" to immigrants and people of color and include them in the OBA actions. Other activists who worked directly or indirectly with the OBA confirmed this perception that the organization worked to include different communities. Activist #42, a Latina activist, noted how the OBA often included the Latino community in their protests and actions, while

Activist #35, an African-American activist, felt the OBA had effectively included the African-American community in their efforts.

On the other hand, many activists discussed the OBA actions as *exclusive* and that the organization was elitist, recruiting select individuals and groups to take part in marches and protests. Activist #41, a Rastafarian activist, claimed to have observed OBA exclusion of young people in the community:

> [The OBA is] kind of elitist. I've seen them be approached by youth who were very interested in becoming involved. And they turned them away more or less. You know? It's almost like certain demographics aren't even welcomed.

She went on to tell stories about how she had witnessed the OBA turn away young African-American activists who had hoped to get involved in activities. In addition, Activist #41 claimed to have experienced such exclusion herself when she attended an OBA meeting and requested for the members of the steering committee to take part in an AIDS walk. She claimed that her request was met with a few kind words and a refusal, "It's like the feeling that you get when you walk in. It's not open arms. It's not opened minds all the way… A lot of times you don't feel—you walk in and you feel awkward." Such claims of exclusion were not limited to merely closing access to events or protests. Many of the activists claimed that they or their organizations were invited to take part in OBA actions, only to be denied the opportunity to speak or take an active role at those actions. For instance, Activist #34, a labor organizer, stated: "I think when it comes to peace rallies particularly, [Labor One is] invited to show, but not invited to speak on the podium."

In part, the fractures about issues and actions that emerged in the interviews constructed an overarching perception held by many activists that the OBA had claimed "ownership" over concepts of social justice. Activist #41 explained, "There's like an ownership thing to [OBA] that, you know—people try to take [social justice] as their own. It's just bad business." Essentially, Activist #41 saw the OBA as owning the concept of social justice, which she felt leads to a "this is the way I want this to work…this is how I want it run" approach to social justice protest and actions. Other activists agreed with this notion of ownership as others described the OBA as "branding" themselves as *the* social justice organization of Erie City. Activist #41 claimed that such ownership/branding made other activists feel "a little bit pushed back…a little bit less welcomed…a little bit less motivated, and a little bit less apt to become involved." Ultimately, the perception of ownership/branding led many activists to feel that they were unwelcome in the Erie City new social movement network dominated by the OBA.

Ultimately, two disparate stories emerged from activists' discussions about the OBA—the central hub of the Erie City network. There was a positive vision of the OBA as an inclusive organization that was open to a diversity of issues and worked collaboratively in their actions throughout Erie City. Direct members of the OBA, most of which were activists who fell with the Reformist Participatory quadrant, held such a view. Conversely, there was a negative vision of the OBA as an elitist organization that used the issues of other organizations to funnel attention to the OBA's primary anti-war issue; Radical Participatory activists held such a Machiavellian view of the OBA. In addition, three Reformist Participatory activists loosely affiliated with the OBA also held the Machiavellian view of the organization. It should also be noted that the Reformist Lay activists and all of the Radical Lay activists were apathetic about the OBA or felt it was in the best interest of their organizations that they avoid OBA actions. Such disparate visions of the OBA—the hub of the network—divided not only the four quadrants, but cut across the Reformist Participatory quadrant.

Such divisiveness is not unheard of, as past research has demonstrated how differing sympathies or tactics create animosities between opposing factions within social movements (see Fantasia, 1988; Gustainis & Hahn, 1988). In fact, fractures over tactics had emerged in the Peace Alliance network described in Chapter 2. However, those fractures emerged during the course of protests and demonstrations, leading to the dissolution of the temporary Multiplex of coordinated performance; such fractures were part of a cycle of building temporary protest communities, protesting together, and then breaking apart. In the case of Erie City, the fractures that emerged stood as an obstacle that prevented the establishment of temporary protest communities altogether. Interestingly, Pickard (2006b) again sheds clues about the nature of the fractures in Erie City. As discussed earlier in this chapter, Pickard's research illustrated "tyrannies" associated with the interactive technology used to coordinate and circulate narratives in new social movement networks: tyranny of ideology, tyranny of structuralessness, and tyranny of editor. The inflexible ideologies held by activists within a network, elites shrouded in a nebulous structuralessness, and the uncertainty associated with vague editorial policies can limit efforts for democratic processes within a new social movement network. Pickard's clues concerning the tyrannies of interactive technology led to a closer investigation of the alternative media used by the Erie City activists, which revealed a significant deviation from the concept of RP described in the previous chapter. When it came to the use of alternative media—particularly their use of the OBA listserv—the interviews with Erie City activists revealed widespread confusion concerning the listserv. As explained in Chapter 2, listservs and other such locally produced interactive media are used to both forward articles about "human rights" and "democracy" to audiences and activists, and circulate a calendar of social justice events that provided opportunities for activists to coordinate protest activities. According to Atkinson and Dougherty (2006) "the information sent out on listservs, such as the Peace Alliance listserv, often brought audience participants together into a forum where they could express their worldviews or perform communicative strategies" (p. 81). Ultimately, listservs were integral to the emergence of the Multiplex because it informed all activists involved with the network about opportunities for the four quadrants to unite and protest an issue that threatened "human rights" and "democracy."

Many of the Erie City activists in the Reformist Participatory quadrant were members of the OBA steering committee who produced the OBA listserv or worked with those producers, and most of the activists in the other three quadrants claimed to be on the listserv. However, when discussing their use of alternative media, many of the activists—particularly activists in the Reformist Participatory quadrant in which the listserv was produced—told conflicting accounts about (1) the functions of the listserv in the network and (2) how the listserv was operated. For some of the activists, the function of the listserv within the network was similar to those functions described in Chapter 2: forwarding articles and a community calendar. For instance, Activist #44, a steering committee member, said about the OBA listserv, "It's consciousness raising. There's articles. It alerts readers about events that are upcoming, events that occurred, and helps to foster notions of peace and justice and non-violence." However, other activists felt the listserv served altogether different functions. Some activists perceived the listserv as a tool that could be used by OBA members to communicate directly with the steering committee. Activist #38, another steering committee member, claimed the listserv was a tool used by the steering committee to gauge what issues were being discussed and raised by OBA members in their postings:

> I think the listserv for us more serves as a kind of flag raising tool. People seem to be talking about this certain thing…It's good just to be aware of—well, people are raising these issues and it can be put on the agenda for us. Makes us aware of something we should think about.

In this excerpt, Activist #38 demonstrates a perception that the listserv is not so much a community calendar, but a device to find out about issues important to members. Therefore, unlike in Chapter 2, in which listservs serve as a community calendar and a source for social justice articles about "human rights" and "democracy," the OBA listserv in Erie City was a medium that seemed to serve different functions within the network according to different activists, with little consensus about those functions.

Furthermore, there were conflicting perceptions among activists about the operation and maintenance of the OBA listserv as they discussed their own use of the listserv. Some activists claimed that the listserv was open; anyone could post comments on the listserv. Conversely, some activists claimed that the listserv was closed; posts for the listserv passed through some kind of a "gatekeeper." In fact, some activists described such a gatekeeping process as physical, in which one had to speak directly to steering committee members about posting messages on the listserv. In particular, Activist #28, a frequent user of the listserv, described the need to make arguments to steering committee members for the inclusion of "after action reports" in listserv postings, "For a long time I have complained to [the steering committee], 'why don't you use the OBA listserv to report about the actions? What the hell happened at some of the events?'" For Activist #28, the listserv was controlled by the steering committee, and any changes to the listserv or materials for the listserv, such as reports about actions, had to be posted by the steering committee. Other activists described a process in which messages could be posted on the listserv, but those messages had to first pass through some "core leaders" in order to be circulated on the listserv. Activist #30, a direct member of the OBA, struggled to provide a description of the process of posting messages to the listserv:

> I don't know. I mean, sometimes I think I know, but I know there's a group of real core leaders who pretty much have a lot to say with how [the listserv]—what [the listserv] responds to, and how [the listserv] responds.

For Activist #30, "core leaders" were integral to the uncertain process of posting of messages on the listserv. Interestingly, even a steering committee member, Activist #44, described a kind of "gatekeeper" who reviewed materials sent along by activists before uploading those materials to the listserv, "I send [an article] on to the OBA listserv. And the gatekeeper probably glances at that to see that it is appropriate and then uploads it on to the list."

Such inconsistencies concerning the function and operation of the listserv in the Erie City network raised a significant question: Why did so many activists, including steering committee members, see such radically different functions and operations? Through further investigation of the website, it was discovered that there were in fact multiple listservs available to anyone who wished to sign up for one: a general listserv that provided the *OBA Times* online, a discussion listserv, a listserv devoted to articles about the economic impacts of the Iraq War, and a community calendar listserv. All of the activists noted the OBA listserv as an alternative media source during the interviews. However, none of the activists ever noted the existence of any other OBA listservs, not even current and former steering committee members. Instead, when activists were asked about their use of alternative media they would report *the* OBA listserv as a primary alternative media source, not *one* of the OBA listservs. Ultimately, it was concluded that the confusion concerning the listserv stemmed from activists' focus on a single OBA listserv, or the fact that they were unaware of other OBA listservs.

Implications for RP and New Social Movement Networks
The research in Erie City revealed fractures within the local level new social movement network that stemmed from activists' perceptions about the social justice issues and protest actions of the OBA. These fractures served as the foundation for an overarching perception by many activists that the OBA had "branded" themselves as *the* social justice organization or claimed "ownership" to the concept of social justice, thus pushing any activists who did not share the OBA visions and goals out of the network. Such a perception helps to explain the lack of a Multiplex necessary for the emergence of temporary protest communities, which left the RP in the Erie City new social movement network "broken."

However, interviews with activists in Erie City, including several members of the OBA and the OBA steering committee, revealed no such attempts at ownership or exclusion. Instead of the Machiavellian methods of the OBA described by several activists, evidence suggested that confusion concerning the OBA listserv was an important factor in the "breaking" of RP in the network. Many of the activists—even steering committee members—were unaware of the multiple listservs used by the OBA in the Erie City network, unsure about the functions of the listserv(s) within the network, or uncertain how the listserv(s) operated altogether. Such uncertainties represent the only significant deviation from the categories and concepts of RP described in Chapter 2, in which listservs or other such interactive media played an integral role in the circulation of narratives necessary for the emergence of the Multiplex. Because the listserv was so important for RP and the emergent Multiplex, the confusion about the multiple listservs in Erie City stands as a problematic factor associated with the fractures in the network. Activist #32, who was affiliated with the before-mentioned Erie City Urban Partnership, spoke at length about this problematic factor, a problem that he called the crisis of "cross-pollination":

> I think the tensions bubble up because we don't cross-pollinate each other. These organizations of five hundred members are actually smaller groups of twenty communicating with each other. And their point of conversation is—maybe they'll read about something in the paper, they'll hear about it on the radio…but they don't hear it in *our* media. We don't know what's going on to go each others stuff very often.

Although he was not speaking about listservs in general or the OBA listserv specifically, Activist #32 claimed that narratives were not adequately circulated, or "cross-pollinated," between the OBA and the different interconnected organizations in the network. He went on to explain that such a lack of narratives "leaves too many unanswered questions" in the minds of activists, which erodes feelings of trust in the network. Consequently, he said that there are many activists pointing at one another "saying that someone's a liar, or they haven't told the whole truth." Activist #32 explained how he had worked with a separate hub-like network years before. In that instance, the different organizations affiliated with the network made efforts to "cross-pollinate" one another through the use of community radio and listservs: "We began to trust one another...That network really began to grow." He noted that such "trust" and "growth" never seemed to emerge in the Erie City network, due in large part to this lack of "cross-pollination." However, most of the activists who participated in the research read or used one of the OBA listservs, but were confused about the role and/or operation of the listservs in the network; in fact, most were unaware that there were multiple listservs.

Ultimately, activists' confusion concerning listservs or other interactive media can hinder the circulation of narratives and play a role in the fractures of the network. The findings from the Erie City research build on the other categories of RP by providing additional evidence of how vital the "cross-pollination" of narratives through a listserv, or any locally produced user-to-user media, can be for the construction and maintenance of a Multiplex where performances of resistance can be coordinated. Such cross-pollination stands as a fifth RP category: the capacity of a network to efficiently circulate common narratives to all of the theatre-like quadrants, or *Narrative Capacity*. The Narrative Capacity of a network can be conceptualized as a dimension that ranges from efficient to inefficient. Those local level new social movement networks that have efficient Narrative Capacity are those in which (1) individuals within one of the RP theatre-like quadrants, operating as a hub organization, are capable of producing some form of media necessary for the circulation of narratives (e.g., stories, articles, and calendars of events) to all of the other quadrants in the network and (2) activists within the other quadrants have knowledge about the functions and operation of the media produced by the hub. The communities in which the original RP research took place, described in Chapter 2, would constitute a network with efficient Narrative Capacity. Inefficient networks are those in which media production is not possible, or the members of the network do not possess the knowledge necessary to accurately read/use the media produced. Such inefficient Narrative Capacity may hinder the construction of a Multiplex, as observed in the Erie City new social movement network.

The fifth category, Narrative Capacity, stands as a form of user-to-user interactivity, in that it entails interactions between multiple individuals through the use of interactive media. In the example of Mystical City discussed in Chapter 2, the interactive media necessary for the emergence of the Multiplex was a listserv. Conversely, in the case of Erie City, multiple listservs proved to be an important tool for the circulation of information and narratives, but the Multiplex did not emerge. Instead, fractures existed in the network that prevented the emergence of the Multiplex. Ultimately, local level networks that are capable of effectively and efficiently circulating narratives through user-to-user interactivity are better capable of constructing the Multiplex and engaging in coordinated performance of resistance. Those networks that lack the capability, or that utilize ineffective user-to-user interactivity, develop no such Multiplex and stand as separate quadrants most of the time.

Conclusion

The research presented in this chapter helps to expand on the concept of RP developed in Chapter 2 by demonstrating the important role of interactivity within the framework. Ultimately, user-to-document Intercreative Capacity has proven to be important for the construction of RP, while user-to-user Narrative Capacity has proven necessary for the long-term maintenance and coordination of performance in RP. In the previous chapter, the portrayals of power in alternative media produced at the global level played an important role in the development of individual and organizational worldviews. Essentially, user-to-document interactivity between local and global networks is important for the intercreative production of alternative media content. Without such Intercreative Capacity, then, RP would not be possible, as alternative media production could potentially become stagnated. Such stagnation, in turn, would make the construction of networks and coordinated resistance altogether difficult. In addition, the capacity for networks to efficiently circulate narratives through listservs and other user-to-user interactive media is important for the emergence of the Multiplex of coordinated performances of resistance. Without such a capacity on the part of a network, fractures can emerge that hold the potential to disrupt any mesomobilization or coordination on the part of activists. In a sense, inefficient Narrative Capacity on the part of a hub organization, or any group within a network, can lead to the permanent separation of the four quadrants.

The previous chapters, including Chapter 3, have provided the reader with insight about the complexities of social movement and alternative media research and demonstrated that the framework of RP can bridge the two fields. Alternative media plays an important role in the construction and maintenance of theatre-like quadrants, in which image events and other such rhetorical strategies are played out through the performance of activists. Narrative Capacity allows for those quadrants to come together and perform resistance together, while Intercreative Capacity aids in the production and circulation of alternative media content. Together, all of these factors give rise to local-level networks that engage in resistance in the political landscape of the early 21st century. Chapters 4 and 5 will explore the alternative media and performances associated with the different RP quadrants, in effect providing examples of the first three categories of RP, while Chapter 6 will explain how the different networks of theatre-like communities constitute an alternative media world.

Chapter 4
"Speaking Truth to Power" and "Amorality": The Reformist Quadrants

The following chapter provides:

1) Descriptions of alternative media titles used by activists within the Reformist Participatory and Reformist Lay quadrants, which includes:

   a. Analysis of the content found within the individual alternative media titles used by reformist activists.

   b. Explication of the collective themes that emerge within both of the quadrants and serve as a backdrop for RP.

2) Examples of different organizations that emerge as vehicles for the resistance performed by activists within the Reformist Participatory and Reformist Lay quadrants.

The previous two chapters introduced and established the theoretical concept of Resistance Performance (RP), which is constructed from five categories. The first two categories, Worldviews and Alternative Media Interactions, intersect to form the four quadrants discussed in Chapter 2. Those quadrants effectively serve as sites in which activists perform the third category, Communicative Resistance. Chapters 4 and 5 will look to different alternative media titles and organizations to provide additional illustration of the first three categories of RP and the emergent theatre-like quadrants. In particular, both chapters will examine the alternative media utilized by activists, the organizations that serve as "vehicles" for Communicative Performance, and specific examples of communicative resistance performed by activists. Chapter 4 focuses on the two reformist quadrants, while Chapter 5 will examine the two radical quadrants.

Alternative Media and Themes

The two reformist theatre-like quadrants of RP utilize a wide variety of alternative media. In cases observed in past research (e.g., Atkinson, 2009a; Atkinson & Dougherty, 2006; Downing, 2003b; Rauch, 2007) alternative media titles such as *Democracy Now!*, NPR's *All Things Considered*, *The Progressive*, *Z Magazine*, the Amnesty International website, and MoveOn.org have been utilized by activists who hold primarily reformist worldviews concerning dominant power structures in society. It should be noted that reformist activists did not exclusively use these titles, as radical activists would also claim to use some of these titles as well. However, these titles were often described by reformist activists as their *primary* sources of information about power structures, resistance, and social justice, whereas radical activists used such titles in a *peripheral* manner (i.e., read only occasionally or skeptically). These titles conform to the concept of alternative media discussed in Chapter 1, in that they (1) are controlled by non-commercial entities (e.g., Atton, 2002a; Downing, 2003b; Downing et al., 2001), (2) entail content that focuses on challenging power structures and/or transforming social roles (e.g., Atkinson, 2005a; Armstrong, 1981; Atton, 2002a; Downing, 2003b; Downing et al., 2001; Meikle, 2002), and/or (3) are constructed as "alternative" through the interpretive strategies of activists (e.g., Rauch, 2007). It is important to note that few titles encapsulate all three definitions, while others encapsulate only one; past research concerning alternative media (e.g., Armstrong, 1981; Atton, 2002a; 2002b; 2004; Downing, 1984; Downing et al., 2001; Meikle, 2002; Rauch, 2007) has typically relied on only one of the above definitions. The research behind the construction of RP described in Chapters 2 and 3 has utilized all three of these definitions in order to bring together the broadest body of alternative media used by activists in any given network; such research has focused on alternative media that meet at least one of the above mentioned definitions.

As briefly discussed in Chapter 2, analysis of alternative media content in past RP research (Atkinson, 2005a; Atkinson & Dougherty, 2006) has examined important themes that emerged from (1) the culmination of *all* of the alternative media used across all four theatre-like quadrants in particular communities, (2) individual alternative media titles, and (3) alternative media that were specific to each individual quadrant.[1] The first set of themes was covered in Chapter 2, in reference to common visions and goals. The second set of themes are largely based on the dominant power structure that is the focus of each alternative media title and the conceptualization of how power functions within that entity (e.g., traditional power v. hegemonic power), and are covered in the following pages. The third constitutes a woven tapestry that stands as a backdrop for the formation of organizations and performances of resistance, which will be discussed later in this chapter.

Democracy Now!

> *Democracy Now!'s* War and Peace Report provides our audience with access to people and perspectives rarely heard in the US corporate-sponsored media, including independent and international journalists, ordinary people from around the world who are directly affected by US foreign policy, grassroots leaders and peace activists, artists, academics and independent analysts. In addition, *Democracy Now!* hosts real debates—debates between people who substantially disagree, such as between the White House or the Pentagon spokespeople on the one hand, and grassroots activists on the other. (www.democracynow.org)

Democracy Now! was established in 1996 by the Pacifica Radio network, a listener supported media organization. Pacifica Radio started the program with journalist Amy Goodman from their WBAI station in New York in order to provide coverage of the presidential election that year with no interference on the part of corporations or private business. Because of immense popularity, the program was extended beyond 1996 and continues broadcasting to this day on over 100 Pacifica Radio affiliates across the United States; the radio program has even developed a syndicated television program that is shown on the DISH Network. Following the attacks of September 11, 2001, *Democracy Now!* began broadcasting the War and Peace Report, a comprehensive examination of government and conflict during times of war. Essentially, the goal of Amy Goodman, Juan Gonzalez, Larry Bensky, and the other journalists at *Democracy Now!* has been to "open up the airwaves" and present a view of current events that is not typically presented by corporate media outlets like NBC and CNN (Goodman, 2001).

Corporations and military agencies are typically the two dominant power structures that are scrutinized within content produced and broadcast by *Democracy Now!* News stories on the radio program often depict corporations, such as Halliburton, as aiding governments (particularly the Administration of former President George W. Bush) to perpetuate acts of war in order to generate corporate and private profits. Essentially, the news stories produced by Goodman and others at *Democracy Now!* focus on collaborations between corporations and government sanctioned military forces that generate enormous profits for all people involved, but often leave civilians dead, wounded, or imprisoned; such actions are defined by the producers of *Democracy Now!* as corporate or military crimes. Such news stories coalesce to form a theme about "crimes against humanity," which stem from any mingling of corporations and military agencies. For instance, the story "Occidental Petroleum Sued for Role in Civilian Massacre in Colombia" that was broadcast on May 2nd of 2003 provides an excellent illustration of the dominant theme found on *Democracy Now!*:

> The lawsuit filed on April 25 by international rights attorneys charges that Occidental Petroleum (OXY) and its private security contractor, Airscan, participated in the air raid that led to the killing of innocent civilians. The suit charges that both OXY and Airscan helped conduct the attack, providing key strategic information, as well as ground and air support to the Colombian military in the bombing raid on the town. Airscan's "Skymaster" plane—which provides aerial surveillance for OXY'S Caño Limon oil pipeline—accompanied the Colombian air force during the bombing, and used its infrared and video equipment to pinpoint targets on the ground. While allegedly targeting suspected rebels, no rebels were in the area. Occidental has been a chief architect of Plan Colombia and a lobbyist for U.S. military aid to Colombia, currently at $131 million this year. Another $110 million is proposed in 2004 for the protection of OXY's Caño Limon pipeline. This unprecedented corporate subsidy of $3.58 a barrel is a handsome payoff for OXY's aggressive lobbying efforts and political contributions. (Goodman, 2003)

The story describes how Occidental Petroleum and Airscan aided in military actions, which killed "innocent civilians" in Colombia. The use of force by the Colombian military is beneficial to OXY and Airscan as the two corporate entities worked as a broker between the US military industrial complex and the Colombian military; conflict in Colombia seems to be profitable to both of these corporations.

National Public Radio's *All Things Considered*

> For two hours every weekday, *All Things Considered* hosts Robert Siegel, Michele Norris and Melissa Block present the program's trademark mix of news, interviews, commentaries, reviews and offbeat features. The program rings with the disparate voices of its commentators, from veteran analyst Daniel Schorr and storyteller Kevin Kling to poet Andrei Codrescu. It hums with the distinctive music that threads between reports—music collected in the online program All Songs Considered. And by the time *All Things Considered* marked its 30th anniversary on the air, the program had earned many of journalism's highest honors, including the Peabody, duPont and Overseas Press Club awards. (www.npr.org)

All Things Considered was first broadcast by National Public Radio (NPR) in 1971 and has since become the primary news program for the network. Every weekday *All Things Considered* presents a wide variety of content in the form of news bulletins, commentaries, and interviews with people who are involved in key political, business, and social issues of the day. Unlike Pacifica Radio described above, NPR is only partially listener supported; funding also comes from underwriting spots, grants from private industry and corporations, and minor government support. The underwriting spots are of particular interest, as they represent a kind of advertising in which statements about products and corporate support for NPR are embedded in the content; such a commercial aspect would normally pose a problem for the program's status as alternative media. However, many activists insist that NPR and *All Things Considered* are "alternative" because of its balanced use of different sources for news, which they often deem to be contrary to corporate media sources. Activists often claim that mainstream news networks like CNN or news programs like *NBC Nightly News* have all become profit driven because of corporate conglomeration. Because of such profit motivation, activists claim that these networks and programs have abandoned the traditional standards of journalism—objectivity and a balanced use of sources—in favor of sensationalism and opinion. Because of such interpretation and differentiation on the part of activists, NPR's *All Things Considered* corresponds with Rauch's (2007) concept of alternative media that emerge from the interpretive strategies.

News stories broadcast on *All Things Considered* often entail a theme of "balanced vision." The theme emerges from the fact that the producers of the program use testimony from corporate representatives, government officials, social justice representatives, and the general public in order to present stories about accountability and potential for reform on the part of dominant power structures in society. Typically, the dominant power structures that are discussed in news stories are corporations and the US government; religious institutions are also often the focus of stories broadcast on the program. The use of multiple sources of information for news stories by NPR is significant, as it is different from other alternative media, such as *Democracy Now!* or *Z Magazine*, as those titles typically rely on the testimony of left-leaning social justice activists and advocates in order to report news and explain issues. Take, for instance, Robert Siegel's (2003) story broadcast on September 18th entitled "Bill George Discusses Richard Grasso's Pay Package and How It Threatens the Reputation of the New York Stock Exchange." The story illustrates how the producers of *All Things Considered* use the testimony of corporate representatives, as Siegel featured an interview with former Medtronic CEO Bill George about the resignation of New York Stock Exchange Chairman Richard Grasso. Grasso resigned from his position because of complaints concerning his exuberant pay package during a time of corporate scandals and a slow market:

> *Robert Siegel*: One lay outsider's view of what just happened is that Mr. Grasso was revealed to be making a huge amount of money. He's not a major-league shortstop, and it's too much, particularly when much of it was earned in a year when the market didn't do all that well. Not the problem, you say.
>
> *Bill George*: Oh, I think it is a problem. I think we have to recognize those of us who lead organizations are really stewards of a legacy, and we have to gain the trust. And if our compensation is beyond the pale, so to speak, in

the eyes of our constituents, it damages the reputation of the institution. So we have to take that into account.

In this excerpt Bill George agrees with the "lay outsider's" notion of what has happened in the Richard Grasso resignation. The exuberant pay package of the former chairman of the New York Stock Exchange generated distrust for contemporary economic institutions. In this instance, *All Things Considered* sought out the testimony of a corporate representative in order to demonstrate a "balanced vision" of the situation with Richard Grasso to their audiences.

The Progressive

Figure 1. *The Progressive* magazine.

> *The Progressive*, a monthly since 1948, has steadfastly stood against militarism, the concentration of power in corporate hands, and the disenfranchisement of the citizenry. It has continued to champion peace, social and economic justice, civil rights, civil liberties, human rights, a preserved environment, and a reinvigorated democracy. Its bedrock values remain nonviolence and freedom of speech. (www.progressive.org)

The Progressive magazine was established in 1909 by Wisconsin Senator Robert La Follette as a forum for news concerning social and institutional "progress" from a liberal perspective. Overall, the magazine tends to focus on issues like civil liberties, the environment, and war. These issues have been highlighted in the magazine through articles contributed by noted authors, journalists, and scholars over the years, like Martin Luther King, Jr., and Upton Sinclair. Today, the current editor, Mathew Rothschild, relies heavily on content written by noted liberal writers and academics, such as Barbara Ehrenreich and Howard Zinn. In addition, the content of the magazine features interviews with liberal and progressive minded politicians, artists, and celebrities such as then-Senator Barack Obama, musician Ani DeFranco, comedian George Carlin, and actor Martin Sheen. As of 2004, circulation of the magazine had reached an estimated level of 66,000 people around the world (Zaleski, 2004), and over the years the magazine has spawned a variety of other media including a website and a radio program.

In *The Progressive*, corporations and the United States government often stand as the two dominant power structures in society. However, unlike the depictions of corporations and governments described in broadcasts by *Democracy Now!*, those structures are depicted in the pages of *The Progressive* as tools that can be used for good or evil. The magazine portrays the dawn of the 21st century, as well as all of American history, as a time in which business leaders have taken power and are constantly devising legislation to help provide their corporate allies with large industrial contracts that will generate profit. Such generation of profit will not benefit common people in any way; instead, only a select few benefit from the profits of these swollen industrial contracts. Although this seems initially bleak, there is a sense of hope embedded in this depiction of corporations: corporations are still at the mercy of the government, and the people can still influence the government. Through elections and political action, progressive activists can take power away from the profit-obsessed business leaders and force corporations to curb their actions, if not outright alter them to be more socially responsible. Ultimately, a theme of "speaking out" develops within the pages of *The Progressive*, in which people point out power discrepancies in society or problems caused by people in power.

First, many of the articles featured in *The Progressive* establish the interrelationship between government and business interests. In this way, corporations are demonstrated as entrenched in government to such an extent that "ordinary" people have little or no voice in issues like global warming. For instance, in the June 2003 article "Unwise Use: Gale Norton's New Environmentalism," David Helvarg wrote:

> In 1999 [Gale] Norton, now working as a lawyer representing the lead industry, became part of the team advising candidate Bush on developing a conservative "environmentalism for the twenty-first century." Among those working with her was David Koch of Koch Industries, which in 2000 paid a $35 million fine for oil pollution in six states, as well as Lynn Scarlett from the libertarian Reason Foundation of Los Angeles.

In this example, Gale Norton and David Koch both played an integral role in the environmental position of the Bush Administration. Koch Industries owns companies that trade and/or produce petroleum, natural gas, gas liquids, chemicals, plastics and fibers, and chemical technology equipment. Koch Industries had been found guilty of pollution infractions, but was nevertheless given a role in the development of environmental policies in the US. Essentially, Helvarg's article makes the claim that the United States government has allowed for corporate interests, rather than public interests, to dictate environmental policy.

Despite the depictions of a tight stranglehold that corporations have over government, the theme presented by *The Progressive* is not entirely hopeless. Within each issue there are stories in which various people fight back against such corporate juggernaughts. For example, the article "Holding the Line at the FCC" by Robert McChesney and John Nichols in the April 2003 issue detailed how some politicians are willing to stand up to corporate interests:

> At a time when the White House and Congress are fully in the grips of corporate America, and when most of the federal bureaucracy seems to bend every rule to serve the interests of the largest campaign contributors, [Michael] Copps is raising the flag of public interest.

McChesney and Nichols go so far as to say that there are "heroes" willing to take a stand against the forces of corporate America, which of course are entrenched in the government power structure. One such "hero" is Federal Communications Commissioner Michael Copps, who challenged the chair of the FCC at that time, Michael Powell, on the issue of media deregulation; ultimately, deregulation would allow corporations to own more media outlets. McChesney and Nichols described how Powell conducted only two public hearings about the issue of media deregulation, while Copps forced several more such hearings around the country.

Z Magazine

Figure 2. *Z Magazine.*

Z is an independent monthly magazine dedicated to resisting injustice, defending against repression, and creating liberty. It sees the racial, gender, class, and political dimensions of personal life as fundamental to understanding and improving contemporary circumstances; and it aims to assist activist efforts for a better future. (www.zmag.org)

Z Magazine was established in 1987 in order to carry on the spirit of resistance as depicted in the movie *Z*, directed by Costa-Gavras, which tells a somber story of repression and resistance in Greece. In the movie, a revolutionary leader called Comrade Z is assassinated by a right-wing dictator, and the letter Z is subsequently outlawed by the military because the it stands as a symbol of resistance. The magazine serves as a forum in which contributors critically examine many different aspects of life in the United States and Western society; usually, such critiques typically focus on the role of the media within society. During the 1990s, the magazine expanded into Z Communications, which includes the print magazine, the online magazine (similar to the print version), ZNet, and Z Video. Both ZNet and Z Video are sites where grassroots activists can produce and circulate additional content through blogs and "ZSpace" sites, which are similar to Facebook profiles. As in the case of *The Progressive*, noted scholars and journalists, such as Noam Chomsky, Edward Herman, Norman Solomon, Barbara Ehrenreich, and Howard Zinn, typically contribute many articles that serve as the content of *Z Magazine*. However, unlike the case with *The Progressive*, the "noted" contributors also serve as "featured" movement intellectuals (see Atton, 2002a), and those "featured" articles funnel readers' attention to additional articles written and submitted by grassroots activists. For instance, Jessica Azulay, a peace and justice activist in New York State who maintains a ZSpace site through ZNet, published an article in the March 2003 issue of the magazine entitled "Resolutions as Resistance."

Articles in *Z Magazine* typically focus on the role of corporate mainstream media in the establishment and maintenance of oppressive ideologies about war, consumerism, sexuality, and race. For the most part, corporate media and the government are viewed as separate power structures that work together on many occasions. Corporate media and the government both desire power and expansion, so the government provides favorable legislation to those corporations that own the media so long as they broadcast and disseminate messages that promote the dominant ideologies in society. In other words, the relationships between corporations and the US government establish a kind of control over the masses. Ultimately, a theme of "identifying propaganda" emerges within the content of *Z Magazine*, in which producers point to instances in which public opinion and beliefs concerning a number of issues are manipulated through the media. An example of this can be found in the article "Hooray for Hollywood" by John Zavesky found in the May 2003 issue:

90   Reformist Quadrants

> This coalition between the media, military, and government appears to be a "win, win" merger. What all three want is a Hollywood ending. The Administration wants Baghdad and the oil it craves. The military wants to use its toys and thus justify a large infusion for the fiscally vampiric military industrial complex. The media wants good ratings and they will get them as long as the war doesn't get too ugly for our side.

The Zavesky article hints at the notion that the media, military, and government all share similar goals and visions. The ultimate implication is that the three different groups working together to meet those similar goals and build a "Hollywood" style ending. With the help of the media, the government and military work together to influence public opinion about the war in Iraq. The dominant theme concerning corporations and media in *Z Magazine* focuses on elites using resources of the media to manipulate and control public opinion, or the elites using media resources to distract the population away from important issues of the day. In this theme the media is the dominant structure in society that influences ideology and hegemony, similar to the concept of the culture industry developed by Horkheimer and Adorno (1972) and Ideological State Apparatus described by Althusser (1971). Both concepts illustrate the role of mass media in the circulation and reification of ideological assumptions in society. It is important to note that unlike any of the other alternative media sources, *Z Magazine* focuses solely on corporate media. Little attention is paid to banks or oil companies, or any other corporations that have few or no connections to mainstream media processes.

Amnesty International Website

> Amnesty International undertakes research and action focused on preventing and ending grave abuses of the rights to physical and mental integrity, freedom of conscience and expression, and freedom from discrimination, within the context of its work to promote all human rights. (http://www.amnestyusa.org)

Amnesty International is a global organization that was established in London in 1961 for the goal of addressing human rights abuses carried out in prisons around the world. Essentially, the organization worked to investigate accusations of torture and illegal imprisonment of people because of their political beliefs. Since the organization's inception, Amnesty International has become affiliated with the United Nations and has become respected and recognized as an authority on human rights by government officials and industry leaders alike (Banks, 2004; Parry, 2005). Over the years, the organization launched a website that now serves as a central site where users can look up Amnesty International documents, research materials, and the findings of the organization's ongoing investigations into human rights abuses. The website also provides information to activists about how they can become involved in the Amnesty International mission. Specifically, the site allows activists to sign online petitions, download letters that they can send along to various political figures, and toolkits for letter writing campaigns in their own communities.

The primary power structure addressed in content found on the Amnesty International website are governments, as those are the entities that actively imprison and torture individuals for their political beliefs. Corporations also stand as dominant power structures in society within content on the website, but without the same powers to detain and torture that are held by governments. Interestingly, the content on the Amnesty International website usually depicts the two power structures working together, but the power of corporations could potentially be used to safeguard against human rights abuses, like torture. For these reasons, the website if dominated by a theme of "guarding human rights" in which governments are closely monitored, their abuses are documented, and corporations are called on to safeguard against torture and immoral imprisonment. Such is the case with the transcript of an oral statement that had been delivered by an Amnesty International spokesperson, Melinda Ching, that was posted on the website on August 1st of 2002. The speech was delivered to the Fifty-Fourth Session of the United Nations Sub-Commission on the Promotion and Protection of Human Rights:

> As states have deregulated their economies and privatized functions traditionally performed by the state to non-state actors, including private sector companies (transnational, multinational or domestic), a lacuna has emerged. Even though states have the primary responsibility to promote and protect human rights, transnational corporations and other business enterprises, as organs of society, are also responsible for promoting and securing the human rights set forth in the Universal Declaration of Human Rights. Transnational corporations and other business enterprises are further obliged to respect generally recognized principles and norms in UN treaties and other international instruments, such as the International Covenants on Civil and Political Rights and on Economic, Social and Cultural Rights, the International Labor Organization (ILO) Declaration on Fundamental Principles and Rights at Work and its Follow-up, and emerging guidelines, like the Organization for Economic Co-operation and Development (OECD) Guidelines for Multinational Enterprises that apply to companies within the framework of OECD membership.

The statement by Ching demonstrates how Amnesty International views both governments and corporations as integral components of society. Because of the enormous role that corporations play in civil society, people should expect that those entities work to guard human rights just when governments fail to act in that regard.

MoveOn.org

> MoveOn is a service–a way for busy but concerned citizens to find their political voice in a system dominated by big money and big media. (www.moveon.org)

MoveOn.org was founded by Silicon Valley entrepreneurs Joan Blades and Wes Boyd due to their frustration about the 1998 impeachment of President Bill Clinton. It was felt by Blades and Boyd that the United States Congress and the American public were dwelling on a subject that had little ramification for the country, the government, or the citizens; namely the Lewinsky scandal. The website and corresponding listserv were both organized to provide users with information about Kenneth Starr's "mishandling" of the independent council and the entire impeachment process, as well as to circulate a petition asking Congress to censure President Clinton and immediately "move on" to important issues facing the US and global community. After the impeachment, the MoveOn website and listserv both remained active in order to provide users with details about government corruption, particularly in terms of the neo-conservative politics at the heart of the Bush Administration (Dawn, 2006; Hamm, 2008).

The primary theme found throughout material posted on MoveOn.org is "rage against the neo-cons," which asserts that neo-conservative politicians and organizations have taken control of power structures, such as corporations and government agencies, in ways that threaten democracy, civil liberties, and world peace. According to various articles and materials on the website, and in emails circulated on the MoveOn listserv, neo-conservative politics are based on the concept that government is only required to run unilateral military actions that will promote American values around the world; government in any other form (e.g., social security, public funded education) is unnecessary and should be eliminated. In order to carry out this goal, neo-conservatives find it integral to divert federal money from social programs, like education and healthcare, to the military industrial complex (Mercer, 2003). Such concern, or rage, for the politics of neo-conservatives is reflected in a MoveOn.org bulletin entitled "The Project for the New American Century" that was posted by MoveOn editor Noah Winer on the website on May 9th of 2003, and circulated through the listserv at the same time.

> The Project for the New American Century (PNAC) is a Washington-based neo-conservative think-tank founded in 1997 to "rally support for American global leadership." PNAC's agenda runs far deeper than regime change in Iraq. Its statement of principles begins with the assertion that "American foreign and defense policy is adrift" and calls for "a Reaganite policy of military through strength and moral clarity." While their tone is high-minded, their proposal is unilateral military intervention to protect against

threats to America's status as the lone global superpower. The statement is signed by such influential figures as Dick Cheney, Jeb Bush, Lewis "Scooter" Libby, Dan Quayle, Donald Rumsfeld, and Paul Wolfowitz....The effect of PNAC's ideology is great on Bush—the presidential candidate who promised a "humble," isolationist foreign policy. The events of September 11, 2001 provided a window of opportunity for furthering PNAC's agenda of American empire. Understanding that agenda can help us anticipate the Bush administration's next steps and organize accordingly.

This excerpt from *MoveOn.org* provides an analysis of neo-conservative ideology, which the website claims is rooted in the Project for the New American Century (PNAC). Within the PNAC the neo-conservative ideology unfolds: unilateral military action is necessary to secure the United States' position as the lone superpower in the world. Through such military action the US can assume a role of global leadership that would not otherwise be achieved through diplomacy or trade.

Each of the alternative media titles discussed in this chapter entail a particular theme, which is based in large part on the depictions in each title of dominant power structures and the ways in which power operates within such structures. Each title presents a view that is slightly different from each of the others in terms of their specific themes, while also conforming to the broader and more nebulous themes of "human rights" and "democracy" that were discussed in Chapter 2. On their own, each title reflects a vision of hegemonic power that would make those titles attractive and/or useful to activists who hold a reformist worldview. As stated in Chapter 2, it is not so much that reformist activists never utilize or talk about power in traditional terms (e.g., control over physical resources), or that reformist activists never utilize alternative media that portray traditional power. Instead, previous research has demonstrated that reformist activists find the before mentioned titles useful for understanding power structures in society and how to address or deal with problems that stem from such power. It should be noted that this is not an exhaustive list and that several other titles such as *Mother Jones* magazine and programming broadcast on Air America Radio are often used by reformist activists. These titles do not stand on their own and are usually read and used by activists in conjuncture with other alternative media and with other activists. In this way, the various themes that emerge from the different alternative media titles often blend together within the context of the theatre-like quadrants and construct a tapestry that serves as a backdrop for those theatres. It is these blended tapestries and backdrops that in many ways shape the Communicative Resistance of RP. The two blended themes associated with activist use of alternative media within the Reformist Participatory and Reformist Lay quadrants will be discussed in the following pages.

Reformist Participatory Quadrant: Speaking Truth to Power
As described in Chapter 2, Reformist Participatory activists not only read the content included in alternative media titles, like *Z Magazine*, but they also interact with those titles by creating content or providing feedback to producers. In many ways, this is similar to the diffused engagement between audience and performers in performance art productions, where audiences often become involved and take part in the performances by interacting with the performers on stage (e.g., Auslander, 1997; Herbert, 1994). Past research has demonstrated that the primary sources of information concerning dominant power structures and social justice often used by Reformist Participatory activists are *Democracy Now!*, *All Things Considered* (NPR), *Z Magazine*, *The Progressive,* and some kind of a clearinghouse website (e.g., Atkinson & Dougherty, 2006; Downing, 2003b; Rauch, 2007). As noted in Chapter 2, the clearinghouse website, like Commondreams.org, proves to be integral as it provides Reformist Participatory activists a glimpse into the worldviews concerning power and social justice associated with the other quadrants. Therefore, in reference to themes that emerge solely within the theatre-like quadrant, the focus will fall on the first four listed above. The theme that emerges from the blending of those four alternative media titles often used by Reformist Participatory activists is "speaking truth to power." This theme is based in large part on the prevalence the Gramscian (1971) notions of hegemony and organic intellectuals within the content of all of the titles.

First, the content in each title is often characterized by the notion that corporations are entrenched in political processes and perpetuate an ideology favorable to the power elites and necessary for the continuation of the current structures in society. Essentially, the corporate dominated media convince the general public that particular roles and behaviors are commonplace and normal, leading to hegemonic participation by those audiences. For instance, in the May 2003 issue of *Z Magazine,* Chomsky discussed how the media make war commonplace and normal: "Right now [war coverage] is cheerleading for the home team. Look at CNN, which is disgusting—and it is the same everywhere. That is to be expected in wartime; the media are worshipful of power" (p. 30). For Chomsky, media "cheerleading" is prevalent everywhere in the media, which makes support for the war in Iraq, and other such conflicts around the globe, commonplace and normal. Second, all of the before mentioned titles often present a view in which it is possible for people to resist the hegemonic power structure by "speaking truth to power." Within these titles, Gramscian organic intellectuals—individuals who examine and articulate power structures, thus making the margins of society visible (Gramsci, 1971)—serve as examples of "notable" figures who have stood up to particular power structures and met with some success. *The Progressive* often includes profiles and interviews with scholars and notable figures such as Kurt Vonnegut (Barsamian, 2003), Janeane

Garofalo (DiNovella, 2003), and Tim Robbins (Steinhardt, 2003); these features within the different titles describe how such "organic intellectuals" stood up to power structures that influenced society through the use of the media and manipulation of ideological assumptions. For instance, the June 2003 issue of *The Progressive* featured a profile of Martha Burk, the chairwoman of the National Council of Women's Organizations, who highlighted the exclusion of women from Augusta National Golf Club. As the article explained:

> Burk successfully pressured some corporations to pull their ads from this year's event. That's when [Augusta National Golf Club] decided to go sponsor free. "Coca-Cola, Cadillac, and Citigroup had already pulled out because they were talking to me," she explained, "and Augusta was trying to preempt that from getting embarrassed." (Lewis, 2003, p. 34)

Within the context of the Reformist Participatory quadrant, then, the alternative media read and used by activists portrays possibilities for people to stand up to the interests and goals of the powerful and make a difference in society. This theme is similar to the themes found within the individual alternative media titles, while also broader than those specific themes. For instance, *Democracy Now!* clearly focuses on power structures and abuses of power, as do articles posted on the Amnesty International website; however, those titles usually provide few examples of people speaking out against those power structures. Combined with *All Things Considered* and *The Progressive*, the content from *Democracy Now!* and Amnesty International are both broadened. As with the diffused audience environment described by Abercrombie and Longhurst (1998), Reformist Participatory activists often co-perform with the alternative media titles by providing feedback to producers or producing their own content, which stands as a kind of performance art theatre. Such co-performance through interactions was described in Chapters 2 and 3.

Reformist Lay Quadrant: Amorality
Unlike the performance art theatre described above, the activists who fall within the Reformist Lay quadrant are similar to the simple audience described by Abercrombie and Longhurst (1998). In this way, the activists rarely co-perform with the alternative media titles through feedback or production on their own. Instead, the activists usually adhere to strict lines between themselves, the audience, and the performances that unfold within the different alternative media titles that they read. Past research has illustrated the Amnesty International website, MoveOn.org, *All Things Considered*, and a clearinghouse website as primary sources for Reformist Lay activists (e.g., Atkinson & Dougherty, 2006; Rauch, 2007). As with the Reformist Participatory quadrant, the primary theme that emerges from

activists' reading of alternative media is based on the content from the first three titles.

The combination of the three titles gives rise to a theme of "amorality," which is in large part based on the notion that power structures are only tools that are controlled by people. In particular, the Amnesty International website and MoveOn.org focused on the enormous role of corporations in society. Corporations appeared to be amoral within the content of the Amnesty International website, which explained to reformist activists the notion that corporations were an integral component of modern society and should protect and promote human rights. For instance, after major combat in Iraq was declared by the Bush Administration, Amnesty International issued a press release on their website entitled "Iraq: On Whose Behalf? Reconstruction Must Ensure Human Rights of Iraqis." The statement by Amnesty International provided eleven points that corporations should observe while operating in Iraq: (1) observe UN human rights rules, (2) observe internationally recognized security norms, (3) consult local communities and solicit women's views, (4) provide essential services in a non-discriminatory manner, (5) do not profiteer, (6) respect the environment, (7) do not perpetuate social divisions, 8) do not offer bribes or encourage corruption, (9) be transparent, (10) support the rule of law and the establishment of a fair justice system, and (11) support the deployment of human rights monitors. For Amnesty International, the corporations as power structures were not necessarily bad; they were amoral. If the people in charge of companies like Haliburton would listen to "the people" and watchdog groups like Amnesty International, they could be persuaded to do good. Similarly, MoveOn.org described corporations as amoral ideological state apparatuses that can be used for good or ill. According to MoveOn.org articles, under the presidency of George W. Bush, neo-conservatives often manipulate both corporate power structures and government agencies to perpetuate the notion that unilateral military adventures are necessary for the United States to be an effective global leader. If neo-conservatives could be driven from corporations and government agencies, those power structures would be cleansed.

The perspective of amorality is different than that which emerged from the theme of "speaking truth to power" associated with the previous quadrant, in that there is little emphasis on resistance or standing up to corporate power. Instead, the theme within the context of the Reformist Lay quadrant depicts power structures as vessels or vehicles that can be controlled by one group or another. The emergent theme even stresses that its not so much important who actually runs those power structures, so long as there are people watching to ensure that abuses and crimes cannot be committed; the presence of the watchdog in society will ensure that power structures obey laws that protect "human rights" and "democracy." For instance, the content on MoveOn.org and the MoveOn listserv contain rage about the neo-conservatives in society and the potential problems that they pose to society through their control of government and industry. The power structures of government and industry themselves are not good or evil, only the people who might control those structures.

Ultimately, the alternative media that are utilized by activists weave together backdrops against which those activists make decisions about how to address power structures in society. Chapter 2 explained how activists within the two reformist quadrants often utilize adjustive tactics in terms of Communicative Resistance. Such forms of resistance make sense when contextualized against the two backdrops of "speaking truth to power" and "amorality." In both cases, breaking laws through militant tactics can be counterproductive as they could potentially alienate audiences who would listen to such truths and alienate the activists themselves as they seek to work as watchdogs over power structures. In addition, the two backdrops fit within the broader concepts of "human rights" and "democracy" that allow for the emergence of the Multiplex of coordinated performances. No activists within either quadrant would ever deny that those things are important for society. However, the two different backdrops might call for slightly different tactics of Communicative Resistance to power structures, which would contribute to the dissolution of that Multiplex. In essence, the backdrop of blended alternative media content is what truly makes the different quadrants theatre-like in nature. In order to illustrate this point, the following pages provide examples of different organizations that typically hold reformist membership, as well as descriptions of different tactics of Communicative Resistance that have emerged from those organizations.

Organizations and Communicative Performances

Before fully engaging in this section concerning organizations, it should be noted that the primary focus is on organizations that exist within local level networks and not those at the global level. It should also be noted that organizations are not themselves classified as Radical Participatory or Reformist Lay. Instead, the activists who make up the different organizations are classified within one of the four quadrants. The organizations are important because they serve as vehicles for the Communicative Resistance performed by activists within their theatre-like quadrants and the overarching Multiplex; it is through their affiliation with such organizations that activists often engage in public performances of resistance against the backdrop constructed from the mixing of different alternative media themes. Therefore, Amnesty International, an organization that is covered in this chapter, is not itself Reformist Lay. However, many activists who join chapters of the organization within local level networks, like Mystical City and Erie City, are classified as such, and for that reason the organization is covered within this chapter. Indeed, many of the leaders and coordinators of

Amnesty International global network, and even a few activists in local level networks, would be classified as Reformist Participatory, but research has demonstrated that most of the core supporters and members of the organization tend to hold reformist worldviews concerning power structures in society, and interact with alternative media in a lay/passive manner. Ultimately, the following discussion about Amnesty International, MoveOn, and Peace Action provides additional examples and further clarification of concepts that have emerged in Chapter 2, as well as the themes that emerged in the previous section of this chapter. The three organizations described in the following pages have been selected because of their prevalence in past research (e.g., Atkinson & Dougherty, 2006; Atkinson, 2009a; Castells, 2004; Rauch, 2007; Stengrim, 2005; Warnick, 2007). For instance, Amnesty International and MoveOn were both present as local level organizations in Mystical City and Erie City. In addition, the Olive Branch Association in Erie City had strong ties to Peace Action, while Peace Alliance of Mystical City had originally been a Peace Action chapter but broke away and became more autonomous in the 1980s.

Amnesty International was established by Peter Benenson, a London based labor lawyer, for the purpose of investigating abuses against "prisoners of conscience" around the globe and bringing those abuses to the attention of the international community. The term prisoner of conscience is a reference to people who have been unfairly imprisoned because of their political beliefs. In 1961, Benenson took up the cause of human rights and prisoners of conscience when he led the "Appeal for Amnesty" campaign that expressed outrage over the arrest of a group of students by the Portuguese government; those students had been toasting their "freedom" in a restaurant at the time of their arrest. The campaign gained international attention from a front-page segment in the *London Observer* produced by Benenson that decried the students' arrest and called for increased information about such prisoners of conscience around the world (see Banks, 2004; Power, 2001). In the following decades, the organization has spawned over fifty regional "sections" in various countries that are coordinated by a centralized International Council (IC) and the International Executive Committee (IEC). The sections are offices or headquarters that are operated by paid staff and usually situated near the capital of the particular country; the sections represent the global network that stretches around the world. The paid staffs affiliated with those sections are responsible for collecting information concerning prisoners of conscience and other political prisoners, getting legal and medical aid to those prisoners, and putting together reports based on their research and interactions with the prisoners. The reports, in turn, are presented to governing bodies within the host country, the United Nations High Commissioner for Human Rights, and in some instances to the International Criminal Court. At the local level, then, within the different countries, grassroots chapters spring up within various metropolitan areas and on college campuses in order to support the regional sections; to date there are over 7,800 local chapters registered with Amnesty International worldwide (Banks, 2004). The local chapters serve as the backbone of Amnesty International work as the volunteers within those chapters provide donations necessary for the funding of the regional sections, the IC, and the IEC. In addition, the activists affiliated with the local chapters conduct much of the routine work that is necessary for Amnesty International's mission; in particular, many of the volunteers sign and circulate petitions and engage in letter writing activities. Often, volunteers can go to the Amnesty International website, or the website of their respective section, and electronically sign petitions or download materials that can be used to write letters to any number of government agencies (see Banks, 2004; Hopgood, 2006; Parry, 2005; Power, 2001). Letter writing campaigns have been instrumental in the release of prisoners of conscience, such as José Gallardo of Mexico and Alpha Condé of Guinea (Banks, 2004). Within local level networks, petition drives and letter writing campaigns stand as Communicative Resistance typically observed in regards to the activists associated with Amnesty International chapters. Typically, the local chapters serve as a site where activists come together and coordinate different letter writing campaigns and discuss their groups' stance on issues involved in petitions that are discussed and described on the Amnesty International website. The activists then set about writing their letters and sending them to the offices of various governmental agencies, and working to get signatures for petitions that their chapter has decided to take up. In Western countries like the United Kingdom and the United States, such petition drives often entail the activists stopping people at strategic points in their community and discussing the particular issue with them in the hopes of getting that person to sign. In addition to those activities, activists within the local chapters also stage candlelight vigils and public workshops (e.g., information booths) at strategic points in their community (e.g., a mall or city hall) in order to provide people with information about prisoners of conscience and abuses of power through prison systems.

Within a local level community like Mystical City or Erie City, then, a small number of Reformist Participatory activists usually establish and maintain the Amnesty International chapters. The participatory activists accomplish this task by sending out press releases to local newspapers, managing a listserv, and producing pamphlets, all for the purpose of circulating narratives that can raise awareness of the group among other activists in the local community. For instance, Activist #2, a Reformist Participatory activist who organized an Amnesty International organization in Mystical City, explained how he received information from Amnesty International listservs, and then passed that information along to other people:

> I'm on several of Amnesty's lists. And so every time that Amnesty has something important to say, it comes to me…So we'll send out information over our list serve and other people will get it. Or if I get something that I think is valuable to another group I know where their offices are, I know where their mailboxes are, I know individuals that I can drop the information off with. And so a lot of it is either emailed or run by foot between organizations. And then when we have some sort of action that involves more than one cause we try to get groups together, and when we get groups together in that way they can share information and then also share it with the public.

The circulation of narratives often includes information and news articles that originate from the Amnesty International website, or some other alternative media source that contains similar information (e.g., MoveOn, NPR's *All Things Considered*); the circulation of the narrative attracts other activists who hold worldviews that correspond with those narratives. Overall, however, many of the activists that come to be affiliated with those local level chapters are classified as Reformist Lay; their worldviews concerning power structures often mirror the mission of the organization and they engage in lay use of the website and other alternative media. Essentially, there is little need for participatory feedback to producers or production of alternative media outside of the actions of participatory leaders of the local chapters, as most of the media work is conducted at the global level and passed directly to the local level. Activist #4 in Mystical City serves as an excellent example of a Reformist Lay activist involved in Amnesty International activities:

> I mainly just go out and do the group activities. I haven't really taken much of a leadership role. I just try and basically be there to be support and kind of be a body in the movement. Help out where I can…I remember last year for Amnesty the really big thing we did, we had a mock refugee camp to raise money for the United Nations High Commission on Refugees. Because around that time the war on terrorism in Afghanistan was really taking off and there was some disregard for refugees there, and for refugees around the world. People weren't thinking about that so we were bringing the issue out under the public eye.

The themes about "amorality" that arise from the blending of information and articles on the Amnesty International website with other alternative media sources constructs a backdrop in which signing petitions, writing letters, or constructing mock refugee camps stand as "appropriate." Such public resistance corresponds with Kowal's (2000) adjustive tactics in that they conform to the laws of the country in which the Amnesty International chapters are found.

The MoveOn organization, which has emerged from the website and listserv discussed previously, in many ways proves to be similar to the

Amnesty International organization; there is a global network that spans the United States, supported by smaller chapters at the local level. Together, both levels work to counter neo-conservative politics that guided US domestic and foreign policy during the administration of George W. Bush; this was accomplished primarily by supporting Democratic candidates and policies (Dawn, 2006; Hamm, 2008). At the global level, MoveOn consists of MoveOn.org Civic Action and MoveOn.org Political Action.

> The MoveOn family of organizations is made up of a couple of different pieces. MoveOn.org Civic Action, a 501(c)(4) nonprofit organization, formerly known just as MoveOn.org, primarily focuses on education and advocacy on important national issues. MoveOn.org Political Action, a federal PAC, formerly known as MoveOn PAC, mobilizes people across the country to fight important battles in Congress and help elect candidates who reflect our values. Both organizations are entirely funded by individuals. (www.moveon.org)

Both organizations work to create advertisements and advocacy campaigns that educate citizens about the problems associated with the neo-conservative agenda and to support Democratic candidates for office. Typically, the organization tries to support Democrats that they deem to be "progressive" or left leaning (e.g., Dennis Kucinich of Ohio, Howard Dean of Vermont), shying away from those that are considered to be "conservative" Democrats (e.g., John Kerry of Massachusetts, Joseph Lieberman of Connecticut); that said, the organization typically rallies behind any Democrat in a two-sided campaign against Republicans (e.g., Bush v. Kerry in 2004). In addition, the organization also works to promote many media projects that have explicit messages that criticize the neo-conservative agenda, such as Michael Moore's movies *Fahrenheit 911* and *Sicko*. The organizations, and the campaigns designed by the organizations, are funded by donations from individuals; much of the donations received by the two MoveOn organizations are generated at the local level. In addition, the global organizations use the local level groups to coordinate the release of certain information pertaining to candidates, issues, and media projects, which is often accomplished through letter writing campaigns. In communities across the US, Reformist Participatory activists plug into the MoveOn global network via the website and listserv; those activists in turn circulate narratives from those sources in their communities. Such narratives explain the problems associated with the neo-conservative agenda in Washington, DC, and call for "house parties" for people to gather and engage in activities. Usually, the house parties entail screenings of movies (e.g., *Fahrenheit 911*) or watching televised debates between candidates. During those parties, activists have the opportunity to make donations to the two main organizations or to the campaigns of progressive candidates and are provided with information about initiatives that they can take up in their own communities, like letter writing campaigns. In his book *The New Blue Media*, Thomas Hamm explained how the primary organizations of MoveOn directed such letter writing campaigns in order to defend the movies produced by Michael Moore, "On its Web site, the group provided form letters that members could send to newspapers across the nation; the process was made even easier because the site also provided addresses for local media outlets" (Hamm, 2008, p. 109).

As with Amnesty International, Reformist Participatory activists in local communities, like Mystical City and Erie City, take up the charge of organizing MoveOn groups and activities. Typically, these activists contact MoveOn.org and apply to be a MoveOn coordinator in their particular region. As the coordinator, then, they organize events (vigils, marches, etc.) and then write about those events on a listserv for the region. For instance, Activist #28 explained his own role as the MoveOn coordinator in Erie City:

> MoveOn has over 800 people on their mailing list in this congressional district. And I added others in addition to what's on the list. So I was the coordinator. And after these events I would write an email letter to everybody saying, "Okay. Thank you for coming yesterday and here's what happened. We were there and so many people showed up and the media were outside." And I would name who was there. Channel Three, channel five, channel nine. "And we went into [the mayor's] office. We met with blank blank blank. And we had discussions for an hour. And etcetera. And I want to thank you very much. And then the next day and that night and the next day the Post Standard—here's the accounts in the Post Standard the next day. And here's what happened." And I would analyze what happened, why it happened, how it happened, what it means, what to do, what the value was, what we should do next time. If there were any screw-ups, and why they happened.

The narratives circulated by the participatory activists attract other reformist activists, many of whom are Reformist Lay activists, who do not provide feedback to the producers of the website or the listserv. Nor do such activists produce any alternative media in their own local communities. The Communicative Resistance that they perform (e.g., writing letters) is classified as adjustive and adheres to the backdrop of "amorality" that emerges from the blending of MoveOn.org content with content from other sources (e.g., *All Things Considered*).

The organization Peace Action provides an interesting case that differs from those discussed above, in that the global network is less structured and provides less direction to activists at the local level. Peace Action came into existence in 1987 when two renowned peace organizations, the Committee for a Sane Nuclear Policy (aka SANE) and the Nuclear Weapons Freeze Campaign (aka Freeze), merged in order to solidify their base and maximize their strengths (Wittner, 2007). SANE was established when a group of well-known and distinguished American citizens, who were also all peace advocates, met in New York in 1957 to discuss the important need to inform people about the catastrophic risks associated with the growing nuclear arsenal. The group decided to run public education campaigns in newspapers nationwide, often utilizing celebrity legitimizers of their cause like Marlon Brando and Dr. Spock. Immediately, local SANE chapters sprung up around the United States, with members often writing letters to the SANE co-chair Norman Cousins at the *Saturday Review* seeking information about how they could get involved in the effort (Jack, 2007). Over the years, those local level groups were used to raise funds and conduct door-to-door canvassing in which the activists would hand out literature prepared by the SANE leadership in New York (Cortright, 2007). Freeze was established in 1979 when Cambridge defense researcher Randy Forsberg proposed that the United States and Soviet Union "freeze" their nuclear arsenals and halt the so-called arms race at the Mobilization for Survival conference; the proposal stood as a theme around which different organizations concerned with world peace could mobilize activists. In 1981, the Freeze Campaign was launched at the first Freeze Conference, in which the gathered activists developed a "strategy paper" that outlined the organization's approach to the nuclear arms race and to peace; the strategy emphasized the importance of grassroots efforts in the campaign to halt nuclear proliferation. From that strategy a National Clearinghouse, or headquarters, of the organization arose, which advised the hundreds of grassroots organizations that emerged as they worked to influence their local communities.

> The national staff role was to support local grassroots organizing. The Freeze office was created as a clearinghouse, not a traditional headquarters, and it was intentionally located away from the coasts in St. Louis. The job of the clearinghouse staff was to nurture and support grassroots organizers across the country, assist in sharing ideas and materials, and report the impact of our collective actions to each other and to the media. (Senturia, 2007, p. 71)

Each local level organization sought to promote anti-nuclear and anti-war resolutions and peace candidates in their own communities, as well as initiate media campaigns to build and broaden their local base (Senturia, 2007; Wittner, 2007).

The modern-day Peace Action established by the merger underscores the strengths of both former organizations: the centralization of SANE and the grassroots empowerment of Freeze. At the global level, the Peace Action's national headquarters are situated in Silver Spring, Maryland; from there, the national staff coordinates a global website that explains the organization's mission, provides information about national Peace Action campaigns and petitions, features blogs written by many of the national staff, and asks users for donations. In this way, the global level of Peace Action is similar to

Amnesty International and MoveOn as the Peace Action website provides centralized information and opinion that can be used by local level organizations in their efforts to help the national staff and raise funds for national campaigns. However, there are significant differences between Peace Action and the two organizations previously discussed as the website instills autonomy on the local organizations, similar to Freeze's emphasis on grassroots organizing. On the website, the blogs by the national staff are subject to commentary by users, a form of interactivity that is not typically observed on the Amnesty International or MoveOn websites. In addition, the national staff provides broad overviews and frameworks of the campaigns that are the organization's current focus, rather than outline specific organizational stances like Amnesty International. For instance, one Peace Action campaign is the Peace Voter campaign that aims to inform voters about the voting record of members of Congress. The overview provides a framework for the campaign:

> Through our Peace Voter campaigns, we inform voters about their choices in both local and national elections, by highlighting different candidates stances on issues relating to peace. Our annual Congressional Voting Record gives credit to those in Congress who voted for a peaceful future, while holding accountable those who voted for larger Pentagon budgets, for spending tax dollars on nuclear weapons, and for wars of aggression and occupation. (www.peaceaction.org)

Essentially, the overview on the site provides a limited amount of information (e.g., voting records) and a basic strategy, or set of goals, for the campaign, but leaves the specific tactics of the campaign to the local level organizations. This is significantly different from Amnesty International and MoveOn, as the tactics for the local level were devised and in part coordinated by the global level.

At the local level, then, in communities like Mystical City and Erie City, Reformist Participatory activists are much more integral in the construction and maintenance of local Peace Action organizations than in the case of Amnesty International and MoveOn. This is not to say that there are no Reformist Lay activists affiliated with Peace Action chapters, but that there are many more participatory activists in Peace Action than had been the case in the previous two organizations discussed. It is often the case that half of the activists that consider themselves to be affiliated with a Peace Action organization fall within the Reformist Participatory quadrant. The global level of Peace Action provides some narratives and frameworks through their website, but it is up to the activists at the local level to ascertain how best to carry out the organization's peace campaigns. Reformists Participatory activists initially plug into the global network of Peace Action, often through the website, and find that the organization reflects many of their own worldviews concerning power and social justice. Those activists then set about circulating narratives taken from Peace Action, as well as similar narratives from other alternative media sources (e.g., *Democracy Now!*, *Z Magazine*) through newsletters, community radio programs, websites, listservs, and/or zines. Activist #22 serves as a good example of such circulation of narratives by Peace Action:

> What I consider what we do at Peace Alliance is advocacy journalism, and I want to make sure that the viewpoint that isn't being seen in mainstream media is getting out there because people can go and turn on the nightly news and hear whatever the Bush administration wants to say, but they don't hear people who are dissenting. People who have alternative viewpoints. So that's what we try to provide...I guess our newsletter goes out to almost six thousand people. And not all of them are in the immediate area, but a majority of them are. I think that our intended audience is supposed to be our members, but I think we're writing this more for people who might not know much about the issues.

As in the case of Amnesty International and MoveOn, the circulation of those narratives draws the attention of other reformist activists in the community to the organization. However, unlike the two former organizations, the Peace Action leadership often puts many of those activists to work on the newsletter or other alternative media produced by the organization. The activists are often asked to take on some of the shifting roles of alternative media production described by Atton (2002a), such as editing, circulation of content throughout the community, or working as reader-writers. Typically, the participatory use of alternative media serves as a tactic to accomplish the overarching Peace Action strategies laid out in the national campaigns within the community (e.g., education about the peace record of political candidates) and to broaden the local organization's base of support. Such alternative media "call out" the different power structures in society, such as the Bush Administration or Halliburton Corporation, for their dangerous roles in nuclear proliferation and war; Peace Action narratives, then, provide to the local community an example of ordinary people standing against such power structures. In addition, the alternative media produced by Peace Action organizations can also aid in the mobilization of local protests and demonstrations that also serve the larger Peace Action campaigns, such as anti-war marches, peace vigils, and festivals. Such activities also serve as an opportunity for Peace Action to not only educate the public about the problems associated with different power structures, but to also demonstrate how ordinary citizens can take a stand against the powerful people in the world. Typically, those demonstrations are lawful and adjustive, so that the organization does not alienate the "average" member of the community, or make them feel that such critiques of power structures are inappropriate. In this way, Peace Action often emerges as the hub of local level networks, as the organization aggressively pursues an agenda of educating the community about problems and corruptions embedded in power structures, like the US government, through the circulation of alternative media and the coordination of lawful demonstrations; such adjustive performance of Communicative Resistance conforms to the backdrop of "speaking truth to power" that emerges from the blending of content from a variety of alternative media titles used by Reformist Participatory activists (e.g., *Democracy Now!*, *Z Magazine*, *The Progressive*).

Conclusion

Overall, the current chapter has provided greater detail to the concepts that emerged in Chapter 2. The chapter illustrates different alternative media titles used by activists within the two reformist theatre-like quadrants, the emergent themes within those two theatres, and organizations that typically serve as vehicles for Communicative Resistance performed by those activists set against their respective backdrops. Within both theatre-like quadrants, then, activists develop a sense about what tactics of Communicative Resistance are appropriate and inappropriate through the use of various alternative media texts that are often produced at the global level (e.g., *Z Magazine*, MoveOn.org); those texts blend together to construct thematic backdrops that contextualize different tactics of resistance. In addition, local level participatory activists circulate narratives, many poached from global alternative media sources, through their own alternative media in order to establish organizations. Reformist Lay activists are in turn drawn to different organizations in local level communities through alternative media that contain narratives that reflect their own worldviews concerning power and social justice. Through those organizations, then, the activists engage in adjustive Communicative Resistance that they shape to fit within the context of the two themes that serve as a backdrop for performances: amorality and speaking truth to power.

It should be noted that tensions sometimes arise within the organizations due to differences concerning the thematic backdrops that emerge from alternative media use. Within more centralized organizations like Amnesty International and MoveOn, there is little tension on the part of the predominately Reformist Lay activists who make up the membership of those organizations. In regards to organizations like Peace Action, however, there are significant tensions that can arise; as stated previously, participatory activists often account for a much larger percentage of Peace Action membership. Often, the Reformist Lay activists are only loosely affiliated with Peace Action due to tensions that arise over differing backdrops constructed from alternative media use. Reformist Lay activists usually put more of their time and efforts into actions by more centralized organizations like MoveOn and Amnesty International; those actions conform more closely to the adjustive watchdog tactics that fit within the context of "amorality" constructed through their lay use of alternative media. Reformist Lay activists often take part in the local level protests and demonstrations organized by Peace Action, as those actions can simultaneously fit within the context of "amorality" and the theme of "speaking truth to power" associated with the Reformist Participatory quadrant. The vigils and marches serve as Communicative Resistance that calls for change or vigilant observation of the current power structures in society like the government or corporations (amorality), just as they also provide examples of citizens standing up to the powerful (speaking truth to power). However, many Reformist Lay activists feel that they are pushed away from the organization, or feel that they that they take a role that is "outside looking in" within the organization as the focus of Peace Action shifts back to the production and circulation of alternative media in the community that fits within the context of "speaking truth to power." Such tensions can lead many of the Reformist Lay activists to distance themselves from Peace Action and pour more of their efforts into groups like MoveOn and Amnesty International.

Chapter 5
Insurrections and Cafés: The Radical Quadrants

The following chapter provides:

1) Descriptions of alternative media titles used by activists within the Radical Participatory and Radical Lay quadrants, which includes:

   a. Analysis of content found within the individual alternative media titles used by radical activists.

   b. Explication of the collective themes that emerge within both of the quadrants and serve as a backdrop for RP.

2) Examples of different organizations that emerge as vehicles for the resistance performed by activists within the Radical Participatory and Radical Lay quadrants.

Similar to the previous chapter, the current chapter explores the alternative media typically utilized by activists in the two radical theatre-like quadrants, as well as organizations that serve as vehicles for the performance of Communicative Resistance by those activists. As discussed in Chapters 2 and 3, the radical activists are those who hold worldviews in which many of the dominant power structures in society are demonized. Institutions like the US government, corporations, or religious denominations are so systemically corrupt that no amount of reform can ever create any positive transformation. Those activists, then, either engage in militant Communicative Resistance, or support such performances by other activists if they do not actually engage in performances themselves. The following section explores the different alternative media titles utilized by such activists and explicates the overarching collective theme that emerges from the blending of those different titles.[1]

Before moving forward, it should first be noted that there is less structure involved with both of the radical quadrants than was ascribed to the reformist quadrants in the previous chapter. Many radical activists circulate narratives in their local communities that are based on anarchist tenets of decentralization, self-sufficiency, and equality related to mutualist associations described by Pierre-Joseph Proudhon (1873), and Communitarian Anarchism developed by Pytor Kropotkin (1899). Proudhon, a French philosopher, conceptualized mutualist associations as collectives in which people all worked together to produce goods that could be bartered and traded to other mutualist associations. In this way, everyone worked for the good of their immediate community and the surrounding communities simultaneously (McElroy, 2003; Proudhon, 1873; Schecter, 1994). Similarly, Kropotkin, a Russian prince, advocated for Communitarian Anarchism in which every member of an anarchist community should be trained in the sciences of agriculture and industry so that they could provide for themselves as well as the collective; each person in the community would be a self-sufficient jack-of-all-trades who could step in at a moment's notice and fill any need of the community (Kropotkin, 1899; McElroy, 2003; Schecter, 1994). In each case, no centralized authority figure was ever in charge of the anarchist community, as members were all equals who played a role in decision-making and operation of the community. Such narratives based on these anarchist principles aid in the construction of theatre-like quadrants that are a part of local-level networks. During major protests such as the 1999 Seattle World Trade Organization protests, the protests at the 2003 Free Trade Area of the Americas protests, and the 2009 Financial Fools' Day protests in London, anarchist concepts of decentralization and self-sufficiency played an important role in the organization and implementation of militant protests that demonstrated contempt for corporate and state power structures (Brecher, Costello, & Smith, 2000; Starr, 2000; Thomas, 2000). In this way, radical activists, their alternative media, and the "organizations" that they construct are all much more decentralized and non-hierarchical—at least on the surface—than those observed within the reformist quadrants, and in this way correspond more with the contemporary new social movements of the networked society envisioned by Castells (1996; 2004; 2006) and Huesca (2001).

Alternative Media and Themes

The activists who fall within the Radical Participatory theatre-like quadrant of RP utilize alternative media titles that have been observed in past research (e.g., Atkinson, 2009a; Atkinson & Dougherty, 2006; Atton, 2002a; 2003; Best, 2005; Downing, 2003a; Meikle, 2002; Pickard, 2006a; 2006b; Rauch, 2007; Stengrim, 2005; Warnick, 2007), like Indymedia.org, *The Nation*, and a wide variety of cheap zines. Such titles are not an exhaustive list of alternative media read and utilized by radical activists, as radical activists use the websites Infoshop.org and Guerilla News Network, and the magazine *Adbusters*, as well. The Radical Lay quadrant, however, proves to be a different case, as there is little alternative media use on the part of those activists and a high reliance on Radical Participatory activists as primary sources for information concerning resistance and social justice. As in the case of the reformist activists illustrated previously, the titles in this chapter were often described by Radical Participatory activists in past research as their primary sources of information concerning power structures and social justice, whereas reformist activists used such titles inconsistently and in a peripheral manner. All of the titles described in this chapter conform to one or more of the definitions of alternative media described Chapters in 1 and 4. As in the case of the previous chapter, two thematic sets will be described in the following pages: themes associated with individual alternative media titles and themes that emerge from alternative media that are specific to only one theatre-like quadrant. Similar to Chapter 4, the first set of themes is based on the dominant power structures that are the focus of each title, and the depictions of power within those entities (e.g., traditional power v. hegemonic power). The latter theme is the woven tapestry that emerges from the blending of all of the before mentioned themes, which stands as the backdrop for the performance of resistance within the two quadrants.

Indymedia.org

> The Independent Media Center is a network of collectively run media outlets for the creation of radical, accurate, and passionate tellings of the truth. We work out of a love and inspiration for people who continue to work for a better world, despite corporate media's distortions and unwillingness to cover the efforts to free humanity. (www.indymedia.org)

The Independent Media Center, also known as Indymedia and IMC, emerged in 1999 when various activists sought to provide timely news coverage of the World Trade Organization protests in Seattle outside of the sphere of corporate influence. The rationale of organizers was that corporate owned media would fail to recognize or publicize the reasons for the protests and demonstrations, thus neutralizing the message conveyed by activists at the event. Activists associated with a myriad of different social justice organizations that travelled to Seattle for the WTO protests were able to place materials onto the new website and promote their particular cause. Meanwhile, activists on the ground at protests throughout the city were able to phone in descriptions of events as they occurred to the website organizers at their downtown headquarters, who in turn put those stories immediately onto the site (Downing, 2003a; Kidd, 2003; Meikle, 2002). Afterwards, Indymedia.org continued to function as a forum where activists could upload news stories from anywhere in the world about protests, actions, or oppressive actions by state or corporate institutions. Due to the enormous web traffic that ensued, a network of regional Indymedia sites sprang up all around the world, from large metropolitan cities like London to more remote areas like Chiapas, Mexico. Today, each of those websites are linked to one another, as well as to the central Indymedia website that was developed in 1999. Indymedia is in no way typical media, as it is far more "alternative" in its nature than any of the other alternative media titles described in the previous chapter. On all of the Indymedia websites, the readers are the producers of content, as open publishing allows for anyone to submit articles, comment on articles, and provide feedback about what others' have written; such feedback often proves to be more interesting than the actual stories because of the debates that spiral out of the articles. In this way, Indymedia reflects the concepts of "readers as writers" and "native reporters" described by Atton (2002a), in that the audiences who are embedded in social justice struggles around the world are the primary producers of content on the website. Indymedia is particularly "anarchist" because of the role of egalitarianism in the online debates, as users often utilize pseudonyms that ensure anonymity as they post articles and responses. The anonymity enhances perceived egalitarianism, which is considered a primary canon of anarchist philosophy (Brecher, Costello, & Smith, 2000; McElroy, 2003).

The articles and commentary posted on Indymedia usually focus on the manner in which power structures in society work to control and manipulate resources. The content of such articles and commentary entail many of the same contentions about the entrenchment of corporations and corporate media in government as found in alternative media like *Democracy Now!* and *Z Magazine*. However, articles on Indymedia often illustrate corporations and military forces as fused, fascist entities that maintain their dominance by seeking to concentrate global resources and leave those outside of their influence in abject poverty. In other words, the focus is not so much on pacifying the masses through hegemony, as in *The Progressive* and the MoveOn website, but pacification through physical means. An example of the fusion of corporations with military forces is evident in an article entitled "Heat on the Prince of Darkness" by an activist named Doug Morris that was posted on April 1st of 2003:

> One of the architects of the Bush regime's invasion of Iraq, nicknamed "The Prince of Darkness" for his dark deeds, is Richard Perle. He served as a foreign-policy adviser in Bush the elder's Presidential campaign, as Assistant Secretary of Defense under Ronald Reagan, is connected to a chain of neo-conservative think tanks, and until the other day was chairman of the Defense Policy Board, which advises the Pentagon. He resigned his chairmanship amid controversy over his financial connections to the military-industrial complex and his potential to gain personally from the US invasion of Iraq.

The excerpt from the Morris article demonstrates the perception that US government and corporate interests have become merged into a single entity.

Rather than a cozy relationship between corporate actors and government officials, as described in alternative media titles in the previous chapter, government and military officials often simultaneously hold positions of power within major industries; from such positions they exercise control over vast resources (e.g., money, oil). Such characters use their multiple positions to advance US imperialism or nationalist interests, which usually involves the acquisition and monopolization of additional resources. The monopoly of resources means that leftist and even moderate organizations that are not part of the fascist agenda are impoverished and cannot advance any alternative interests or worldviews. If such groups do attempt to advance alternative viewpoints or to act in opposition to corporate/military fascism, brute force is subsequently used. An example of such brute force and protection of "imperialism" is evident in an article entitled "Indigenous Activists Beaten by Police" posted by an activist with the international social justice organization Action for Community and Ecology in the Regions of Central America (ACERCA) named Brendan on May 21st of 2003. In the article, Brendan documented the efforts by local people in Mexico to protest against the police forces that patrolled the Pan American highway—a stretch of highway through Mexico and Central America that is used by transnational corporations to move products and raw materials:

> On May 15, 2003, 300 people peacefully blocked the Pan American highway north of the town Unión Hidalgo, in the state of Oaxaca, Mexico. They were demanding the immediate release of political prisoner Carlos Manzo. It's reported that at approximately 4 pm police forces fired tear gas on the protestors and began to brutally beat women and children in an attempt to break up the protest. The protesters had closed down traffic on the highway from 10 am to 3pm to denounce the actions of the Juchitán police forces.

The views of the indigenous protesters in Oaxaca and their attempts to stop the movement of products and materials stood in stark contrast to the interests of transnational corporations in the area. In response, the police, acting under orders of the mayor of Unión Hidalgo, brutally attacked the protesters. Activists like Brendan and Morris claim that such brutality awaits all who defy the militaristic corporations, or stand in their way of resource acquisition. The only way to resist the fascist forces and their brutality is by challenging their control over resources. This is a difficult task considering that such an opponent already controls the majority of resources, leaving opposition depleted and weak. Many writers on Indymedia describe sheer numbers of activists and bodies as a means to challenge such power structures. An example of such a challenge is found in an article by an activist called Krishna entitled "US Try to End Nepal's Peace Process" that was submitted on May 9th of 2003. The article describes how Maoist insurgents in Nepal have managed to challenge US domination in the region:

In fact the Maoists pose no threat to the national interest of America but they pose a serious threat to American imperialism and the globalised world economic order. This is the main reason of US keenness in Nepalese affairs since the beginning of People's War in 1996. Initially [the US] expected the early death of the movement but contrary to it movement's base started becoming pervasive and it registered unprecedented increase among its supporters. Not only this, in the span of just three years [the Maoist movement] expanded its organizational base in most of the 75 districts of Nepal and created liberated zones in more than 25 districts. American establishment got alarmed. After disintegration of Soviet Union the American imperialism intoxicated with the end of communism could not accept this phenomenon. At a time when it was celebrating the 'end of history' and inaugurating the era of 'clashes of civilizations,' the emergence of a powerful peoples movement disturbed its festivity.

Ultimately, a theme of "radical resistance" is associated with the content found within the many articles and comments on Indymedia. The US government and governments around the world are a fusion of military, police force, and corporations. Standing up to those powers is not an easy task, however, and the role of localized groups or organic intellectuals does not seem to be enough to loosen that grasp; especially outside of the United States and Europe. What is required to throw off the yoke of such fascism is militant action, such as the efforts by protesters in Mexico and Maoist insurgents in Nepal. Only through the militant efforts of insurgents can there be any hope of change. In a sense, Indymedia is more radical than most alternative media titles because revolution by the proletariat is often described as the only viable solution to problems posed by dominant power structures in society.

The Nation

Figure 1. *The Nation* magazine.[2]

> *The Nation* will not be the organ of any party, sect, or body. It will, on the contrary, make an earnest effort to bring to the discussion of political and social questions a really critical spirit, and to wage war upon the vices of violence, exaggeration, and misrepresentation by which so much of the political writing of the day is marred.
>
> —From *The Nation's* founding prospectus, 1865 (www.thenation.com)

The Nation magazine was established in 1865 by abolitionists Joseph Richards and Edwin Godkin. In the time since it was first published, the magazine has established international offices around the world and developed into a weekly periodical. During that time, the magazine has critiqued economic structures, including capitalism and socialism, and challenged the rationales for most wars waged by the United States government. In addition, the magazine has provided insight and critiques concerning popular culture, gender, and the environment (Armstrong, 1981). In recent years, *The Nation* has stressed that progressive grassroots movements can equal the accomplishments of conservative grassroots movements over the course of the past twenty years; namely, they can change beliefs and attitudes on the local level by working closely with communities. Such a process is going to take time and patience, but in the end social justice ideals can win out on the local level. This process is different than the "speaking to power" theme associated with the Reformist Participatory quadrant because common people are leading the efforts of resistance, rather than the celebrity organic intellectuals found in titles like *The Progressive*.

Many articles found in *The Nation* describe the entrenchment of corporate interests in government, much like *The Progressive* and other alternative media titles discussed in Chapter 4. However, the focus of those articles are not so much on the hegemonic control through the relationship between government and corporate entities, but instead the control of physical resources (e.g., money, medicine, arms) through such relationships and entrenchment—similar to Indymedia described above. For instance, in the article "ALEC Meets His Match" in the June 9th, 2003, issue of *The Nation*, John Nichols described the impact of the American Legislative Exchange Council (ALEC) on government. ALEC is a conservative organization that bills itself as the "largest bipartisan, individual membership association of state legislators" (Nichols, 2003).

> ALEC was remolded by corporate lobbyists to implement their agenda. Flush with $6 million a year in funding from Amoco, Chevron, Texaco, Phillip Morris, RJ Reynolds, Cargill, AT&T, Wackenhut Corrections, the American Nuclear Energy Council, the Chlorine Chemistry Council, the American Petroleum Institute, the Pharmaceutical Research and Manufacturers of America, and, until recently, Enron, ALEC has drawn a

membership of 2400 legislators—one-third of the nation's total—with "junkets and other largesse," according to "Corporate America's Trojan Horse in the States: The Untold Story Behind the American Legislative Exchange Council," a study released last year by the Defenders of Wildlife and the Natural Resources Defense Council. ALEC sets up task forces of legislators and corporate lobbyists who draw up "model legislation," dealing with everything from expanding spending on prisons, to removing barriers to the genetic modification of food, to supporting the Bush Administration's push to create a Free Trade Area of the Americas. The bills are then introduced by the legislators and promoted by the lobbyists.

Much like the content found in *The Progressive*, this excerpt explains that corporate America is deeply involved in the legislative process. In fact, it seems that corporate influence is so entrenched that there is little chance the cause of social justice will prevail within the halls of Congress. However, rather than focus on the construction and maintenance of ideology, the primary focus is on the use of vast sums of money by the corporate controlled government to create legislation that will produce corporate friendly legislation; such legislation will, in turn, generate more resources (e.g., money, lobbyists) for those corporate systems. In addition, the influence of corporate interest is not limited to government and legislation in the United States, as another article from the June 9th issue entitled "Offering Hope—at a Price" by Katharine Greider described the impact of the drug industry on American society:

> Generally speaking the drug industry does not expend resources to develop medicines that might be an enormous boon for public health but offer little prospect for commercial gain. For example, a tiny percentage of new drugs brought to market are to treat diseases like malaria that kill huge numbers of poor people around the world. If this seems natural enough—these are business people after all, not public-health activists—then perhaps it will seem more surprising that American taxpayers support a portion of the research to develop drugs over which drug companies claim sole proprietorship. Proprietorship and, of course, the right to charge whatever they please.

The above excerpt once again stresses the control of resources by corporations in society, namely control over the production and marketing of drugs. Essentially, the drug industry has little concern for manufacturing drugs that will help people who suffer from diseases such as malaria or typhoid, but rather drugs with limited health value, such as Viagra, that will generate additional resources in the form of profit.

For the most part, the only hope to stand against the corporate interests that have become entrenched in the government and society comes from grassroots movements; that is, mobilization and resistance from below. Resistance against such power structures can only be achieved through the efforts of citizens and activists in local communities, as the US Congress and national assemblies have been corrupted by the influence of corporate resources, such as money and gifts. Take, for instance, the article "Toward a Global Movement" by Medea Benjamin in the April 21st issue of 2003:

> While in the anticorporate globalization movement we had already formed impressive ties with grassroots movements overseas, antiwar organizing has given us the opportunity to expand geographically to areas such as the Middle East, where we had less-developed contacts; to multiply our ranks with a dazzling array of new sectors, from city councils to women's and civil rights organizations such as NOW (National Organization for Women) and the NAACP (National Association for the Advancement of Colored People); and, most important, to merge the peace movement with the movement to fight corporate-dominated globalization.

In the article, Benjamin explains the wars in Afghanistan and Iraq are two projects designed and perpetuated by corporate power structures. She claims that resistance to such projects will not come about through Congress, but rather through the construction of relationships between grassroots groups and established global networks, like the NAACP. Essentially, it is important to piece together a patchwork coalition of people and groups that represent the interests of common people from different walks of life around the world. Together, such coalitions, or networks, can work to pressure the corporate entrenched government in such a way to end the two wars. Such a sentiment was echoed by Nichols in his previously discussed article, as he explained how to thwart the agenda of ALEC, "groups are able to build tight knit networks of [local level] legislators who use close ties to grassroots groups— and whatever foundation funding they can scrape together—not just to battle ALEC but to pass progressive legislation."

As with many of the themes discussed in Chapter 4, the government and the vast majority of resources are controlled by corporate interests within the pages of *The Nation*; corporations perpetuate their position through their monopoly over resources in society. In this way, then, the magazine appeals to many radical activists, as that worldview focuses on traditional notions of power. Rather than the organic intellectuals described in *The Progressive*, however, those who resist the machinery of such domination are common people working in their local communities to make significant changes. These common people working at the local level are the basis for the theme of "resistance from below." It is the people in local communities who must resist. The odds are stacked against these common people, but there is some hope for change from the bottom up.

118 The Radical Quadrants

Zines

Figure 2. Two zines: *Beginners guide to sexuality* and *After the Fall.*

> Zine publishing stands in for meeting people: it can be explained as an instance of material culture that instantiates lived experience, a set of social relations. At the same time it presents an individual's declaration and construction of self-identity and invites others to engage in dialogue about that identity. (Atton, 2002a, p. 67)

In addition to the above-mentioned alternative media titles, many radical activists read "zines" written by individuals, organizations, and anarchist collectives. The term "zine" is derived from "fanzines" that, in the past, often focused on particular music, activities, television programs, or celebrities. Zines are inexpensive magazines that are written and printed using conventional personal computers and printers, and often photocopied for easy circulation within an immediate local community (Armstrong, 1981; Atton, 2002a; Downing, 1984; Downing et al., 2001). Such alternative media are often deemed to be of substandard quality, relegated to what Atton (2002a) describes as the "ghetto sphere," a concept that he claims has emerged from the corporate domination of the airwaves and media production resources for commercial purposes. Essentially, such corporate domination has led to the privatization of Jurgen Habermas' (1974; 1989) public sphere, which is the space where ideas are exchanged and democracy is enacted. Many scholars and activists feel that such privatization and the subsequent corporate "filtering" of the media content have tainted the potentials for democracy in the public sphere and placed greater emphasis on commercial products over the exchange of ideas (e.g., Herman & Chomsky,

1988; McChesney, 1998). In response, many citizens and activists have turned to zines as a means to produce and circulate narratives outside of the sphere of corporate influence. Since production takes place outside of the corporate domain, and because many producers harbor deep suspicions about commercial interests, the politics of zine production often leave the final product "underdeveloped." As discussed in Chapter 1, the lack of resources requires that zine producers turn to the use of organizational tactics, such as decentralization of production, anti-copyright policies, and reliance on "movement intellectuals." The results are simple sheets of paper folded together and sometimes stapled, which feature artwork, photographs, stories, commentary, poetry, songs, or just about anything else that can be printed.

According to Atton (2002a), most zine production stands as a form of letter writing on the part of producers, and social interaction on the part of audiences. For the producers, they are able to lay pen to paper (or fingers to keyboard) and generate a manifesto in which they provide their own particular critique of power structures in society through analysis, poetry, artwork, or storytelling. On the part of the audience who read those zines, the critiques stand as a social interaction and invites further social interaction through the audiences' very possession of the zine. The audiences not only read the critiques written by the producer, but also often gain insight into many details about the producer(s) through their stories and art. In addition, the possession of such media demonstrates to others that the owner has a critical, often radical, worldview. Essentially, zines symbolize what Atton (2002a) and Castells (2004) call a "resistance identity" that is defined in terms of stigma and marginalization, often because they live in defiance of the powerful in society. Atton claims that ownership of such zines generates interest on the part of other people and helps to initiate social interactions about particular topics (e.g., war, corporate crime), which provides for opportunities to build organizations and community. Ownership of zines also create a kind of authenticity, as the owner can demonstrate that they are truly radical and outside of the domain of mainstream media and dominant power structures.

The beginners guide to sexuality and *After the Fall* are two examples of zines produced and circulated by radical activists, mainly anarchists.[3] The first, *the beginners guide to sexuality*, is a small booklet printed on three sheets of paper folded into eleven pages of text. According to a disclaimer found in the pamphlet, the material was produced by an unnamed anarchist collective situated in the Denver area. The content of the pamphlet describes sexual discrimination which "wimmin" face within a patriarchical society and what men should do to reverse many of those problems. The pamphlet also discusses how men should respect the boundaries of women and make steps toward responsible sexuality.

We are taught to "make the first move," and crap like "her mouth says no, but her body says yes." We can get off in two minutes flat if we want to. We don't have to worry about looking like a sex object everyday, or realize that every other dipshit we pass each day will be jerking off over what's beneath our pants...Since men play the oppressor it becomes necessary for us to become accountable for our actions/mistakes...it is our responsibility as people who identify as experiencing male privilege to deconstruct internalized ways of thinking and acting towards wimmin as well as how we think and act towards each other.

The second zine, *After the Fall*, was produced by a New York City anarchist collective who called themselves After the Fall; the zine was named after the group. The zine appeared to be a make-shift newspaper that comprised of seven pages of fine print stories, drawings, and cartoons. Unlike the previous zine, *After the Fall* dealt with a variety of different topics, such as an anarchist's journey to Israel and Palestine, comics that featured fun and joy associated with dumpster diving for food, and an "editorial" that critiqued corporations. The central feature of the zine, however, involved many stories that described efforts of the New York based More Gardens! activists to transform the Cabo Rojo area of the city into a community garden, how those efforts were met by authorities, and activists' reaction to the authorities.

In the last 30 years, the city tore down perfectly fixable homes, stopped trash pick ups and closed down our fire houses—letting paid arsonists burn down our neighborhoods. There wasn't a single police officer when you needed one, the side walks where kids could fall into were never fixed. The people themselves responded to this neglect by creating the community gardens. The gardens are clean, and with them the kids are safer and the people have a place to come together...Amidst a dozen police escort, two garden activists found their way up to the 27 feet high Sunflower (steel structure with a chair and lock down at the top) and the Sleeping Dragon (steel tube encased in a 50 gallon concrete drum) laying on the front ceiling of the casita.

The content of both zines involve personal worldviews (*the beginners guide*), personal narratives (*After the Fall*), and artwork (*After the Fall*), which fits Atton's (2002a) description of zines. Both of the zines, and many other zines like them, entail a theme of "clash of cultures" in contemporary society. On the one side are anarchist producers of the zine, who describe relationships and communities that are based on tenets of anarchism, such as decentralization, self-sufficiency, and equality. On the other side are oppressive outsiders (e.g., US government, police, corporations) who perpetuate abuse, exploitation, and destruction of the environment; such people are often depicted as threatened by the culture of anarchism and other alternative worldviews. The worldviews and personal narratives of the producers of such zines stand in stark contrast to the backdrop of oppression and injustice and serve as a basis for alternative lifestyles in which community bonds are stronger, safer, and more respectful. As the rejection of oppressive power structures is not a society-wide phenomenon, the zines, particularly *After the Fall*, describe how important it is for anarchists and other radical activists to stand in solidarity, to form alternative relationships, and to fight to protect fragile communities that stand in resistance.

Radical Participatory Quadrant: Insurrection!
As discussed Chapter 2, the Radical Participatory activists not only read alternative media content, but they co-perform with that content through their own production and feedback to global producers. Similar to the Reformist Participatory activists discussed in the previous chapter, the Radical Participatory activists perform as a diffused audience. In this way, the Radical Participatory quadrant also functions as a performance art production, in which audiences take part in the performances found in alternative media through their own production and/or feedback to producers. Past research has demonstrated that Indymedia.org, *The Nation*, and a variety of zines serve as primary sources of information about resistance and social justice for Radical Participatory activists (e.g., Armstrong, 1981; Atkinson & Dougherty, 2006; Atton, 2002a; 2004; Downing, 2003a; 2003b). These are not the only alternative media titles used by Radical Participatory activists as other titles, like the anarchist news website Infoshop.org, have emerged from additional research projects (e.g., Atton, 2003). In addition, Chapters 2 and 3 demonstrated that clearinghouse websites, like Commondreams.org, and local level listservs are also important to Radical Participatory activists, as they provided those activists with glimpses into the other quadrants and aided in the construction of the Multiplex through the coordination of common visions and goals. In reference to themes that emerge solely within the theatre-like quadrant, the focus, then, falls on the alternative media titles and zines described above. The theme that emerges from the blending of such alternative media titles often used by Radical Participatory activists is "insurrection!"

Indymedia and *The Nation* generated a theme in which corporate forces are entrenched in politics and world governance through their monopolization and manipulation of resources. Essentially, corporations utilize resources (e.g., money, arms, lobbyists) to control government processes to such an extent as to leave little hope for any reform through democratic processes. It is often argued in articles found within *The Nation* that grassroots movements are needed to produce change, which can be a slow and arduous process. For instance, in Nichols' (2003) article about ALEC, he describes corporate influence as so entrenched in politics that there is little hope that social justice can prevail through national level politics. Instead, grassroots progressive groups need to make arguments to local legislatures. If change does not occur, the next step is a militant revolution, such as the insurgent action in Nepal and Chiapas described in Indymedia, or mass protests like the demonstrations against the WTO in Seattle. According to Brendan and Krishna, whose postings on Indymedia were described above, militant strategies performed by large numbers of activists are one of the few options available for people who live under blatant, repressive state apparatuses, such as US corporate imperialism. Ultimately, the theme from these two primary sources is about corporations as enemies that must be resisted in a way that typically hinders or reverses corporate monopoly over resources. Such a theme also emerges from many of the makeshift zines found throughout local level networks, in communities like Erie City and Mystical City. Anarchist zines like *After the Fall* and *the beginners guide to sexuality* demonstrate the producers' perceptions about the nature of the world by contrasting the oppressive cultures that grow from the different power structures in society with the egalitarian tenets of anarchism.

Within the context of the Radical Participatory theatre-like quadrant, then, the alternative media read and used by activists portrays a world in which corporate power structures use their resources to control governments and policy. Such content contends that wars and other government actions are carried out for the benefit of elites and not for the citizenry. This is not altogether different from the themes of "speaking truth to power" and "amorality" associated with the two reformist quadrants, except that the domination of resources takes center stage. Within the pages and pixels of the primary alternative media titles used by activists who fall within the Radical Participatory quadrant, speaking out against power structures and educating people about hegemony in society will accomplish very little. Instead, it is important to strike at the resources controlled by those power structures, and hinder the ability to accumulate and control resources in general; such militant strategies are especially evident through Indymedia and zines like *After the Fall*.

Radical Lay Quadrant: A Café
Radical Lay activists often pay little attention to alternative media; instead, they collect information about resistance and social justice from social interactions with Radical Participatory activists. Past research has demonstrated that the only alternative media used by these activists are radio programs like *All Things Considered* on NPR. As described in the previous chapter, *All Things Considered* uses testimony from corporate representatives, government officials, social justice advocates, and the general public to present stories about power structures in society, which gives rise to the theme of "balanced visions." For instance, in a May 7, 2003, broadcast of *All Things Considered*, entitled "South African Businesses Battle AIDS," addressed health problems related to HIV/AIDS for people who worked in the gold and diamond mines in South Africa managed by the

Anglo-Gold Corporation. Throughout the broadcast, multiple visions and voices from representatives of Anglo-Gold Corporation, South African workers at Anglo-Gold, medical experts, and social justice advocates are all used to examine the social justice issue of AIDS in South Africa (Beaubien, 2003) and provide a more "balanced" story about the situation than stories presented in the mainstream news media. As titles like *All Things Considered* are usually the only alternative media used by Radical Lay activists, it would then seem that "balanced visions" would be the backdrop of the quadrant.

At first glance, the theme of balanced visions seems problematic, as it does not really match the radical worldviews associated with the Radical Lay activists. How could the voices of "corrupt" Anglo-Gold representatives strike a balance for radical activists? However, such a first glance does not take into account the social interactions in which these activists engage. In past research, several Radical Lay activists have claimed that much of their information about resistance and social justice came from interactions with Radical Participatory activists in their community and not from alternative media—even media that they used, like *All Things Considered*. The Radical Lay activists do not engage within a theatre like the other three activist types discussed in Chapter 2; instead, they rely on social interactions with other radical activists for information concerning power structures and resistance in society, and claim that their use of alternative media, like *All Things Considered*, merely plays in the background.[3] Such activists claim that they choose such programs and broadcasts for their background because they deem them to be at least partially independent from corporate and government influence, although not entirely. However, such activists feel that it is better to play NPR or other such titles in the background, than more corporate/government friendly media like CNN or Fox News. In this way, the Radical Lay quadrant is more like a café, in which little attention is paid to the music drifting in the background as patrons sit and interact with one another. The Radical Lay café-like quadrant, then, can be envisioned as a site where activists engage in conversation together, talking about the power structures and resistance while a radio plays NPR or Pacifica Radio in the background, like music on a jukebox. For this reason, the Radical Lay activists performs more like Abercrombie and Longhurst's (1998) concept of a mass audience rather than as a diffused or simple audience.

"Organizations" and Communicative Performances

As discussed previously in this chapter, there is much less structure in terms of the radical quadrants because of many activists' reliance on tenets of anarchism. Emphasis on decentralization and self-sufficiency often makes formal establishment and maintenance of an organization within a local level network difficult, if not often impossible; authority figures and rules of conduct can violate those anarchist tenets. That is not to say that rules and hierarchy are outside of the bounds of radical activists. As discussed in Chapter 3, rules and hierarchy often exist within groups formed by radical activists as deep structures that are not codified in any way. Nevertheless, many radical activists consider the very concept of organization to be contrary to the social justice goals of a movement, as organizing is a step toward bureaucracy and co-optation by the dominant power structures that are the nemesis of a movement. According to Activist #40, a Radical Participatory activist in Erie City, "All movements go through two phases. The street phase and the bureaucratic phase...As soon as the Democrats get it or the Republicans get it, it gets institutionalized, bureaucratized, and the movement element of it is over." Such institutionalization seems offensive to Activist #40, as well as other radical activists, because of their demonization of corporations and government. Instead, many Radical Participatory activists within local level communities, such as Erie City and Mystical City, "plug into" global level networks, like Indymedia or Infoshop, and learn of radical groups like Black Bloc Anarchists and Radical Cheerleaders. It is important to note that such radical groups depicted in the alternative media of global level networks are not so much defined by issues or goals, but by the tactics that are utilized in their protests against power structures in society. Radical Participatory activists, in turn, produce zines in order to circulate narratives about the clash of cultures that exist within society, as well as within the community. In this way, the radical activists at the local level come together into informal groups and co-opt tactics used by other radical groups for their own issues and goals within their communities. The following "organizations"—Black Bloc Anarchists and Radical Cheerleaders—have been selected because of their prevalence in past research (e.g., Atkinson & Dougherty, 2006; Atton, 2002a; Downing, 2003a; Paris, 2003; Starr, 2006). As with alternative media titles, this is not an exhaustive list of "organizations" with which radical activists often become involved. DeLuca (1999), for instance, has written extensively about radical activist groups like Green Peace and Kentuckians for the Commonwealth, while Harold (2004) has closely examined the Culture Jammers and the Biotic Baking Brigade.

Black Bloc is the name used in reference to radical groups that engage in militant protest tactics at major demonstrations, like the 1999 World Trade Organization protests in Seattle and the Financial Fools Day protests in London of 2009. Oftentimes, such groups are comprised of activists who claim to be anarchists, or who adhere to anarchist tenets described previously in this chapter. It should be noted that not all anarchists are Black Bloc or involve themselves in militant actions, as Amory Starr (2000) has indicated in her book, *Naming the Enemy*, that many anarchist collectives disdain violence and avoid militant confrontations with police and authorities; such anarchists deem militant actions to be contrary to social justice goals.

Nevertheless, many anarchists or anarchist-oriented activists do consider themselves to be Black Bloc and often engage in militant tactics that involve confrontation with authorities and property destruction. In an article published in *Social Movement Studies*, Starr (2006) indicated that Black Bloc developed from Abbey Hoffman's calls for "monkeywrenching" in the 1970s, which involved putting metal spikes into trees and sabotaging logging equipment. In turn, radical activists affiliated with groups such as the Animal Liberation Front, Earth Liberation Front (ELF), and Earth First! adopted those tactics in their efforts to rescue animals from laboratories and hinder logging efforts in the northwestern US. These Black Bloc groups are quite different from many of the organizations described in Chapter 4, such as Amnesty International and MoveOn local chapters, in that issues or topics are not their focal interest. Instead, the Black Bloc, in local communities like Mystical City and Erie City, are drawn together because of their interest in militant tactics for resistance against dominant power structures in society. In fact, Jeffrey Paris, an anarchist scholar and professor of philosophy, claims Black Bloc itself is a protest tactic first and foremost:

> [T]he Black Bloc is not a group or a movement; it is a tactic open to anyone who seeks to escalate the social and economic costs of repressive governmental activity. Affinity groups engaged in Black Bloc tactics come from a large spectrum of ideologies, though many or most identify as anarchists. (Paris, 2003, p. 321)

Essentially, Black Bloc, as a tactic, involves wearing black clothing from head to toe in order to mask the number of activists, while simultaneously making many activists appear as one large body. Black ski masks and/or bandanas used to cover the face also provide activists with anonymity that can protect them from legal repercussions for militant protest actions, such as storming police lines and throwing tear gas canisters back at police. These militant tactics serve a practical function, which is to influence the allocation of resources by power elites who are in control of government and other institutions in society. In other words, militant tactics force those in power to move resources that they would otherwise use in other oppressive efforts elsewhere. Past research concerning activists who claim to be "Black Bloc" or "Black Bloc Anarchists" (e.g., Starr, 2000; 2006) reflect Paris' tactic-oriented definition. For instance, Activist #9, a Radical Participatory activist in Mystical City, described his social interactions with other radical activists in the community:

> I guess the main thing that we really discuss is tactics. How in the world are we going to fight these huge entities that have so much more power than we do? We share outrage about what's going on. But as far as really getting deep into the issues—since there's a lot of agreement about the inherent

trouble with the system and the way it is, a lot of what we talk about is how do we change it? How do fight the system? Fight corporations?

Militant tactics utilized by Black Bloc groups have been documented by a variety of scholars and writers. In her book *The Battle in Seattle*, Janet Thomas (2000) explained how such anarchist groups broke the windows of Nike and Gap stores in downtown Seattle during the WTO protests of 1999. By throwing rocks and other objects through windows of those businesses, the anarchists were able to force police to move from one location to another; the activists had in effect influenced the allocation and distribution of resources by the authorities within the city. In her book *Webs of Power*, the anarchist activist Starhawk (2002) described her own role in multiple Black Bloc actions at the Seattle protests. In one instance, a group of anarchists witnessed a line of police mounted on horseback brutalizing peaceful activists and pushing them from the street. Working together, Starhawk and her compatriots blocked Constitution Avenue by lying down in the middle of the street in an effort to halt the police line. Later, her Black Bloc "cluster" worked to block another intersection downtown, which resulted in their arrest. Naomi Klein (2002), author of *Fences and Windows*, explained the tactics utilized by a Black Bloc contingent at the Free Trade Area of the Americas (FTAA) protests in Quebec City in 2001. According to Klein, the Black Bloc, acting separate from more adjustive and "peaceful" protesters, donned gas masks and took up positions at the front of anti-FTAA marches. As the multiple marches progressed nearer to police lines within the city, the police launched tear gas canisters toward the protesters; the Black Bloc retaliated by grabbing up the tear gas canisters and throwing them back at the police. Starr (2006) provided a list of tactics often utilized by Black Bloc groups: property destruction, barricading streets and property, throwing lightweight materials and trash at police, and attempting to cross police lines. Ultimately, in the bigger picture of protests and resistance, these actions by Black Bloc groups forces the power elites and authorities to allocate money and move resources to globalization conferences and events in cities like Seattle and Miami, and away from oppressive enterprises like the war on drugs and the "imperialist" wars in Iraq and Afghanistan.

Similar to the Black Bloc, Radical Cheerleading emerged in the mid-1990s as a tactic used to protest against a wide variety of issues, from war to gender discrimination. Often, Radical Cheerleading, as a tactic, involves performances on the part of activists that mimic or parody cheerleaders typically seen at American sporting events (Kantrowitz, Springen, & Hontz, 2003; Thompson, 2003). Starr (2006) refers to such tactics as "Pink Bloc." As in the case of Black Bloc groups, radical activists that form Radical Cheerleading groups in local communities often come together because of their fascination and interest in the tactic. Activist #18, a Radical

Participatory activist in Mystical City, illustrates the "tactic-orientation" associated with Radical Cheerleading:

> We were kind of bored one day and we went on the Internet and looked up some files and downloaded these cheers. It was so fun. Just actually reading through the cheers they had, they were so hilarious. Just so creative in their rhetoric discussing these ideas. Like globalization, or just anything. It's just so funny. That was probably what drew me to [Radical Cheerleading] the most.

Although little academic attention has been paid to Radical Cheerleading and Radical Cheerleaders, a number of news articles and essays have examined such activists and their protest tactics. According to Barbara Kantrowitz, Karen Springen, and Jenny Hontz (2003) in an article published in *Newsweek* magazine, Radical Cheerleading was first developed by two sisters in Florida as an effort to cheer on and encourage other activists. The tactic was often featured in various alternative media, like Indymedia, and was quickly adopted across the United States by several other activist groups. In recent years, Radical Cheerleading groups have emerged with names like the Memphis Dirty Southern Belles and the Rocky Mountain Rebels (Cosgrove-Mather, 2003). Such groups took the tactic of Radical Cheerleading beyond mere encouragement for other activists and turned it into a form of nonviolent confrontation. As a tactic, Radical Cheerleading can be classified as militant, but is quite different from the militant tactics of the Black Bloc described above; Black Bloc tactics are categorized as militant because they are confrontational in nature and usually violate laws. The activists who engage in Radical Cheerleading rarely, if ever, violate laws, but often violate "societal rules." According to Kowal (2000), militant tactics are those that break rules and threaten dominant groups, which can include breaking laws or engaging in activities that violate traditions or mores; Radical Cheerleading involves the latter. The breaking of such social traditions and mores can often deeply agitate people outside of a movement, as well as reformist activists who are interested in more adjustive tactics of resistance. Ultimately, the commotion stirred by these Radical Cheerleading squads can have the same effects as Black Bloc tactics. Specifically, the agitation often leads to people calling security or police forces so as to remove the activists (e.g., Nichols, 2005; Starr, 2006). As in the case of the Black Bloc, the allocation of such forces—and the money that they cost—means that those resources will not be used in other oppressive enterprises on the part of dominant power structures.

The performances of Radical Cheerleaders often involve makeshift costumes similar to those worn by "traditional" cheerleaders, which subvert the clean-cut image of the American sports icon while drawing the gaze of onlookers. Some costumes worn by members of Radical Cheerleading squads are well coordinated, while in other squads the activists hardly match

(Cosgrove-Mather, 2003). Using props, like pom-poms made from trash bags, the Radical Cheerleaders dance about and recite chants in front of audiences at public places, such as malls, schools, and outside of businesses and government offices (Cosgrove-Mather, 2003; Kantrowitz, Springen, & Hontz, 2003; Thomas, 2000). The chants and cheers sang by Radical Cheerleaders are similar to the concepts of diatribe (Windt, 1972), as they often involve language or performances that are deemed to be offensive or obscene by onlookers. In addition, the militant tactics of such activists can serve as image events (DeLuca, 1999) that challenge ideographs (e.g., ideological assumptions) like the importance of consumerism, the necessity of war, and heteronormative sexuality. In their *Newsweek* article, Kantrowitz, Springen, and Hontz (2003) explained how a Milwaukee based Radical Cheerleading squad wore cheerleaders-as-pirates costumes and travelled to various malls in the area to perform cheers about body image and motherhood. Elizabeth Nichols (2005), an activist-writer for *Off Our Backs* magazine, wrote about her participation in a Radical Cheerleading squad that protested at Inauguration of President George W. Bush in January of 2005. In mismatched uniforms, Nichols' squad cheered at an anarchist march, and then went to cheer and chant for crowds in downtown Washington, DC. Cheers like "Take it to the Streets," "Resist," and "Cheerleaders National Anthem" apparently angered many of the police who were nearby, as the cheerleaders were met with jeers and pepper spray from those police.

"Cheerleaders National Anthem":
(*To the tune of the Star Spangled Banner*)
Oh say can you see
By the blue TV's light
When democracy failed
And Wall Street was scheming
The jail stripes and iron bars
Left the ghettos in scars
From our sofas we watched
As the nation was screaming
And the missiles red glare
Star Wars nukes in the air
If you're not rich and white
Then your rights are stripped bare.
Oh, say will that blood spattered dollar sign still reign
In the land of corporate greed
And the home of the slave. (Nichols, 2005, p. 16)

In the previous chapter, global networks, like Amnesty International, played an integral role in the construction of organizations by reformist activists. In the case of radical activists, however, global networks play a different role. In local communities, like Mystical City and Erie City, Radical Participatory activists "plug into" alternative media, like Indymedia and Infoshop; past research has designated such online/interactive alternative media as networks (see Atton, 2003; Atkinson, 2008; Best, 2005; Pickard, 2006a; 2006b; Stengrim, 2005). Through such alternative media networks, radical activists witness militant performances like Radical Cheerleading and Black Bloc efforts. The depictions of dominant power structures that monopolize resources and utilize brute force against opposition, coupled with the depictions of militant resistance by Black Bloc anarchists and insurgents in places like Nepal and Mexico, give rise to the theme of "insurrection!" within that quadrant. Those Radical Participatory activists, in turn, reflect such themes in their own production of zines, as well as their social interactions with Radical Lay activists. The Radical Lay activists, conversely, do not utilize alternative media like the other types of activists. For those activists, alternative media like NPR's *All Things Considered* are used as a substitute for media sources that have been "corrupted" by the corporate sphere; their primary source of information about power and resistance comes from their social interactions with the Radical Participatory activists. Working together, then, the two activist types collaborate together and utilize many of the tactics that the Radical Participatory activists have found through global alternative media networks. Such work develops into Black Bloc groups or Radical Cheerleading squads. Unlike the tensions that develop between Reformist Participatory and Reformist Lay activists, as discussed in Chapter 4, there is little tension between the two radical quadrants as they work together utilizing such militant tactics. In fact, through the use of alternative media like Indymedia, Radical Participatory activists learn about sites for protest outside of their local community so that their respective groups can take their militant performance to other communities and protest against multiple power structures. One Radical Participatory activist in Mystical City, Activist #10, called such travelling protest "the demo circuit." Throughout their protests and their journeys the Radical Participatory activists photograph and record their efforts, which later serves as the basis for content that they contribute to interactive alternative media networks.

Conclusion

The current chapter has helped to provide more detail concerning many of the concepts discussed in Chapter 2. In particular, the chapter has explicated the themes associated with individual alternative media titles used by Radical Participatory activists and has illustrated the overarching theme that emerges from the blending of alternative media titles within the Radical Participatory quadrant. It is important to keep in mind the mass audience-like use of alternative media within the Radical Lay quadrant and those activists' reliance on the Radical Participatory activists for information that is integral to the development of their worldviews. Ultimately, the alternative media utilized by Radical Participatory activists construct a thematic backdrop against which militant Communicative Resistance is the most effective way to hinder the ability of dominant power structures to monopolize and manipulate resources in society.

Overall, Chapters 4 and 5 have effectively provided many details that should help the reader to conceptualize the first three categories of RP: Critical Worldviews, Alternative Media Interactions, and Communicative Resistance. In addition, the details in both chapters aid in the conceptualization of Intercreative Capacity and Narrative Capacity *within* local networks. Through descriptions of alternative media used by activists, and examples of organizations that those activists build, the reader should now have more insight into what goes on within and between the four theatre-like quadrants of RP in local communities. The following chapter describes the emergent "alternative media world," which builds on Nick Couldry's (2000; 2003) concepts of the "media world" and the "ordinary world." In many ways, the alternative media world serves to illustrate the role of Intercreative Capacity and Narrative Capacity beyond the local level. The emergence of the alternative media world holds important implications for the conceptualization of resistance in the political landscape of the 21st century.

Chapter 6
Alternative Media World

The following chapter provides:

1) A description of the alternative media world concept, as well as the role of RP within that concept.

2) Illustration of the role of the alternative media world concept in contemporary political communication.

The previous four chapters have explained and demonstrated the five categories that give rise to Resistance Performance, and explored the alternative media and Communicative Resistance associated with the four theatre-like quadrants of RP. Overall, the four preceding chapters should help students and researchers of new social movements to better understand the role of alternative media in local level activist networks. The current chapter focuses on the role of RP in the larger global networks beyond local communities, by illustrating the concept of the alternative media world. Past research concerning new social movements and RP have elaborated on the interactive collaboration that produces many alternative media titles, which often makes the audience a part of alternative media production. The blurring of the line between the audience and the producer, as described by Atton (2002a), hints at the construction of an alternative media world, which builds on concept of media ritual developed by Nick Couldry in his books *The Place of Power* (2000) and *Media Rituals* (2003). The following sections explore the concept of the alternative media world and its connection and contrast with Couldry's research.

Alternative Media World Defined

Past research by Couldry concerning the concept of media ritual has addressed distinctions between the "ordinary world" and the "media world." The ordinary world is the social space where "regular" people live and work, engaging in activities that are mundane. In contrast, the media world is the larger-than-life social space of media production that is much more intense, populated by people who are "special." The distinction, as well as the hierarchy of the mundane versus special, is maintained through various audience rituals that create a common-sense distance between the two social spaces. Such concepts have contributed to debates and research concerning mainstream audiences' interactions with mainstream media and performance (e.g., Couldry, 2004; Sandvoss, 2005). Much of the research concerning new social movements described in previous chapters has also begun to address issues of media/ordinary worlds through the exploration of alternative media (e.g., Atton, 2002a; 2004; Downing, 2003a; 2003b; Meikle, 2002). The concept of RP explored throughout this book effectively bridges research concerning social movements and new social movements in the field of Communication, with the research concerning the alternative media utilized by activists within the fields of Journalism and Media Studies. This bridge concept illustrates how activist interactions with alternative media texts and alternative media producers construct multiple perceptions about reality concerning power structures in society and resistance. The use of alternative media, as well as the themes found within alternative media content, stands as theatre-like quadrants where activists perform resistance. Essentially, the concept of RP helps to illustrate a distinction between the ordinary world and an *alternative media world* that is different from the media world alluded to by Couldry, in that the alternative media world is a place where the audience takes part in media production as they create and circulate content (e.g., Atkinson, 2008; Atton, 2002a; Caldwell, 2003), interact with producers of alternative media (e.g., Atkinson & Dougherty, 2006; Atton, 2002a), or pass information through networks via the Internet (e.g., Best, 2005). In other words, the interactivity of the audience with alternative media texts and networks places them *within* the boundaries of the alternative media world.

Media World v. Ordinary World
The concepts of media world and ordinary world emerged from Couldry's critical research concerning media and audiences published in his books *Places of Power* and *Media Rituals*. In both of those publications, Couldry explored how the use of media in the everyday lives of audiences constructs the illusion of an interconnected world that has a center. There are three primary concepts associated with the construction of such an illusion: media ritual, framing, and hierarchy. Couldry illustrated how rituals performed by audiences imbue "the media" with symbolic power, which creates the "myth" that society has a central point. Media rituals are formal, almost ceremonial actions that are performed by audiences in relation to people, events, or places depicted in the media, or associated with media production. Examples of media rituals include the parties or gatherings for special events that are broadcast on television (e.g., the Superbowl), jumping to attention when a celebrity enters the room and asking for their autograph, and turning to media coverage as a primary source of information about major events in society (e.g., coverage of election returns). Such media rituals performed by

audiences help to frame people and places portrayed in the media and associated with media production as separate from the rest of the world. In a sense, rituals create boundaries between the audience and the people and places associated with "the media."

> It is better to think of the ritual process as stretched across multiple sites, indeed across social space as a whole. This wider landscape, which for convenience I call the ritual space of the media, is highly uneven. It is formed around one central inequality (the historic concentration of symbolic power in media institutions) but is shaped locally through many detailed patterns, particularly the categories through which we understand our actions in relation to the media. (Couldry, 2003, p. 13)

Media rituals on the part of audiences, along with the subsequent framing associated with those rituals, help to create a hierarchy between these two spaces, in which one is special and the other is mundane. Such separation and hierarchy stands as the foundation for the concepts of media world and ordinary world. The "specialness" associated with the media world, in turn, stands as a symbolic form of power; once someone or something crosses the boundary and becomes a part of the media world, they/it become special. However, one must first draw the gaze of the media world in order to gain such access. Ultimately, media rituals performed by audience help to establish the distinction between the two spaces—one space special—while also reinforcing the boundaries. In this way, then, society appears to have a center that holds the symbolic power to categorize people and places based on "the differential symbolic resources they possess" (Couldry, 2003, p. 38). The mythic center is inherently interconnected with media production, in that the media are responsible for the differentiation between the special and the ordinary.

One example that serves as an excellent illustration of Couldry's concepts, as well as the illusions that stem from those concepts, is the ritual that he calls "media pilgrimage." The media pilgrimage is a trip taken by a person to visit someplace that has been made special because of its portrayal in media content; this could be a site covered in the news, or a site where a movie was filmed. As a ritual, the media pilgrimage allows the person to momentarily cross the boundary between the two worlds and "play" with the boundaries. Such "play" does not result in the collapse or breaking of those boundaries, but instead reinforces the distinction between ordinary and media. In his research, Couldry (2000) studied the pilgrimages concerning a British soap opera called *Coronation Street*. The set stood as a part of the special media world because it had been portrayed on television. Because of the set's prominent place in society, many fans of the program took "pilgrimages" to see the place firsthand. In his interviews with people who toured the set, he found that such visits allowed audiences the opportunity to compare the mediated vision of *Coronation Street* with the actual set, and to experience the "reality" of the program by touching the set and seeing the stars of the program. The pilgrimage allowed the audience to momentarily "experience" the excitement of the media world from the other side of the boundary, all the while legitimizing the notion that the worlds are separate and that the media world is a "special" place. Experiencing the reality of the set did not destroy the hierarchy of media world v. ordinary world, but rather reinforced such distinction. The act of traveling to the site served as a ritual that reified for the pilgrims, and others whom they spoke to later, that the set was in fact special and important. It should be noted that the pilgrimage only provided a small window of access into the media world for the audiences. Such a glimpse did not allow them to actually become a part of the media world, as they were ordinary people surrounded by the special people and objects that make up the media world.

Alternative Media World
The concept of the alternative media world is similar to Couldry's media world, as both involve the differentiation between the special and the ordinary. However, such hierarchy is the only similarity between the two. The concept of alternative media world differs sharply from Couldry's theories concerning media ritual and the construction of the center of society because of two factors: intercreative production and nebulous narratives in alternative media content. Together, these factors construct a decentralized world that is defined by larger-than-life issues and struggles, and populated by participatory activists who become "special" because of their role in the production and circulation of the alternative media that are integral for the emergence of RP.

First, the intercreative production associated with many alternative media titles plays an important role in the alternative media world. As discussed in Chapter 3, interactivity can take on three forms: user-to-system, user-to-user, and user-to-document (McMillan, 2002). User-to-document interactivity constitutes the Intercreative Capacity of RP, in which audiences have some influence over content of a media text through direct input or feedback to producers. Many alternative media titles rely heavily on intercreativity as a strategy for production. Atton (2002a) describes such reader-writers as a strategy necessary for the production within the "ghetto sphere" of alternative media. Therefore, alternative media producers often rely on suggestions from their audience for ideas about news stories and "minor" content contributions (e.g., *Z Magazine*), or they rely on the audience for all of the content altogether (e.g., Indymedia). In a sense, this strategy also constitutes a ritual on the part of the participatory audience; activists witness something that they deem important, and either make suggestions to producers, or submit their own content. Whether the audience is making suggestions, providing minor contributions, writing full-length news stories, or commenting about news stories, the line between audience and production becomes blurred. Such a blurred line between the audience and producers not only contributes to the concept of diffused audience described by Abercrombie and Longhurst (1998), but also radically differs from the concept of media world described by Couldry (2000; 2003). Rather than the audience engaging in rituals that frame the media as special and themselves as separate and ordinary, rituals like providing feedback or writing content frame the alternative media and the participatory audience as special. In fact, the blurring of the line between audience and producer associated with reader-writer rituals frames the audience within the alternative media world. The framing of the audience as special and a part of the alternative media world is not something that is exclusive to participatory activists. Many lay activists also engage in rituals that blur the lines between audience and producer, framing the alternative media in such a way that they are a part of the process. Although they do not regularly contribute content or commentary, many lay activists utilize tools found on alternative websites like the Amnesty International site and MoveOn.org. Activists are often able to download fliers, pamphlets, stickers, and other materials from such alternative websites that they can, in turn, hand out and circulate at protests or events in their local communities. In this way, lay activists become part of the process of narrative circulation, which again blurs the line between audience and producer. Such blurring is not as distinct as in the case of participatory activists and their production-oriented rituals, but important nonetheless. By downloading materials from alternative media sites and circulating them in some fashion, the lay activists are able to frame themselves as part of the alternative media world as well.

Second, many alternative media titles utilize nebulous narratives in their depictions of social justice issues and resistance by activists, particularly in relation to portrayals of efforts set in international locations. As demonstrated through the analysis of themes in Chapters 4 and 5, many alternative media titles focus on social justice issues and resistance carried out by activists. Often, producers of alternative media focus their content on the actions of activists in international locations, far from many of their audiences; Brendan's and Krishna's posts on Indymedia concerning Mexico and Nepal in Chapter 5 serve as good examples. Much of the content found within alternative media, like the articles posted by Brendan and Krishna, rely on broad concepts and language, such as "principles of unity" (Pickard, 2006a) and "human rights" (Atkinson, 2009a; Atkinson & Dougherty, 2006), in order to describe social justice and resistance. As described in Chapter 2, such broad narratives are important for the construction of a Multiplex of coordinated performance. However, the use of nebulous narratives also holds important implications for social construction of the resistance that is portrayed in those titles by people who are involved in one or more activist networks, particularly resistance in places outside of the United States and western Europe. It is these narratives that are passed around activist networks, at both the local and global levels, that aid in the differentiation between special and ordinary. The use of vague language and ambiguous concepts in alternative media content construct "mythic" representations of larger-than-life social justice issues and resistance to oppression. Such representations in alternative media present a romanticized, adventurous image of resistance that is both appealing to audiences and deceptive in the way in which the subjects' lived experiences of resistance are characterized. The appeal associated with these representations are important as they attract audiences to take part in such exciting endeavors, and, thus, create the possibility for multiple communities to come together and resist dominant power structures. In part, this appeal is similar to the mesomobilization of networked activism described by Best (2005). However, the deceptive nature of the adventurous, mythic representations of resistance is much more important for the concept of the alternative media world. The vague descriptions and ambiguous concepts distort, or even hide from sight, both the oppression associated with power structures experienced by people depicted in alternative media content, as well as their lived resistance against those power structures.

In part, many of the images that give rise to such romanticism comes from the activists who are portrayed in alternative media content. In his book *The Marketing of Rebellion*, Clifford Bob (2005) explains how many insurgent groups and international movements must organize and perform in such ways so as to "match" the agendas of nongovernmental organizations (NGOs) that are sources of financial and humanitarian aid. Examples of NGOs would be Amnesty International, Green Peace, and the Sierra Club. Most NGOs produce alternative media, such as websites, that are integral for RP; the Amnesty International website was covered in detail in Chapter 4. These NGOs and their alternative media constitute the global level networks that have been discussed in previous chapters. For organizations to merely request aid from these global level NGOs is not enough, as there are literally thousands of groups around the world that struggle against government and corporate power structures within their home countries; there are few resources and high demand. Therefore, Bob claims that such groups and movements must organize and perform in such a way that will attract the attention of global level NGOs and bring much needed resources to their cause. Once these insurgent groups and movements have attracted the attention of the NGOs, they become the focus of alternative media content. The performances on the part of the insurgent groups and movements, coupled with the nebulous concepts and ambiguous language utilized by the producers, create a vision of the insurgents and their movements in alternative media content that is quite different from their lived experiences.

The alternative media world, thus, is a place that is special because of the extraordinary and exciting visions of resistance presented to audiences. The performances of international insurgent groups and the nebulous visions of oppression and resistance hide from the sight of audiences many of the real problems associated with dominant power structures in society, which allows for the emergence of overly romanticized images of resistance to such power. Through intercreative processes, these images are circulated and recreated in local level alternative media by participatory activists. In addition, many lay activists aid in the circulation of these romanticized images as they download pamphlets, leaflets, and stickers from the NGO websites. In this way, then, US and Western activists are often closer to the romanticized resistance than the people portrayed in alternative media content; the Western activists are part of the special alternative media world. The lived experiences of oppression and resistance of people in countries like Mexico and Nepal constitute the "ordinary world" that is separate and distinct from the alternative media world. The ordinary world is a place that is neither exciting nor romantic, and can only occasionally be glimpsed via testimonial narratives of the "ordinary" people in places like Mexico and Nepal that experience oppression of their governments, and live in resistance. Testimonial narratives are "told in the first person by a narrator who is also the real protagonist or witness of the events he or she recounts, and whose unit of narration is usually a 'life' or a significant life experience" (Beverly, 1992, p. 92). Such narratives are rich, detailed stories that are told by people who have experienced marginalization, oppression, and resistance; the stories are told in order to break the silence about their plight (Beverly, 1992; 2000; Tierney, 2000). The testimonial narratives of insurgent groups and movements, who are subjects of alternative media content, often stand in stark contrast to their representations in the alternative media world.

Alternative Media World in Political Communication: An Example

The concepts of alternative media world and RP both impact the landscape of political communication in the early 21st century. The performances and rhetoric of insurgent groups and social movements in international locations around the world serve as the content for alternative media produced by global-level NGOs. Local level activists "plug into" the global-level NGO networks, usually through the Internet, and access alternative media featuring such international movements. The content of alternative media produced by those global-level networks simultaneously raise awareness about problems that exist well beyond local communities, while aiding in the construction and maintenance of worldviews concerning power and resistance within such local communities. The nebulous concepts and vague language used to describe the international movements and their resistance allow for the local level activists to utilize those groups in their own arguments about the environment, corporate corruption, and war. Through protest actions and participatory alternative media use, the images and narratives about international movements like the Maoists in Nepal are circulated among audiences who would have likely never heard about them. However, the resistance and oppression that is featured in such protest and local level alternative media are usually nothing like the lived experiences of people within those international movements.

The Zapatista Movement of Chiapas, Mexico, serves as an excellent example of the alternative media world concept and its role of that concept in political communication. Many websites, like the Amnesty International website and Indymedia, feature news stories written by activists and "movement intellectuals" concerning the problems faced by the Zapatista Movement in Chiapas, Mexico, and their resistance to the transnational corporations that drive contemporary globalization. The movement, named after the Mexican revolutionary Emilio Zapata, began as a movement for civil rights and equality for indigenous people living in southern Mexico. Bob (2005) claims that during those early years, the movement failed to gain any attention from NGOs; they had not engaged in any activities or performances that "matched" them to groups like Green Peace or Amnesty International. The movement grabbed international attention on January 1st, 1994, with an uprising that coincided with the enactment of the North American Free Trade Agreement (NAFTA) between the United States, Mexico, and Canada. The sudden uprising captured small towns across the Chiapas countryside, such as San Cristobal de las Casas. The violence of the initial uprising was short lived, as the Zapatistas retreated back into highlands of the Lacandon Jungle, where they declared their communities autonomous from the Mexican government (e.g., Bob, 2005; Klein, 2002; Marcos, 2001). Afterwards, the movement took a peaceful turn as the Zapatistas sought to build bridges with the international community in order to educate people outside of Mexico about the problems faced by the indigenous people. Through the communiqués of the mysterious Subcomandante Insurgente Marcos that were circulated across the Internet and reprinted in a variety of alternative media titles, the Zapatistas explained to the world their rationale for resistance: economic and racial oppression imposed on the indigenous people by NAFTA, multinational corporations, and the Mexican government. What is just as important to understanding the Zapatistas—if not more important—is their colorful rhetoric and performance following the uprising. Taking the name of Emilio Zapata, the Zapatistas don black ski masks and speak (often through Marcos) in vagaries and poetics about multiple dreaming worlds and Mayan gods. They wear the masks because, as Marcos claims, no one can see the indigenous people until they hide their faces—and when their faces are hidden they present a mirror in which all people can see themselves. They speak in vague language about dreaming worlds held up high by Mayan gods of earth and wind because this one world contains countless voices and experiences co-existing and colliding together (e.g., Bob, 2005; Carrigan, 2001; Klein, 2002; Marcos, 2001). Essentially, such performances stand as an image event that challenges the ideographs of globalization and free trade. Such colorful rhetoric and performances serve as the primary portrayal of the Zapatistas in alternative media titles produced by global level NGOs (e.g., Amnesty International) and global level alternative media networks (e.g., Indymedia).

In an article published in *New Media and Society*, Adrienne Russell (2005) examined the depictions of the Zapatista Movement on websites used by activists around the world. In his analysis, he revealed the various "myths" of the Zapatistas that emerged from the images and descriptions of the movement that were posted by participatory activists who were on the ground in the midst of the Zapatistas, who had been to Chiapas and returned to their homes in the United States or Europe, or who had become interested in the movement and were passing information along. These myths included (1) the masked "universal" Marcos who could simultaneously be anyone and everyone, (2) the autonomous communities inhabited by exotic "noble warriors" who engage in a romantic struggle against tyranny, and (3) the faceless, colonial-like "neoliberal beast" that exploits and dehumanizes people in order to generate profits. These broad themes that emerged from images and ambiguous language used on websites and other alternative media are similar to the broad narratives of "be the media" and "principles of unity" (Pickard, 2006a; 2006b) and "human rights" and "democracy" (Atkinson, 2009a; Atkinson & Dougherty, 2006) that allow for the rise of networked activism (Best, 2005) and the Multiplex of RP. Such narratives constitute a kind of *mythic resistance*, which entails heroic actions by romanticized activists against simplistic "cartoon-like" villains who threaten broad concepts like democracy (Atkinson, 2009b). Mythic resistance proves important for drawing attention to international movements that seek support from NGOs and for the construction of the Multiplex described in Chapter 2. The use of the different myths of the Zapatistas described by Russell (2005) frames the alternative media producers and the subjects of their content as adventurous and romantic; alternative media and processes of production become a special place. In a tactical sense, the images of mythic resistance associated with the Zapatistas often make for more exciting alternative media content, thus drawing larger audiences. Such a tactic can help to overcome many of the limitations associated with the ghetto sphere of alternative media production described by Atton (2002a) and increase circulation and readership because of the appeal to "enthusiast infatuation." The concept of enthusiast infatuation was posited by Dwight Conquergood (1985) as an explanation of potential risks of qualitative and ethnographic research. Essentially, ethnographic researchers must keep their interest and enthusiasm concerning their research in check; as such enthusiasm will influence their perceptions and skew their observations. In the case of alternative media content, the nebulous concepts and vague language associated with mythic resistance taps into general interests of the audience, while the images of mythic resistance (e.g., the ski masks worn by Zapatistas) can create enthusiasm concerning the subject.

As an example, a story called "MEXICO: The Zapatistas Started the 'Other Campaign'!" by an activist called Zapatista Esperanza was circulated to different Indymedia cites (Indymedia UK, Indymedia Ireland, Indymedia Portland) in January of 2006. The story focuses on a political campaign that served as a substitute for the Mexican political elections of 2006; Marcos served as Delegate Zero in the alternate campaign. During an event coordinated by members of the Other Campaign, Marcos and many other Zapatistas spoke to crowds in San Cristobal de las Casas.

> At about 1 pm Zapatistas and supporters from all over the world met in San Cristobal. At 5 pm more than 20,000 Zapatistas with masks over their faces stood there without talking. It was a very strange moment. Then "Delegado Zero" arrived: People began to cheer and moved into the city centre, shouting slogans like "Zapata vive. La lucha sigue" "Zapata lives. The struggle goes on." A few hours later the City centre was full with Zapatistas. From a stage, 5 people, 3 men, and 2 women talked to them. The speeches were held against capitalism, "the culture of death", and aimed towards equality of men and women and towards an anarchist society. The last who spoke was "Delegado Zero", Subcomandante Marcos, who stressed that the "Other Campaign" is not political mainstream, is not on the side of the institutionalized left, but is anticapitalist, anarchist and free. He shouted: "Viva la otra campaña!" At the moment the whole city of San Cristobal is full with Zapatistas wearing masks, talking, eating, sleeping. A truly surreal scenery.

The story manages to draw attention in two ways. First, the author makes note of the Zapatista masks, which are a signature part of their performance and rhetoric. As discussed previously, Marcos has claimed that the indigenous people of Chiapas are invisible until they wear such masks; the masks make the Zapatistas visible (Bob, 2005; Carrigan, 2001; Klein, 2002; Marcos, 2001). Essentially, the masks make the "ordinary" unusual and interesting for the audience. In addition to the descriptions of the masked Marcos and masked Zapatistas within the text, Zapatista Esperanza also provides links to photographs of the event posted on the Indymedia Chiapas site by activist/photographer Tim Russo; the photographs feature the masked Marcos/Delegate Zero, as well as other masked Zapatista people.

Figure 1. Photograph of the "Other Campaign," taken by Tim Russo and posted on Indymedia Chiapas.

Second, Zapatista Esperanza focuses on broad concepts that emerged within the speeches at the Other Campaign event and also utilizes ambiguous terms and language to describe the event. Within the story, she draws attention to Marcos' emphasis of the Other Campaign as "anticapitalist" and "free," and the crowds' outburst of "the struggle lives on." She goes on in the article to sum up the different speeches, claiming that they were "against capitalism" and "aimed toward equality" in a setting that was "truly surreal." Anticapitalist is a broad concept that can have wide appeal, from radical anarchists to progressives who have been disenchanted with trade policies that have developed under corporate-oriented globalization. Concepts like "free," "struggle," and "equality" are similarly broad, in that radical and reformist activists (in both the right-wing and left-wing) all value freedom and admire people who struggle.

However, such a vision of resistance stands in stark contrast to testimonial narratives that have emerged in past research concerning the Zapatistas. Oral histories of indigenous people who live in the autonomous communities and are allied with the Zapatistas have revealed categories of resistance that are based on personal examples of oppression and resistance and match established theories concerning resistance. In an article published in *Communication, Culture and Critique*, Atkinson (2009b) described three testimonial narratives presented to a group of American and European activists visiting different autonomous communities in Chiapas.[1] In each case, the testimonial narratives were presented to those activists by the general assembly that acted as community leaders. In the first testimonial narrative, community leaders explained to the activists how they had attempted to start a transportation cooperative that would allow people to move efficiently between the community, the nearby fields, and the markets. The cooperative proved to be controversial, as an affluent bus company petitioned the Mexican government to have the cooperative shut down in order to eliminate competition. After the cooperative was closed, members of the community detained buses and drivers of the affluent company as a form of protest; they planned to hold the drivers until the company and the Mexican government eased off of their restrictions on the cooperative. As retaliation against the community, the police and army carried out an "action" that resembled an invasion; the community leaders claimed that a thousand troops and hundreds of trucks entered the small town. Several houses in the community were burned to the ground, and many members of the community were herded into a barn and tortured. During the testimonial narrative, many of the community leaders showed scars that they had received during the action (e.g., bullet wounds). The descriptions of poverty in the community, the petition by the bus company, and the detainment of drivers as protest all demonstrated the concept of militant resistance described by Kowal (2000); such resistance met with militaristic backlash that hurt the community even worse. In the second narrative presented to the activists, the leaders of a separate community explained how they had been engaged in legal conflicts with the Mexican government over the rights to the surrounding lands. The government claimed that the people of the community should have access to the lands only if they renounce their status as indigenous, or native, people; the community leaders found such demands to be demeaning and indignant. In response, the community sought aid from an oppositional political party in order to play what they called "the political game." The leaders explained how they promoted the oppositional party within their community, asking that people vote for those politicians. In return, the opposition leaders had promised that they would reward such aid by making the community's land claims a political and legal issue in upcoming state elections. Unfortunately, no such support from the oppositional party materialized. Their personal accounts about plans to work with the oppositional party corresponded with Kowal's concept of adjustive resistance; such resistance met with little or no success. In the final testimonial narrative presented to the activists, community leaders explained to the activists the serious problems that they faced. Over the years, the community had been flooded with refugees that were forced from their homes by paramilitary forces carrying out orders of the Mexican government. The community leaders presented a horrific and tragic narrative that illustrated oppressive forces laying siege to their community. Interestingly, resistance was not a component of the narrative, but rather the presentation of the narrative itself constituted a form of resistance. According to Bettina Aptheker (1989) and Robin Clair (1998), resistance is often conceptualized as a "masculine" power struggle. Mechanisms of coping and survival, such as retelling stories and interacting with strangers from outside, may also constitute resistance as community members can engage in those activities in order to create a sense of hope or dignity while "under siege" (Aptheker, 1989). In communities like the Nazi occupied Jewish ghettos, telling stories and maintaining traditions "was the bedrock that gave meaning to life and served as the underpinning that made all else possible" (p. 190). By directing attention to oppressive practices, describing to a group of outsiders the lived experiences under such oppression and working to build relationships with outsiders (e.g., the activists), community leaders engaged in a category of resistance based on coping and survival. Ultimately, three testimonial narratives presented by the leaders of the different communities provided a glimpse into the "ordinary world" of the indigenous people of Chiapas and the Zapatista Movement.

The distinction between the alternative media world associated with mythic resistance and the ordinary world of the Zapatista Movement is maintained by many of the rituals performed by activists. Intercreative alternative media use by participatory activists, such as production of content about the Zapatistas and commentary posted on websites that focus on their movement, constitute rituals that aid in such distinction. Other audience rituals, like the alternative media pilgrimage, help to reconstruct and reinforce the boundaries between the alternative media world and the ordinary world. In the case of the activists travelling through Chiapas, those activists were engaging in a "pilgrimage" to explore the resistance associated with the Zapatista Movement that had been featured in a variety of alternative media titles. During their pilgrimage, the activists visited Zapatista communities, where they heard the testimonial narratives described previously. As the pilgrimage to the Zapatista communities came to an end, the activists were conflicted about what they had discovered. On the one hand, they were all familiar with the images of mythic resistance presented in numerous alternative media titles like Indymedia and *Z Magazine*. Conversely, they had glimpsed into the ordinary world of the Zapatista communities through the testimonial narratives that they had heard during the pilgrimage. The activists were at a loss as to how to discuss or describe the Zapatistas after crossing the boundary between the two worlds. As they struggled with this dilemma, however, they began to tell personal narratives about their own experiences with resistance and social justice "back home," which often dealt with broad topics like "ethical consumerism" (e.g., buying fair trade products). Weaving such stories helped the activists to relate the testimonial narratives to forms of resistance with which they were all more familiar, resistance associated with alternative media content and the new social movements with which they were affiliated. In this way, the Zapatistas, their communities, and their resistance came to be seen by the activists in terms of the products that were present in their communities and the ethical way that they made their own products; the activists often commended the Zapatistas for their hard work and efforts. By weaving stories, then, the activists built a blindfold-like conceptualization of the pilgrimage that hid from sight the specific instances of militant resistance, adjustive resistance, and coping/survival demonstrated in the testimonial narratives; only broad and nebulous mythic resistance remained. As one of the activists proclaimed at the end of the pilgrimage: "We need more democracy. We need more justice. We need all of these things the Zapatistas are for" (Atkinson, 2009b, p. 154). Therefore, rather than breaking down the boundary between the alternative media world and the ordinary world, the alternative media pilgrimage had in fact reinforced the distinction between the two. Mythic resistance remained romanticized in the eyes of the activists, while the resistance and oppression in the ordinary world remained largely invisible.

The alternative media world plays an important role in political communication of the early 21st century. Activists in places like Chiapas and Nepal work to construct performances and rhetoric that will "match" with global level networks like Amnesty International and Indymedia. Such performances and rhetoric often attract attention through the use of broad, nebulous concepts (e.g., equality and freedom), while utilizing symbols and trappings that attract the gaze of the audience. In this way, the activists and their cause can serve those global level networks that seek to challenge and transform ideographs in society (e.g., free trade) or to construct more militant resistance against dominant power structures. Once such activists have effectively matched with a global network, their performances and rhetoric become the subject of alternative media produced by the network and circulated to broad audiences around the world. It is such alternative media that activists in local level communities, like Erie City and Mystical City, "plug into" and use in the production of local alternative media and the establishment of RP.

Conclusion

The current chapter has introduced the concept of alternative media world, and explained how it functions within contemporary political communication. In relation to the concept of RP, the chapter has provided information to help the reader to conceptualize the role of Intercreative Capacity and Narrative Capacity between local level and global level networks. Essentially, the Narrative Capacity of a local level network is not only important for the construction of the Multiplex of coordinated performance, but also for the circulation of narratives from global level networks within local communities. For instance, activists within local level networks that have efficient narrative capacity are more likely to have heard of the Zapatistas and their conflict in Chiapas than activists within networks with inefficient Narrative Capacity. The accumulation of narratives like those about the Zapatistas help to shape the worldviews and theatre-like communities found within local communities and also draws activists' attention to resistance and social justice in international locations like Chiapas and Nepal. In addition, Intercreative Capacity, as a ritual performed by participatory audiences of alternative media, places local level activists (both participatory and lay) within the special alternative media world that is distinct from the ordinary world of marginalized groups that are the subject of alternative media content.

Overall, the preceding chapters of the book provide a framework that allows students and scholars of new social movements and political communication to understand alternative media. In this way, these chapters serve as a roadmap for any scholarly pursuits that aim to understand and explore the role of alternative media within the structures of contemporary new social movement networks and the political resistance that is carried out by networked activists. The following chapter summarizes the main points of the book and explains how the concept of RP fits within the competing areas of rhetoric and social science, as well as the different fields of Communication, Media Studies, and Journalism.

Conclusion

The following chapter explains:

1) Implications of RP for research in the field of Communication concerning social movements and new social movements.

2) Implications of RP for research concerning alternative media within the fields of Communication, Journalism, and Media Studies.

The first chapter of this book provided the reader with a brief history of the research concerning social movements and alternative media within the fields of Communication, Journalism, and Media Studies. In reference to social movements, the review of literature examined the debate between social scientists and rhetoricians and demonstrated how scholars turned to concepts like "new social movements" and the network metaphor to address the changing face of social movements. In reference to alternative media, the review of literature demonstrated the way in which scholars in the fields of Journalism and Media Studies focused their efforts on defining alternative media, as well as exploring the processes of alternative media production. Overall, Chapter 1 demonstrated rich, rigorous lines of research that have helped scholars and students to better understand both topics.

However, past research conducted within the fields of Communication, Journalism, and Media Studies have not effectively combined both lines of research, or demonstrated the role of alternative media within the political resistance carried out by activists that struggle against dominant power structures in contemporary society. Chapters 2 through 6 have worked to accomplish this task by introducing and illustrating the concept of Resistance Performance, a concept that is situated within the larger Audience Performance Paradigm. The concept of RP illustrates a symbiotic relationship between the local and global levels of networked activism; the processes of alternative media production and the content that is produced effectively connect both levels. Essentially, activists at the global level produce alternative media content, much of which focuses on international insurgents and movements that have formulated rhetorical and performance tactics to draw attention of resource laden NGOs and groups. The alternative media content is then used by activists in local level communities to construct the four theatre-like quadrants in which they perform resistance.

148 Conclusion

The participatory activists in those local-level communities engage in two rituals: local level production and global level feedback. The local level production notifies all of the activists within the network about protests and other events in which they can perform resistance and engage in social interactions together; such local level alternative media is integral for the emergence of the Multiplex of coordinated resistance. Meanwhile, the global level feedback aids producers associated with global networks in their search for topics and refinement of arguments. In this way, then, the two levels cannot exist without one another. In addition to the symbiotic relationship, RP holds important implications for research concerning social movements and alternative media. In the following pages, I will briefly explain how the concept of RP advances theories and frameworks that have emerged in past research.

Social Movement Research

Overall, the concept of RP holds important implications for theories and frameworks associated with social movements that have developed from research of rhetoricians and social scientists. In addition, the concept proves integral for the study of new social movements and new social movement networks. To begin, Chapter 1 illustrated the origins of social movement research that stemmed from the efforts of rhetoricians like Griffin (1952) and developed into long running debates between those scholars and social scientists. In large part, social scientists like Smelser (1962) and Gurr (1970) made the contention that social movements were the product of collective behavior that developed in stages or phases. Conversely, rhetoricians like Bowers and Ochs (1971) and Windt (1972) studied the strategies of agitation used by activists, while others like McGee (1975; 1980a; 1980b) focused on the transformation of meaning and ideographs because of the rhetoric of social movements. The concept of RP works within the framework of both and can be useful to scholars and students within both camps. First, the cyclical nature of RP within the context of local level networks can prove to be quite useful for scholars and students of the social sciences. In particular, the ongoing cycle of circulating narratives through alternative media, constructing the Multiplex of coordinated performance between the multiple theatre-like quadrants, and the dissolution of that Multiplex fits much of the past research that has developed from the social science quarter. The role of alternative media in this cycle—particularly locally produced alternative media—can provide such social scientists with new insight into the emergence of collective behavior within 21st century social movements. Second, the notion of theatres constructed from the use of alternative media content can advance research of rhetoricians. The theatre-like quadrants stand as text-centered sites where specific actions are required and appropriate. These actions are the strategies of agitation and rhetoric that generates meanings that can challenge and transform ideographs, which has emerged from past research by rhetoricians. The alternative media, then, are integral for the development of activist agitation and rhetoric.

In addition, Chapter 1 addressed how several Communication scholars and rhetoricians turned to the concept of new social movements in order to explore the issue of identity politics in the programmed society described by Touraine (1978). From the theoretical perspective first developed by Touraine, social movements were not so much about creating political or legal change, as much as efforts to shape political identity. Communication scholars and rhetoricians like DeLuca (1999), Calafell (2007), and Pezzullo (2003) worked within the framework of the new social movement in order to explore the image events and performances of activists who sought to challenge ideographs and stereotypes in society. DeLuca's concept of image event built on past research of McGee and others concerning the role of rhetoric in the transformation of ideographs in society; the image event was an action that drew the gaze of the media and could, thus, be circulated in society and challenge traditional ideographs like "progress" and "industrialism." Conversely, Calafell examined the ways in which the performances of activists like El Vez simultaneously accepted and rejected stereotypes of Latinos in order to build cross-cultural bridges that could challenge negative perceptions about Latinos. The concept of RP is valuable for these two lines of research, in that both stand as tactics of Communicative Resistance performed by activists within the context of their respective theatre-like quadrant. In addition, the image events and performances are often photographed by activists and subsequently used within alternative media content produced at the local and global levels. As alternative media content, then, such image events and performances become part of the thematic backdrop within the four quadrants. Also, the concept of alternative media world holds important implications for Pezzullo's research, which focused on activist tours of Cancer Alley. In her research, Pezzullo examined the stories told by activists, tour guides, and community members during the bus tour through communities in Louisiana devastated by corporate pollution; these stories were cultural performances that constructed a shared memory that connected the activists and the marginalized communities. The concept of alternative media world helps to illustrate how activists came to be a part of the tour (e.g., alternative media content produced by global networks like Sierra Club), as well as the potential blindfolds and pitfalls that activists face during such journeys (e.g., the stories that they tell to relate to their experiences on the tour). Overall, such tours stand as alternative media pilgrimages across the boundary between the ordinary world of marginalized communities and the alternative media world associated with local and global activist networks.

Finally, the review of literature in Chapter 1 explained the rise of the network metaphor in the study of new social movements. In particular, many

150 Conclusion

Communication scholars turned to concepts developed by Castells (1996; 2004; 2006) and Huesca (2001), such as network society. Through their research, scholars like Arquilla and Ronfeldt (2001), Best (2005), Pickard (2006a; 2006b), and Stengrim (2005) demonstrated that new social movements function as networks that contain a multitude of nodes around the world; Indymedia and Amnesty International are examples of such networks. The research conducted by these scholars had, in fact, demonstrated the concept of global level networks described in this book. The framework of RP illustrates the role of alternative media and the construction of resistance within local level networks, and thus builds on past research concerning new social movement networks. The framework of RP not only demonstrates existence of the local level networks, but also illustrates the symbiotic relationship between both levels, as discussed previously. In fact, the symbiotic relationship between the two levels associated with RP can be conceptualized as a *universal network*, in which the two levels support one another.

Alternative Media Research

The concept of RP also holds important implications for past research concerning alternative media. The literature review in Chapter 1 explained how most research conducted by scholars in the fields of Journalism and Media Studies had focused on defining alternative media and illustrating processes of alternative media production. In reference to the former, the concepts and frameworks in this book should help to build a stronger definition of alternative media that can be used by scholars and students in the fields of Journalism and Media Studies, as well as the field of Communication. In past research, alternative media has been defined *primarily* in terms of content (e.g., Armstrong, 1981; Downing, 1984; Downing et al., 2001), organization of media production (e.g., Atton, 2002a; 2004; Meikle, 2002), or interpretive strategies (e.g., Rauch, 2007). In some instances, past scholars have utilized these different definitions, but within different research projects. For instance, in both versions of *Radical Media* (1984; 2001) Downing and Downing et al. worked from the content definition of alternative media, and then later from the production definition in the edited volume *Contesting Media Power* (Downing, 2003a); in the first Downing classified different forms of content, while in the second he examined the role of anarchism in alternative media production. The point here is that past research has usually been anchored to only one definition. Within the context of RP, alternative media has been defined using all three of the concepts associated with past research: content produced by noncommercial sources that focuses on social change or transformation of social roles, and is interpreted by the audience as "alternative." Such a definition is not absolute, as only a few of the alternative media titles described in this book adhere precisely to all three. Indymedia.org and anarchist zines fit all three points, while others like *The Nation* and MoveOn.org do not. *The Nation* entails content that clearly advocates for social change and the transformation of various roles in society, and is understood by most activists to be "alternative" as it "goes against the mainstream media." However, the production of the magazine tends to be "traditional" in that there is a hierarchy (e.g., editor, editorial staff, writers) and limited advertising to fund the magazine. Conversely, MoveOn.org is a noncommercial source that is organized in such a way to overcome many of the limitations associated with the "ghetto sphere" that emerges from the subsequent lack of sources. However, the content produced through MoveOn does not advocate for much in the way of change to the political system; they simply advocate for one political party, the Democrats, over another. Nevertheless, many activists understand MoveOn to be "alternative" because it challenges particular powerful elites in society. Ultimately, this flexible three-point definition is important for research concerning alternative media because it provides a broad framework that brings together the largest possible mosaic of content and production that takes place within the context of new social movement networks.

The concept of RP is also important for research concerning processes of production. In particular, both concepts help to build on past research concerning the tactics of production that take place within the so-called ghetto sphere, as well as the intercreative processes of production and blurred lines between audience and producers. First, past research by Atton (2002a; 2004), Curran (2003), Downing (2003a), and Meikle (2002) has addressed many of the tactics utilized by alternative media producers to overcome limitations imposed by their stance against commercial interests in media, such as anti-copyright policies, reader-writers, and reliance on content written by "movement intellectuals." The concept of RP adds an additional tactic to the list provided by past researchers: the use of nebulous narratives and vague language to describe problems associated with dominant power structures and those who challenge such power. Often, the subjects of portrayal within alternative media content add to such ambiguity and abstraction through their own rhetoric and performances as they seek to "match" with outside agencies to gain resources. However, as noted in the example of the content produced by Zapatista Esperanza and circulated on Indymedia, many alternative media producers use vague language and broad concepts in order to describe such rhetoric and performances. Alternative media producers often use concepts like "democracy" and "freedom," as well as narratives about "struggle" and "equality." As a tactic, the use of nebulous narratives and ambiguous language is important, as it allows for the content to appeal to broader audiences. Radical and reformist audiences, as well as those who would be considered mainstream, all value "democracy" and "freedom." All of those audiences admire people who "struggle" and seek "equality." In this way, then, many alternative media producers are able to attract audiences who might not otherwise agree with their point of view on many specific issues and policies and therefore increase circulation of their narratives. Also, the intertwined concepts of RP and alternative media world build on past research concerning reader-writers and the blurring of the line between audiences and producers by providing insight into the interactions between the local and global levels. It was noted in Chapter 3 that alternative media production is typically accomplished through user-to-document interactivity. Such interactivity includes direct production of content on the part of audiences, as well as feedback to producers through personal interactions. Therefore, the reader-writer concept developed by Atton (2002a) is expanded through the framework of RP to include activists who engage in some form of interactions with global and local producers. At the local level, participatory activists who produce newsletters and listservs in their communities often receive feedback from their audiences that involves encouragement and little else. Many of those local level producers, in turn, provide feedback and input to producers affiliated with global level networks like Amnesty International and MoveOn. The reader-writers, then, are audiences who write and submit their own content to alternative media titles, as well as audiences who interact and provide feedback to the producers of such titles. Those activists who write content and interact with producers cross the line between the ordinary world and into the larger-than-life alternative media world defined by romanticized images of resistance and narrative concepts like "freedom" and "equality."

Looking to the Future

The concepts, definitions, and examples provided in this book can prove valuable to scholars and students who study alternative media, social movements, and politics of resistance in contemporary society. The concept of RP, its characteristics, and the intertwined concept of alternative media world can all be used to understand alternative media content, alternative media use, grassroots organizations within local communities, protests, and dissent. However, RP and all of its related components and characteristics should not be viewed as the end of the line concerning such research; instead, they represent one step in a larger line of questions and study. There are a number of issues that scholars and students of social movements and alternative media need to address in order to build on RP. First, almost all of the past research on social movements and alternative media that preceded this book, as well as the research that developed RP, focused on left-leaning and progressive movements and media. There has been little research to date that had examined and explored the use of alternative media by radical right-wing groups, or even analysis of the content of radical right-wing media like the racist website Stormfront.org. It is unclear at this point whether the concept of RP adequately addresses political resistance within the context of those groups and their media. In addition, social networking sites like Facebook and MySpace only play a small role within the framework of RP; Chapter 4 briefly alluded to the role of ZSpace profiles on ZNet in the production of content for *Z Magazine*. Beyond such a use, it is unclear what role social networking sites play in the construction of the theatre-like quadrants and Communicative Resistance. Also, the foundational research and data collection in past research concerning social movements, alternative media, and RP have been conducted within the United States, and in some instances Western Europe. There has been little research in the fields of Communication, Journalism, and Media Studies concerning these topics within eastern nations like Japan and South Korea, or in repressive states like Iran. Research by Bob (2005) has indicated how groups within "developing countries" or countries dominated by repressive regimes work to "match" international NGOs in order to gain resources. Material presented in Chapter 6 illustrates how such matching plays a role in the alternative media world and RP. However, it is still unclear whether the framework of RP accurately illustrates social movements, alternative media, and the formation of resistance in such "developing countries."

Finally, one issue that could be problematic for understanding social movements and their relationship to alternative media is one of the principal concepts examined within this book: resistance. The framework of RP and the related concept of alternative media world are based almost entirely on the idea of resistance: resistance portrayed in alternative media and resistance performed by activists who use alternative media. This is nothing new, as much of the past literature concerning social movements and alternative media in the fields of Communication, Journalism, and Media Studies has focused on agitation, rhetoric, and alternative media content used to challenge powerful groups. Therefore, it seems that social movements and new social movements are resistance to power structures, while alternative media is a means of such resistance. Does this mean that all social movements, new social movements, and alternative media should be defined in terms of their resistance? Increasingly, it is becoming evident that some grassroots groups place resistance to power structures second, while their lifestyles and lived experiences takes center stage. One such example would be the DetroitYES! community in the city of Detroit, Michigan. The organization was formed around an online art project called the Fabulous Ruins of Detroit, which features various photographs of abandoned and dilapidated buildings within the city. These photographs are all framed within a contextualizing narrative about Rome and Athens presented by the site's producer at the beginning of the tour. In this way, Detroit is not an economically burned out city in decline that needs to be rebuilt or deserted, but an archaeological site worthy of inspection and exploration. The DetroitYES! community that has sprung up around this virtual tour organizes activities and events online that promote local artists and the historical legacy of the city; they advance a vision of Detroit that is alternative to visions presented in popular media. These networked activists are not so much interested in resisting the large media organizations that portray Detroit as dangerous and burned out, but rather, they are concerned with constructing an alternative conceptualization of their city and living their lives within the context of that alternative city. In this way, the activists, their use of websites like the Fabulous Ruins of Detroit, and their actions all hint at something different from Resistance Performance, just like the use of alternative media by activists hinted at something different from Abercrombie and Longhurst's (1998) Spectacle Performance. The case of the DetroitYES! activists hints at something like Standpoint Performance, in which audiences use media to communicate with others and build an informed understanding about their cultural location. Clearly, these activists understand their differences with people in different cultural locations, even those people who hold power over them. However, resistance against those other people is not first and foremost, as in the case of many of the organizations and much of the alternative media described in this book. Organizations like MoveOn and Peace Action operate from the understanding that there are dominant power structures in society and that those structures create problems. In order to remedy those problems, such organizations work to identify power structure, explain the problems associated with their power, and motivate people to engage in resistance. Such perspectives are evident in those groups' actions, as well as the alternative media that they produce and circulate. Exploration of Standpoint Performance associated with groups like the DetroitYES! community is essential to gain a stronger understanding of alternative media and social movements in contemporary society.

Notes

Chapter 1

1. Smelser (1962) and Gurr (1970) are used here as examples of sociologists and other scholars who operated from a purely social scientific position. Their work, as well as the work of a multitude of other researchers, preceded Ralph Turner and Lewis Killian's (1972) book *Collective Behavior*, which became the standard for social scientific research concerning social movements. Later research by Smelser, in fact, built on Turner and Killian's seminal work.

2. *The Rhetoric of Agitation and Control* has expanded since its initial release in 1971. Since that time a second edition by Bowers, Ochs, and Jensen was published in 1992, followed by a third edition by Bowers, Ochs, Jensen, and Schultz in 2009.

3. McGee's theories were a response to Herbert Simons' (1970; 1972) arguments concerning leaders, resources, and persuasion in social movements. According to Simons, leaders within social movements must find ways to manage scarce resources in an effort to address important social issues so as to draw new members into the movement. McGee, and later DeLuca (1999), argued that such a position was based on material resources and thus grounded in social science. Simons' position, they argued, ignores rhetoric and therefore ignores meaning.

4. Indymedia.org and the Indymedia network are covered in greater detail in Chapter 5.

Chapter 2

1. Depictions and conceptualizations concerning power in alternative media emerged from Atkinson's (2005a) qualitative content analysis of 80 alternative media titles published in *Qualitative Research Reports in Communication*. The following

discussion concerning traditional and hegemonic power is based on that article.

2. "Nation Cover: Block Bush," by John Carr, from the September 13, 2002, issue of *The Nation*. Reprinted with permission from the September 13, 2002, issue of *The Nation* magazine.

3. The first three categories emerged from interviews with activists in the Midwestern community of Mystical City conducted by Atkinson and Dougherty (2006) and published in *Western Journal of Communication*. The fourth category emerged from interviews with activists in Mystical City and global level producers conducted by Atkinson (2008) and published in *Mass Communication and Society*. The fifth category emerged from interviews conducted by Atkinson (2009a) with activists in the northeastern community of Erie City and was published in *Communication Studies*. The following discussion concerning the first three categories of RP is based on the 2006 article in *Western Journal of Communication*.

4. Atkinson and Dougherty's (2006) initial RP research in Mystical City featured qualitative content analysis (see Altheide, 1996; Krippendorff, 2004; Mayring, 2000) of alternative media used by activists. The analysis focused on over 80 articles and news stories from a variety of alternative magazines (*The Nation, The Progressive, Z Magazine*), radio programs (*Democracy Now!*), websites (Commondreams.org, Indymedia.org, InfoShop.org) and several emails from a local listserv (Peace Alliance listserv). The findings from that content analysis corresponded with additional analysis conducted in regards to the activists and network in Erie City. The following discussion concerning common visions and goals in alternative media content is based on the 2006 article in *Western Journal of Communication*.

5. The emergence of two levels of new social movements corresponds with the multilevel position developed by Pan and McLeod (1991). The epistemological view developed by Pan and McLeod references media communication at two levels (production and audience) connected by content and feedback; four aspects in all. First, the organizational scope of media operations produces the media content. Corporate strategies and economic pressures affect the form of content (e.g., McChesney, 1998; Turrow, 1992), organizational goals and structures impact program themes (e.g., Gitlin, 1983; Tuchman, 1978), or

individual producers with a track record of success are key in the construction of media content (e.g., Newcombe & Alley, 1983; Pekurny, 1982). Next, the content circulated by producers constitutes the second aspect of the multilevel concept. The third part of the multilevel concept is the audience level. The audience expresses particular behaviors (e.g., Cantor, 1994) or socially constructs reality and identity by using the media content (e.g., Berger & Luckman, 1966; Denzin, 1997; Gamson & Modigliani, 1989). The final aspect includes the feedback, or audience interactions with the level of media production. Multilevel analysis, whether used to create a new theory or modify an old one, is accomplished by connecting producers with audiences through these four aspects using specific concepts designated by the data.

Chapter 3

1. The fourth category, Intercreative Capacity, emerged from interviews with local level activists in Mystical City and eight global level producers conducted by Atkinson (2008) and published in *Mass Communication and Society*. The eight global producers were identified in past interviews with activists that focused on the reading of resistance (see Atkinson, 2007). The following discussion concerning Interactive Capacity is based on the 2008 article in *Mass Communication and Society*.

2. *Global Producer #1* wrote for magazines such as *The Nation*, *Z Magazine*, the Internet site Commondreams.org, and engaged in discussions on *Democracy Now!* radio. *Global Producer #2* wrote for Internet sources such as Alternet, Commondreams.org, Counterpunch, and ZNet. *Global Producer #3* published articles in *New Left Review* and the *UK Guardian* and wrote articles for websites such as Commondreams.org and Dissidentvoice.org. *Global Producer #4* wrote articles for magazines such as *Mother Jones* and *The Nation* and for websites such as Opendemocracy.net, Salon.com, and TomPaine.com. *Global Producer #5* had written two books that were widely recognized by the social justice activists in Center City. *Global Producer #6* was the web administrator of the Citizen Engagement website, a nonprofit organization dedicated to facilitating democracy by bolstering the public's capacities for self-governance. He had written articles for websites such as Alternet, Commondreams.org, and TomPaine.com. *Global Producer #7* was the web administrator of the Worldwide Outreach website, a

nonprofit organization that provided information to activists concerned about the environment and social justice. He had written articles for Commondreams.org. *Global Producer #8* was an artist and activist organizer. She had also written articles that were featured on the Worldwide Outreach website and had submitted several articles to Indymedia.org.

3. The fifth category, Narrative Capacity, emerged from interviews conducted by Atkinson (2009a) in the northeastern community of Erie City, and published in *Communication Studies*. The following discussion concerning Narrative Capacity is based on that article.

Chapter 4

1. During interviews with activists in Mystical City (Atkinson, 2007; Atkinson & Dougherty, 2006) and Erie City (Atkinson, 2009a), activists were typically asked questions concerning which alternative media titles that they used to aid them in their efforts for social justice and resistance. In the case of the Atkinson and Dougherty (2006) study, lists of different alternative media were compiled and examined using qualitative content analysis (i.e., Altheide, 1996; Krippendorff, 2004; Mayring, 2000).

Chapter 5

1. The themes of alternative media used by radical activists emerged from the same research that gave rise to the themes described in the previous chapter. Specifically, alternative media titles were identified in Mystical City (Atkinson, 2007; Atkinson & Dougherty, 2006) and Erie City (Atkinson, 2009a). In the Atkinson & Dougherty (2006) study, lists of the different alternative media were compiled and examined using qualitative content analysis (i.e., Altheide, 1996; Krippendorff, 2004; Mayring, 2000).

2. The research concerning zines was conducted by Atkinson (2006) and published in *Journal of Communication Inquiry*. In that research, Atkinson attended the 2002 North American Anarchist Gathering in Lawrence, Kansas. There he collected a number of anarchist zines for analysis. *After the Fall* and *the beginners guide to sexuality* were both collected at the site. The following discussion concerning the content of both is based on the 2006 article in *Journal of Communication Inquiry*.

3. Such a finding concerning Radical Lay activists has proven consistent in both Mystical City (Atkinson, 2005; 2007; 2008; Atkinson & Dougherty, 2006) and Erie City (Atkinson, 2009a).

Chapter 6

1. Atkinson (2009a) travelled to Chiapas with a group of activists engaged in a "Truth Excursion" organized by a global network called Worldwide Outreach. There were seven activists involved in this Truth Excursion. During the trip, Atkinson conducted narrative excavation (see Krizek, 2003) by interviewing the activists and recording the public oral histories of different Zapatista groups that they encountered. The research was subsequently published as an article in *Communication, Culture, and Critique*. The following discussion concerning Zapatista testimonial narratives and alternative media pilgrimage is based on that article.

References

Abercrombie, N., & Longhurst, B. (1998). *Audiences: A sociological theory of performance and imagination*. Thousand Oaks, CA: Sage.

Allen, M. (1995). Communication concepts related to perceived organizational support. *Western Journal of Communication, 59*, 326-346.

Altheide, D. (1996). *Qualitative media analysis*. Thousand Oaks: Sage.

Althusser, L. (1971). *Lenin and philosophy and other essays*. New York: Monthly Review Press.

Amnesty International. (2003, October). Iraq: On whose behalf? Reconstruction must ensure the human rights of Iraqis. Retrieved April 15, 2009, from http://wwwamnesty.org/en/library/asset/MDE14/172/2003/en/efd5679d-d679-11dd-ab95-a13b602c0642/mde141722003en.html

Anderson, J. A. (1996). *Communication theory: Epistemological foundations*. New York: Guilford Press.

Ang, I. (1985). *Watching Dallas*. London: Routledge.

Aptheker, B. (1989). Tapestries of life: Women's work, women's consciousness, and the meaning of daily experience. Amherst, MA: University of Massachusetts Press.

Armstrong, D. (1981). *A trumpet to arms: Alternative media in America*. Boston: South End Press.

Arquilla, J., & Ronfeldt, D. (2001). The advent of netwar (revisited). In J. Arquilla & D. Ronfeldt (Eds.), *Networks and netwars: The future of terror, crime, and militancy* (pp. 1-25). Santa Monica, CA: RAND.

Atkinson, J. D. (2005a). Towards an understanding about complexities of alternative media: Portrayals of power in alternative media. *Qualitative Research Reports in Communication, 6*, 77-84.

Atkinson, J. D. (2005b). Conceptualizing global justice audiences of alternative media: The need for power and ideology in performance paradigms of audience research. *Communication Review, 8*, 137-157.

Atkinson, J. D. (2006). Analyzing resistance narratives at the North American Anarchist Gathering: A method for the analysis of social justice alternative media. *Journal of Communication Inquiry, 30*, 251-272.

Atkinson, J. D. (2007). Contemporary crusaders and timeless elders: Building cultural capital through alternative media texts. *Popular Communication, 5*, 171-190.

Atkinson, J. D. (2008). Towards a model of interactivity in alternative media: A multilevel analysis of audiences and producers in a new social movement network. *Mass Communication & Society, 11*, 227-247.

Atkinson, J. D. (2009a). Networked activism and the broken multiplex: Exploring fractures in the resistance performance paradigm. *Communication Studies, 60*, 49-65.

Atkinson, J. D. (2009b). Networked activists in search of resistance: Exploring an alternative media pilgrimage across the boundaries and borderlands of globalization. *Communication, Culture, and Critique, 2*, 137-159.

Atkinson, J. D., & Dougherty, D. S. (2006). Alternative media and social justice movements: The development of a resistance performance paradigm of audience analysis. *Western Journal of Communication, 70*, 64-88.

Atton, C. (2002a). *Alternative media.* Thousand Oaks, CA: Sage Publications.

Atton, C. (2002b). News cultures and new social movements: Radical journalism and the mainstream media. *Journalism Studies, 3*, 491-505.

Atton, C. (2003). Infoshops in the shadow of the state. In N. Couldry & J. Curran (Eds.), *Contesting media power: Alternative media in a networked world* (pp. 57-70). New York: Rowman & Littlefield Publishers.

Atton, C. (2004). An alternative Internet: Radical media, politics and creativity. Edinburgh University Press.

Auslander, P. (1997). From acting to performance: Essays in modernism and postmodernism. New York: Routledge.

Banks, D. (2004). *Amnesty International.* Milwaukee, WI: World Almanac Library.

Barsamian, D. (2003, June). The Progressive interview: Kurt Vonnegut. *The Progressive*, 35-38.

Bauman, R. (1977). *Verbal art as performance.* Prospect Heights, IL: Waveland Press.

Beaubien, J. (Executive Producer). (2003, May 7). South African businesses battle AIDS. *All Things Considered* [Radio broadcast]. Washington, DC: National Public Radio.

Benjamin, M. (2003, April 3) Toward a global movement. *The Nation* [Online]. Retrieved April 15, 2009, from http://www.thenation.com/doc/20030421/benjamin.

Berger, P. L., & Luckman, T. (1966). The social construction of reality: A treatise in the sociolgy of knowledge. Garden City, NY: Doubleday.

Berners-Lee, T. (1999). *Weaving the web.* London: Orion Business Books.

Bernthal, K. (1995). Online transmission of inflammatory remarks. *PC Novice, 6*, 39-40.

Best, K. (2005). Rethinking the globalization movement: Toward a cultural theory of contemporary democracy and communication. *Communication and Critical/Cultural Studies, 2*, 214-237.

Beverly, J. (1992). The margin at the center: On testimonio (testimonial narrative). In S. Smith & J. Watson (Eds.), *De/colonizing the subject: The politics of gender in women's autobiography* (pp. 91-114). Minneapolis: University of Minnesota Press.

Beverly, J. (2000). Testimonio, subalternity, and narrative authority. In N. Denzin & Y. Lincoln (Eds.) *Handbook of qualitative research* (pp. 555-565). Thousand Oaks: Sage Publications.

Bob, C. (2005). The marketing of rebellion: Insurgents, media, and international activism. Cambridge University Press.

Bowers, J., & Ochs, D. (1971). *The rhetoric of agitation and control.* Longman Higher Education.

Bowers, J., Ochs, D., & Jensen, R. (1992). *The rhetoric of agitation and control* (2nd ed.). Prospect Heights, IL: Waveland Press.

Brecher, J., Costello, T., & Smith, B. (2000). *Globalization from below: The power of solidarity.* Cambridge, MA: South End Press.

Butler, J. (1990). Gender trouble: Feminism and the subversion of identity. New York: Routledge.

Calafell, B. (2007). Latina/o communication studies: Theorizing performance. New York: Peter Lang.

Caldwell, J. (2003). Alternative media in suburban plantation culture. *Media, Culture & Society, 25*, 647-667.

Cantor, J. (1994). Fright reactions to mass media. In J. Bryant & D. Zillmann (Eds.), *Media effects advances in theory and research* (pp. 213-245). Hillsdale, NJ: Lawrence Erlbaum Associates, Publishers.

Carrigan, A. (2001). Afterword: Chiapas, the first postmodern revolution. In J. Ponce de Leon (Ed.), *Our word is our weapon: Selected writings of Subcomadante Insurgente Marcos* (pp. 417-444). New York: Seven Stories Press.

Castells, M. (1996). The rise of the network society, the information age: Economy, society and culture, volume I. Cambridge: Blackwell.

Castells, M. (2004). *The power of identity.* Malden, MA: Blackwell Publishing.

Castells, M. (2006). The network society: From knowledge to policy. In M. Castells & G. Cardoso (Eds.), The network society: From knowledge to policy (pp. 3-22). Washington, DC: Center for TransAtlantic Relations.

Ching, M. (August 1, 2002). Amnesty International oral statements: 55th session of the Sub-Committee on the Promotion and Protection of Human Rights. Retrieved April 15, 2009, from http://www.amnesty.org/en/library/info/IOR40/ 014/2003/en.

Clair, R. P. (1998). *Organizing silence: A world of possibilities.* Albany: State University of New York Press.

Conquergood, D. (1985). Performing as a moral act: Ethical dimensions of the ethnography of performance. *Literature in Performance, 5*, 1-13.

Conquergood, D. (1991). Rethinking ethnography: Towards a critical cultural politics. *Communication Monographs, 58*, 179-194.
Cortright, D. (2007). SANE reborn. In G. Stassen & L. Wittner (Eds.), *Peace Action: Past, present, and future* (pp. 47-58). Boulder, CO: Paradigm Publishers.
Cosentio, V. J. (1994). Virtual legality. *Byte, 19*, 278.
Cosgrove-Mather, B. (2003, November 14). Radical cheerleaders raise ruckus. *CBS News Online*. Retrieved May 15, 2003, from http://www.cbsnews.com/stories/2003/11/14/national/ main583821.shml
Couldry, N. (2000). The place of power: Pilgrims and witnesses of the media age. London: Routledge.
Couldry, N. (2003). *Media rituals: A critical approach*. London: Routledge.
Couldry, N. (2004). Theorising media as practice. *Social Semiotics, 14*, 115-132.
Curran, J. (2003). Global journalism: A case study of the Internet. In N. Couldry & J. Curran (Eds.), *Contesting media power: Alternative media in a networked world* (pp. 227-242). New York: Rowman & Littlefield Publishers.
Dawn, L. (2006). It takes a nation: How strangers became family in the wake of Hurricane Katrina. San Rafael, CA: Earth Aware.
Debord, G. (1967). *The society of the spectacle*. Paris: Editions Buchet-Chastel.
Debord, G. (1988). *Comments on the society of the spectacle*. Paris: Editions Gerard Lebovici.
Deetz, S. A. (1992). Democracy in an age of corporate colonization: Developments in communication and the politics of everyday life. Albany, NY: State University of New York Press.
DeLuca, K. (1999). Image politics: The new rhetoric of environmental activism. New York: Guildford Press.
Denzin, N. (1997). Interpretive ethnography: Ethnographic practices for the 21st century. Thousand Oaks, CA: Sage Publications.
DiNovella, E. (2003, May). *The Progressive* interview: Janeane Garofalo. *The Progressive*, pp. 35-39.
Downing, J. (1984). Radical media: The political experience of alternative communication. Boston, MA: South End Press.
Downing, J. (2003a). The Independent Media Center movement and the anarchist social tradition. In. N. Couldry & J. Curran (Eds.), *Contesting media power: Alternative media in a networked world* (pp. 243-258). New York: Rowman & Littlefield Publishers.
Downing, J. (2003b). Audiences and readers of alternative media: The absent lure of the virtually unknown. *Media, Culture & Society, 25*, 625-645.
Downing, J. D. H., Ford, T. V., Gil, G., & Stein, L. (2001). *Radical media: Rebellious communication and social movements*. Thousand Oaks, CA: Sage.

Durlak, J. T. (1987). A typology for interactive media. *Communication Yearbook, 10,* 743-757.

Eliasoph, N. (1988). Routines and the making of oppositional news. *Critical Studies in Mass Communication, 5,* 313-334.

Elin, L. (2003). The radicalization of Zeke Spier: How the Internet contributes to civic engagement and new forms of social capital. In M. McCaughey & M. Ayers (Eds.), *Cyberactivism: Online activism in theory and practice* (pp. 97-114). New York: Routledge.

Endres, D., & Warnick, B. (2004). Text-based interactivity in candidate campaign Web sites: A case study from the 2002 elections. *Western Journal of Communication, 68,* 322-343.

Evan, W. (1972). An organization-set model of interorganizational relations. In M. Tuite, R. Chisholm, & M. Radnor (Eds.), *Interorganizational decisionmaking* (pp. 181-200). Chicago: Aldine.

Fairhurst, G., & Sarr R. (1996). *The art of framing: Managing the language of leadership.* San Francisco: Jossey-Bass.

Fantasia, R. (1988). *Cultures of solidarity: Consciousness, action, and contemporary American workers.* Berkeley: University of California Press.

Fish, S. (1980a). *Is there a text in this class? The authority of interpretive communities.* Cambridge, MA: Harvard University Press.

Fish, S. (1980b). Interpreting the variorum. In J. Tompkins (Ed.), *Reader-response criticism: from formalism to post structuralism* (pp. 164-184). Baltimore, MD: Johns Hopkins University Press.

Fiske, J. (1987). *Television culture.* London: Routledge.

Foucault, M. (1975). *Discipline and punish: The birth of the prison.* Paris, France: Gallimard.

Gamson, W., & Modigliani, A. (1989). Media discourse and public opinion on nuclear power: A constructionist approach. *American Journal of Sociology, 95,* 1-37.

Garrido, M., & Halavais, A. (2003). Mapping networks of support for the Zapatista Movement: Applying social-networks analysis to study contemporary social movements. In M. McCaughey & M. Ayers (Eds.), *Cyberactivism: Online activism in theory and practice* (pp. 165-184). New York: Routledge.

Geddes, D., & Linnehan, F. (1996). Exploring the dimensionality of positive and negative performance feedback. *Communication Quarterly, 44,* 3, 326-344.

Gerbner, G., Gross, L., Morgan, M., & Signorelli, N. (1980a). Aging with television: Images on television drama and conception of reality. *Journal of Communication, 30,* 37-47.

Gerbner, G., Gross, L., Morgan, M., & Signorelli, N. (1980b). The mainstreaming of America: Violence profile #11. *Journal of Communication, 30,* 10-29.

Giddens, A. (1984). *The constitution of society*. Berkley: University of California Press.
Gitlin, T. (1978). Sociology: The dominant paradigm. *Theory and Society, 6*, 205-253.
Gitlin, T. (1983). Hill street blues: "Make it look messy." In T. Gitlin (Ed.), *Inside primetime* (pp. 273-324). New York: Pantheon.
Goffman, E. (1956). *The presentation of the self in everyday life*. Edinburgh University Press.
Goffman, E. (1963). *Behavior in public places*. London: Free Press of Glencoe.
Goffman, E. (1971). Relations in public: Microstudies of the public order. London: Harper Colophon Books.
Goodman, A. (2001). Democracy now: Challenging power on the air. In N. Welton & L. Wolf (Eds.), *Global uprising: Confronting the tyrannies of the 21st century* (pp. 76-79). Gabriola Island, Canada: New Society Publishers.
Goodman, A. (Executive Producer). (2003, May 2). *Democracy Now!* [Radio broadcast]. New York: Pacifica Radio.
Gorsevski, E. (2004). *Peaceful persuasion: The geopolitics of nonviolent rhetoric*. Albany, NY: State University of New York Press.
Gramsci, A. (1971). The formation of intellectuals. In Q. Hoare & G. Smith (Eds.), *Selections from the prison notebooks of Antonio Gramsci* (pp. 5-14). New York: International. (Original work published 1951)
Gray, J. (2005). Antifandom and the moral text: Television without pity and textual dislike. *American Behavioral Scientist, 48*, 840-858.
Greider, K. (2003, June 9). Offering hope—at a price: U.S. drug firms make the choice clear; our outrageous profits or your life. *The Nation* [Online]. Retrieved April 15, 2009, from http://www.thenation.com/doc/20030609/ greider.
Griffin, L. (1952). The rhetoric of historical movements. *Quarterly Journal of Speech, 38*, 184-188.
Griffin, L. (1980). On studying movements. *Central States Speech Journal, 31*, 225-232.
Gurr, T. (1970). *Why men rebel*. Princeton University Press: Princeton, NJ.
Gustainis, J. J., & Hahn, D. F. (1988). While the whole world watched: Rhetorical failures of anti-war protest. *Communication Quarterly, 36*, 203-216.
Habermas, J. (1974). The public sphere: An encyclopedic article (1964). *New German Critique, 1*, 49-55.
Habermas, J. (1989). *The structural formation of the public sphere*. Cambridge, MA: MIT Press.
Hall, S. (1980). Encoding/decoding. In S. Hall, D. Hobson, A. Lowe, & P. Willis (Eds.), *Culture, media, language* (pp. 128-138). London: Hutchinson.

Hamm, T. (2008). *The new blue media: How Michael Moore, MoveOn.org, Jon Stewart and company are transforming progressive politics.* New York: New Press.

Harold, C. (2004). Pranking rhetoric: "culture jamming" as media activism. *Critical Studies in Media Communication, 21,* 189-211.

Hebdige, D. (1979). *Subculture: The meaning of style.* London: Pluto Press.

Helvarg, D. (2003, June). Unwise use: Gale Norton's new environmentalism. *The Progressive* [Online]. Retrieved April 15, 2009, from http://www.progressive.org/node/1196.

Herbert, S. (1994). Bread and circuses. In N. Hodges (Ed.), *Performance art into the 90's* (pp. 6-35). London: Art & Design.

Herman, E. (2003, June). Normalizing godfatherly aggression. *Z Magazine,* 34-39.

Herman, E., & Chomsky, N. (1988). *Manufacturing consent: The political economy of the mass media.* New York: Pantheon Books.

Hills, M. (2005). Patterns of surprise: The "aleatory object" in psychoanalytic ethnography and cyclical fandom. *American Behavioral Scientist, 48,* 801-821.

Holmes, S. (2004). "But this reality you choose!": Approaching the "interactive" audience of reality TV. *International Journal of Cultural Studies, 7,* 213-231.

Holstein, J. A., & Gubrium, J. F. (1995). *The active interview.* Thousand Oaks, CA: Sage.

Hopgood, S. (2006). *Keepers of the flame: Understanding Amnesty International.* Ithaca, NY: Cornell University Press.

Horkheimer, M., & Adorno, T. (1972). *Dialectic of enlightenment.* New York: Seabury Press.

Huesca, R. (2001). Conceptual contributions of new social movements to development communication research. *Communication Theory, 11,* 415-433.

Jack, H. (2007). The beginnings of SANE. In G. Stassen & L. Wittner (Eds.), *Peace Action: Past, present, and future* (pp. 15-24). Boulder, CO: Paradigm Publishers.

Jenkins, H. (1992). Strangers no more we sing. In L. Lewis (Ed.), *The adoring audience: Fan culture and popular media* (pp. 208-236). London: Routledge.

Jensen, J. (1992). Fandom as pathology: The consequences of characterization. In L. Lewis (Ed.), *The adoring audience: Fan culture and popular media* (pp. 2-29). London: Routledge.

Kantrowitz, B., Springen, K., & Hontz, J. (2003, Sept. 29th). We're here! We cheer! Get used to it! *Newsweek* [Online]. Retrieved April 15, 2009, from http://www.radicalteencheer.com/press/03-newsweek.htm

Kellner, D. (1995). *Media cultures.* London: Routledge.

Kidd, D. (2003). Indymedia.org: A new communications commons. In M. McCaughey & M. Ayers (Eds.), *Cyberactivism: Online activism in theory and practice* (pp. 47-70). New York: Routledge.

Kiousis, S. (2002). Interactivity: A concept explication. *New Media & Society, 4*, 355-383.

Klein, N. (2002). Fences and windows: Dispatches from the front lines of the globalization debate. New York, NY: Picador.

Kowal, D. (2000). One cause, two paths: Militant vs. adjustive strategies in the British and American women's suffrage movements. *Communication Quarterly, 48*, 240-255.

Krippendorff, K. (2004). *Content analysis: An introduction to its methodology* (2nd ed.). Thousand Oaks: Sage.

Krishna. (2003, May 9). *U.S. government interfering in Nepal negotiation.* Retrieved May 2, 2003, from http://www.indymedia.org/en/2003/05/108822.shtml

Krizek, R. (2003). Ethnography as excavation of personal narrative. In R. Clair (Ed.), *Ethnography: Novel approaches to qualitative methods* (pp. 141-152). Albany: State University of New York Press.

Kropotkin, P. (1899). *Fields, factories, and workshops.* London: Hutchinson.

Landow, G. (2006). Hypertext 3.0: Critical theory and new media in an era of globalization. Baltimore, MD: The Johns Hopkins University Press.

Langellier, K. (1983). A phenomenological approach to audience. *Literature in Performance, 3*, 34-39.

Lazarsfeld, P., Berelson, B., & Gaudet, H. (1949). *The people's choice: How the voter makes up his mind in a presidential election.* New York: Columbia University Press.

Lewis, A. (2003, June). Martha Burk takes a swing. *The Progressive*, 32-34.

Lindloff, T. (1988). Media audiences as interpretive communities. *Communication Yearbook, 11*, 81-107.

Longhurst, B., Bagnall, G., & Savage, M. (2004). Audiences, museums and the English middle class. *Museum and Society, 2*, 104-124.

Lucas, S. (1980). Coming to terms with movement studies. *Central States Speech Journal, 31*, 255-266.

Machin, D., & Carrithers, M. (1996). From "interpretive communities" to "communities of improvisation." *Media, Culture & Society, 18*, 343-352.

Marcos. (2001). War! First declaration of the Lacandon Jungle. In J. Ponce de Leon (Ed.), *Our Word is our weapon: Selected writings of Subcomadante Insurgente Marcos* (pp. 13-16). New York: Seven Stories Press. (Originally published 1994)

Mayring, P. (2000). Qualitative content analysis. *Forum: Qualitative Social Research* [Online Journal], *1*(2). Retrieved October 1, 2002, from http://www.qualitative-research.net/fqs-texte/2-00/2-00mayring-e.htm

McChesney, R. (1998). The political economy of global communication. In R. McChesney, E. Wood, & J. Foster (Eds.), *Capitalism and the*

information age: The Political economy of the global communication revolution. New York, NY: Monthly Review Press.
McChesney, R., & Nichols, J. (2003, April). Holding the line at the FCC. *The Progressive* [Online]. Retrieved April 15, 2009, from http://www.progressive.org/node/1265.
McElroy, W. (2003). *The debates of liberty: An overview of individualist anarchism, 1881-1908.* New York, NY: Lexington Books.
McGee, M. (1975). In search of "the people": A rhetorical alternative. *Quarterly Journal of Speech, 61,* 235-249.
McGee, M. (1980a). The ideograph: A link between rhetoric and ideology. *Quarterly Journal of Speech, 66,* 1-16.
McGee, M. (1980b). "Social movement": Phenomenon or meaning? *Central States Speech Journal, 31,* 233-244.
McMillan, S. (2002). Exploring models of interactivity from multiple research traditions: Users, documents, and systems. In L. Lievrouw & S. Livingstone (Eds.), *The handbook of new media* (pp. 163-182). Thousand Oaks, CA: Sage.
Meikle, G. (2002). *Future active: Activism and the internet.* New York: Routledge.
Melucci, A. (1992). Frontier land: Collective action between actors and systems. In M. Diani & R. Eyerman (Eds.) *Studying collective action* (pp. 238-258). London: Sage Publication.
Mercer, I. (2003, September 10). Bush is a neoconservative. Worldnetdaily Exclusive Commentary. Retrieved December 6, 2003 from http://www.worldnetdaily.com/news/article.asp?ARTICLE_ID=34517
Mumby, D. (1988). *Communication and power in organizations: Discourse, ideology, and domination.* Westport, CT: Ablex Publishing.
Mumby, D. (1997). The problem of hegemony: Rereading Gramsci for organizational communication studies. *Western Journal of Communication, 61,* 343-375.
Murphy, P. D., & Kraidy, M. M. (2003). International communication, ethnography, and the challenge of globalization. *Communication Theory, 13,* 304-323.
Newcombe, H., & Alley, R. (1983). *The producer's medium.* New York: Oxford University Press.
Nichols, E. (2005, April). J20: A radical cheerleader reflects on the inauguration. *Off Our Backs,* 15-16.
Nichols, J. (2003, June 9). Taking it to the states: Fighting the right at home. *The Nation,* 11-17.
Olesen, T. (2005). *International Zapatismo: The construction of solidarity in the age of globalization.* London: Zed Books.
Olson, K., & Goodnight, G. T. (1994). Entanglements of consumption, cruelty, privacy, and fashion: The social controversy over fur. *Quarterly Journal of Speech, 83,* 28-48.

O'Sullivan, P. B., & Flanagin, A. J. (2003). Reconceptualizing "flaming" and other problematic messages. *New Media & Society, 5*, 67-93.

Owens, L., & Palmer, L. (2003). Making the news: Anarchist counter-public relations on the world wide web. *Critical Studies in Media Communication, 20*, 335-361.

Pan, Z., & McLeod, J. (1991). Multilevel analysis in mass communication research. *Communication Research, 18*, 140-173.

Paris, J. (2003). The black bloc's ungovernable protest. *Peace Review, 15*, 317-322.

Parry, A. (2005). *Amnesty International*. Philadelphia, PA: Chelsea House Publishers.

Patraka, V. (1996). Spectacular suffering: Performing presence, absence, and witness at the US Holocaust Memorial Museum. In E. Diamond (Ed.), *Performance and cultural politics* (pp. 89-107). London: Routledge.

Patraka, V. (1999). *Spectacular suffering: Theatre, facism, and the Holocaust*. Bloomington, IN: Indiana University Press.

Pekurny, R. (1982). Coping with television production. In D. Whitney & J. Ettema (Eds.), *Individuals in mass media organizations: Creativity and constraint* (pp. 131-143). Thousand Oaks: Sage.

Pezzullo, P. (2003). Touring "cancer alley," Louisiana: Performances of community and memory for environmental justice. *Text and Performance Quarterly, 23*, 226-252.

Pfeffer, J. (1992). *Managing with power: Politics and influence in organizations*. Boston, MA: Harvard Business School Press.

Pickard, V. W. (2006a). United yet autonomous: Indymedia and the struggle to sustain a radical democratic network. *Media, Culture & Society, 28*, 315-336.

Pickard, V. W. (2006b). Assessing the radical democracy of Indymedia: Discursive, technical, and institutional constructions. *Critical Studies in Media Communication, 23*, 19-38.

Pierce, T., & Dougherty, D. S. (2002). The construction, enactment, and maintenance of power-as-domination through an acquisition. *Management Communication Quarterly, 16*, 129-164.

Porter, W. M., & Catt, I. (1993). The narcissistic reflection of communicative power: Delusions of progress against organizational discrimination. In D. Mumby (Ed.), *Narrative and social control: Critical perspectives* (pp. 164-185). London: Sage.

Power, J. (2001). *Like water on stone: The story of Amnesty International*. Boston, MA: Northeastern University Press.

Proudhon, J. (1873). *De la capacite politique des classes ouvrieres*. Paris: Librarie Internationale.

Puopolo, S. T. (2001). The web and US Senate campaigns 2000. *American Behavioral Scientist, 44*, 2030-2047.

Rafaeli, S. (1988). Interactivity: From new media to communication. In R. Hawkins, J. Wiemann, & S. Pingree (Eds.), *Sage annual review of communication research: Advancing communication science: Merging mass and interpersonal processes, 16* (pp. 110-134). Beverly Hills: Sage.

Rauch, J. (2007). Activists as interpretive communities: Rituals of consumption and interaction in an alternative media audience. *Media, Culture & Society, 29*, 994-1013.

Rhoades, L., & Eisenberger, R. (2002). Perceived organizational support: A literature review. *Journal of Applied Psychology, 87*, 698-714.

Rossiter, C. (1962). *Conservativism in America*. New York: Vintage Books.

Ruddock, A. (2001). *Understanding audiences: Theory and method*. London: Sage Publications.

Russell, A. (2005). Myth and the Zapatista movement: Exploring a network identity. *New Media & Society, 7*, 559-577.

Sadler, W. J., & Haskins, E. V. (2005). Metonymy and the metropolis: Television show settings and the image of New York City. *Journal of Communication Inquiry, 29*, 195-216.

Sanchez, J., & Stuckey, M. (2000). The rhetoric of American Indian activism in the 1960s and 1970s. *Communication Quarterly, 48*, 120-136.

Sandvoss, C. (2005). One-dimensional fan: Toward an aesthetic of fan texts. *American Behavioral Scientist, 48*, 822-839.

Schecter, D. (1994). *Radical theories: Paths beyond Marxism and social democracy*. Manchester: Manchester University Press.

Scott, A., & Street, J. (2001). From media politics to e-protest? The use of popular culture and new media in parties and social movements. In F. Webster (Ed.), *Culture and politics in the information age: A new politics* (pp. 215-240). London: Routledge.

Searle, J. (1995). *The construction of social reality*. New York: Free Press.

Seigle, R. (Executive Producer). (2003, September 18). *All things considered*. [Radio broadcast]. New York: National Public Radio.

Senturia, B. (2007). The Freeze grassroots strategy: Building the movement. In G. Stassen & L. Wittner (Eds.), *Peace Action: Past, present, and future* (pp. 67-78). Boulder, CO: Paradigm Publishers.

Shanock, L. R., & Eisenberger, R. (2006). When supervisors feel supported: Relationships with subordinates' perceived supervisor support, perceived organizational support, and performance. *Journal of Applied Psychology, 91*, 689-695.

Shugart, H. (2005). On misfits and margins: Narrative, resistance, and the poster child politics of Rosie O'Donnell. *Communication & Critical/Cultural Studies, 2*, 52-76.

Sillars, M. (1980). Defining movements rhetorically: Casting the widest net. *Southern Speech Communication Journal, 46*, 17-32.

Simons, H. (1970). Requirements, problems, and strategies: A theory of persuasion for social movements. *Quarterly Journal of Speech, 56*, 1-11.

Simons, H. (1972). Persuasion in social conflicts: A critique of prevailing conceptions and a framework for future research. *Speech Monographs, 39*, 227-247.

Smelser, N. (1962). *Theory of collective behavior*. New York, NY: The Free Press.

Starr, A. (2000). *Naming the enemy: Anti-corporate movement confront globalization*. London: Zed Books.

Starr, A. (2006). "...(Expecting barricades erected to prevent us from peacefully assembling)": So-called "violence in the global north alterglobalization movement. *Social Movement Studies, 5*, 61-81.

Steinhardt, D. (2003, June). Tim Robbins, defiant. *The Progressive*, pp. 30-31.

Stengrim, L. A. (2005). Negotiating postmodern democracy, political activism, and knowledge production: Indymedia's grassroots and e-savvy answer to media oligopoly. *Communication and Critical/Cultural Studies, 2*, 281-304.

Stewart, C. (1980). A functional approach to the rhetoric of social movements. *Central States Speech Journal, 31*, 274-281.

Stromer-Galley, J. (2000). On-line interaction and why candidates avoid it. *Journal of Communication, 50*, 111-132.

Sundar, S., Kalyanaraman, S., & Brown, J. (2003). Explicating Web site interactivity: Impression formation effects in political campaign sites. *Communication Research, 30*, 30-59.

Thomas, J. (2000). *The battle in Seattle: The story behind and beyond the WTO demonstrations*. Golden, CO: Fulcrum Publishing.

Tierney, W. G. (2000). Undaunted courage: Life history and the postmodern challenge. In N. Denzin & Y. Lincoln (Eds.), *Handbook of qualitative research* (pp. 537-553). Thousand Oaks: Sage Publications.

Touraine, A. (1978). *The voice and the eye: An analysis of social movements*. New York: Cambridge University Press.

Tuchman, G. (1978). *Making news: A study in the construction of reality*. New York: Free Press.

Turner, R., & Killian, L. (1972). *Collective behavior*. Englewood Cliffs, NJ: Prentice-Hall.

Turrow, J. (1977). Another view of "citizen feedback" to the mass media. *Public Opinion Quarterly, 41*, 534-543.

Turrow, J. (1992). *Media systems in society: Understanding industries, strategies, and power*. New York: Longman.

Vegh, S. (2003). Classifying forms of online activism: The case of cyberprotests against the World Bank. In M. McCaughey & M. Ayers (Eds.), *Cyberactivism: Online activism in theory and practice* (pp. 71-96). New York: Routledge.

Warnick, B. (1998). Appearance or reality? Political parody on the Web in campaign '96. *Critical Studies in Media Communication, 15*, 306-324.

Warnick, B. (2007). *Rhetoric online: Persuasion and politics on the World Wide Web*. New York: Peter Lang Publishing.

Warnick, B., Xenos, M., Endres, D., & Gastil, J. (2005). Effects of campaign-to-user and text-based interactivity in political candidate campaign web sites. *Journal of Computer-Mediated Communication, 10* (3), article 5.

Weick, K. (1979). *The social psychology of organizing*. New York: McGraw-Hill.

Winer, N. (May 9th, 2003). The project for the new American century. Retrieved April 15, 2009, from http://www.moveon.org/ moveonbulletin/ bulletin13.html

Windt, T. O. (1972). The diatribe: Last resort for protest. *Quarterly Journal of Speech, 58*, 71-91.

Wittner, L. (2007). A short history of Peace Action. In G. Stassen & L. Wittner (Eds.), *Peace Action: Past, present, and future* (pp. 1-14). Boulder, CO: Paradigm Publishers.

Wolin, S. (2003, May 19). Inverted totalitarianism. *The Nation*, 13-15.

Zaleski, R. (2004, April 30). Bush raises left's circulation and magazine's. *Capital Times* [Online]. Retrieved April 15, 2009, from http://www.theleftcoaster.com/archives/001659.php

Zavesky, J. (2003, May). Hooray for Hollywood. *Z Magazine* [Online]. Retrieved April 15, 2009, from http://www.zmag.org/zmag/ viewArticle/ 14144

Zinn, H. (2003, June). Dying for the government. *The Progressive*, 16-17.

Index

Abercrombie, Nicholas, 25-34, 41, 54
All Things Considered, 22, 82, 84-86, 94-96, 122-123, 129
Alternative media
  Definition, 13-17, 22, 150-151
  Strategies for production, 17-19, 22-23, 118-119, 151-152
Alternative Media Interactions, 37, 40-46
Alternative media pilgrimage, 143-144, 149
Alternative media world, 134-137, 150
Amnesty International, 45-46, 90, 97-100, 136, 138
Amnesty International website, 35, 46, 82, 90-91, 95-96, 138
Anarchist, xvii, 11, 19-20, 38-39, 44, 110, 112, 118-121, 124-126
Armstrong, David, 13-14, 17, 40, 82, 115, 118, 121, 150
Arquilla, John, 10-11, 56, 150

Atkinson, Joshua, xii-xiii, xvii-xviii, 32, 40, 56, 74-75, 82, 94, 95, 98, 110, 121, 124, 129, 132, 135, 139, 141-144
Atton, Chris, xii, 15, 16-19, 22, 32, 40-41, 60, 82, 89, 105, 110, 112, 118-120, 121, 124, 129, 131-132, 134, 139, 150-152
Audience Performance Paradigm, 33-34, 147
Best, Kirsty, xii, xiii, 11-13, 21, 45, 54-55, 70, 110, 129, 133, 136, 139, 150
Black bloc, 124-127, 129
Bowers, John, xi, 3-4, 7, 22, 47-48, 149
Calafell, Bernadette, 9-10, 22, 47, 149
Caldwell, John, 15-17, 132
Castells, Manuel, xii, 11-13, 41, 44, 56-57, 98, 110, 119, 150
Commondreams.org, 23, 49, 52-54, 65, 68, 94, 121
Communicative Resistance, 37, 46-49, 70, 95, 97, 99, 102, 106-107, 130, 149, 153
Couldry, Nick, 19, 28, 131-134
Critical Worldview, 37-40, 42-46

176   Index

DeLuca, Keven, xii, 8-10, 20-22, 39, 46, 64, 124, 128, 149
Democracy Now!, xvii, 22, 32, 34-35, 41, 67, 82-84, 94-95
Denzin, Norman, 9, 21, 40, 46, 60, 82, 94
Downing, John, xii, 13-17, 19, 29, 32, 40, 48, 110-111, 118, 121, 124, 132, 150-151
Evan, William, 10-11, 56
Goffman, Erving, 28-29
Griffin, Leland, 1-3, 5, 148
Gurr, Ted, 2-3, 148
Gustainis, Justin, 6, 33, 74
Habermas, Jurgen, 17, 118
Hahn, Dan, 6, 33, 74
Harold, Christine, xii, 20-21, 33-46, 124
Hebdige, Dick, 27, 30
Huesca, Robert, xi, 7, 11-13, 21, 40, 56-57, 110, 150
Indymedia.org, xvii, 12-13, 16, 18-19, 23, 32-34, 40-42, 44, 51-53, 56, 60, 110-114, 121-122, 124, 135, 138, 140-141, 144, 150-151
Interactivity
  Conceptualizations, 60
  User-to-Document, 60-70
  User-to-User, 60, 70-79
  Social Movement Research, 13, 19-20
Intercreative Capacity, 37, 61, 79, 130, 134, 144
Kowal, Donna, 6, 46-47, 100, 127, 142
Longhurst, Brian, 25-34, 41, 54
Lucas, Stephen, 4-6
McGee, Michael, 4, 8, 148-149
McMillan, Sally, 40, 60, 134
Meikle, Graham, xii, 16-19, 22, 40, 60-61, 82, 110-111, 150-151
Mesomobilizaton, 12-13, 79, 136

MoveOn.org
  Website and listserv, 20, 35-36, 39-40, 82, 92-93, 95-96, 104, 151
  Organization, 98, 100-102
Multiplex
  Construction, 50-53, 69-70, 121, 135-136, 139-140, 144, 148
  Definition, xiii, 49-50, 54
  Hindrance, 70, 74-75, 77-79
  Narrative Capacity, xiv, 37, 70-79, 130, 144
Nation, The, xvi, 22, 32, 34-35, 51, 66, 110, 114-117, 121-122, 151
Networked activism, xviii, 10-13, 20-21, 45, 54, 136-139, 147-148
New social movement
  Defined, xi-xii, 7-8
  Performance, xiii, 9-10, 21-22, 32-33, 37-38, 132, 149
  Rhetoric of Image, xii, 8-9, 21-22, 149
New social movement networks, xviii, 10-13, 21, 52, 56-57, 64-65, 69, 74-75, 77-78, 149-150
Ochs, Donovan, xi, 3-4, 7, 22, 47-48, 149
Owens, Lynn, 19-21
Palmer, Kendall, 19-21
Peace Action, 46, 98, 102-106, 154
Pezzullo, Phaedra, 9, 21, 29, 149
Pickard, Victor, xii, xvii, 11-13, 21, 32, 45, 51, 54, 56, 65, 69, 74, 110, 129, 135, 139, 150
Power, xiii, 8, 15, 34-38, 44-46, 50, 56-57, 63-64, 69, 79, 82, 94-97, 106-107, 110-111,

121, 124-126, 132-133, 142, 153-154
Progressive, The, 35, 44-45, 51, 82, 86-88, 94-95, 106
Radical cheerleaders, 62, 124, 126-129
Rauch, Jennifer, 16-17, 40, 82, 85, 94-95, 98, 110, 150
Resistance, xvii, 3, 15, 32-33, 119, 135-144, 151-154
Ronfeldt, David, 10-11, 56, 150
Rossiter, Clinton, 38
Ruddock, Andy, 25-26
Sanchez, John, 48
Shugart, Helene, xii, 7, 9
Sillars, Malcolm, 4-7
Smelser, Neil, 2-3, 5, 148
Stengrim, Laura, 12, 21, 41-42, 45, 56, 69, 98, 110, 129, 150
Stewart, Charles, 6
Stuckey, Mary, 48
Touraine, Alain, 7-8, 149
Warnick, Barbara, xii, 20-21, 39-40, 60, 98, 110
Windt, Theodore, 4, 33, 128, 148
Zapatistas, xv, xvi, 19, 42, 138-144
Zines, xii, xvii, 16-18, 22, 31, 40-41, 110, 118-122, 124, 129, 151
Z Magazine, xiv, xvii, 23, 34-36, 44, 68, 82, 85, 88-90, 94, 143, 153

General Editors
Lynda Lee Kaid and Bruce Gronbeck

At the heart of how citizens, governments, and the media interact is the communication process, a process that is undergoing tremendous changes as we embrace a new millennium. Never has there been a time when confronting the complexity of these evolving relationships been so important to the maintenance of civil society. This series seeks books that advance the understanding of this process from multiple perspectives and as it occurs in both institutionalized and non-institutionalized political settings. While works that provide new perspectives on traditional political communication questions are welcome, the series also encourages the submission of manuscripts that take an innovative approach to political communication, which seek to broaden the frontiers of study to incorporate critical and cultural dimensions of study as well as scientific and theoretical frontiers.

For more information or to submit material for consideration, contact:

BRUCE E. GRONBECK	LYNDA LEE KAID
Obermann Center for Advanced Studies	Political Communication Center
N134 OH	Department of Communication
The University of Iowa	University of Oklahoma
Iowa City, IA 52242-5000	Norman, OK 73109

To order other books in this series, please contact our Customer Service Department:

        (800) 770-LANG (within the U.S.)
        (212) 647-7706 (outside the U.S.)
        (212) 647-7707 FAX

Or browse online by series:
        WWW.PETERLANG.COM

www.ingramcontent.com/pod-product-compliance
Ingram Content Group UK Ltd.
Pitfield, Milton Keynes, MK11 3LW, UK
UKHW021838210426
5322IPUK00021B/354